Thinking with Literature

Towards a Cognitive Criticism

TERENCE CAVE

OXFORD
UNIVERSITY PRESS

OXFORD
UNIVERSITY PRESS

Great Clarendon Street, Oxford, OX2 6DP,
United Kingdom

Oxford University Press is a department of the University of Oxford.
It furthers the University's objective of excellence in research, scholarship,
and education by publishing worldwide. Oxford is a registered trade mark of
Oxford University Press in the UK and in certain other countries

First Edition published in 2016

Impression: 1

Published in the United States of America by Oxford University Press
198 Madison Avenue, New York, NY 10016, United States of America

British Library Cataloguing in Publication Data
Data available

Library of Congress Control Number: 2015947354

ISBN 978-0-19-874941-7

Printed in Great Britain by
Clays Ltd, St Ives plc

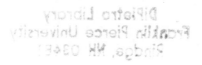

This book is dedicated to 'Mr B.', as we like to call him, and to his daughter Angela Lina Balzan, whose generosity and vision continue to inspire research unfettered by an obsession with strictly quantifiable outcomes.

Preface

This book grew out of a series of public lectures and draft essays. They were written over the three-year span of a project known familiarly as 'Thinking with Literature' and officially as the Balzan Interdisciplinary Seminar 'Literature as an Object of Knowledge'. It grew, above all, out of the many conversations afforded by the project, and those conversations are still audible here and there, especially perhaps in Chapters 6 and 9. In the mode of its presentation, it is a direct response to the final session of our concluding colloquium, also called 'Thinking with Literature', where the project participants addressed the particular problem of giving cognitive literary study a status which is neither subservient to 'science' (or any other non-literary discipline, for that matter) nor merely opportunistically coloured with the veneer of those disciplines. Many of those present on that occasion agreed that such an approach should be cognitively *informed*, that is to say argued in a way that would be regarded as acceptable by cognitive scientists, psychologists, linguists, and philosophers; but that, at the level of expression, it might aim to be cognitively *inflected*. In other words, it should be a literary criticism worthy of the name, resisting integration into extraneous agendas for which literature would provide mere illustrative examples, but at relevant points inflected by frames of reference, terminology, conjectures, and the like drawn from across the spectrum of cognitive disciplines. Others may choose a different balance, but it is the one I have attempted to achieve here.

This is therefore neither an introductory handbook, nor a systematic account of one or more cognitive approaches to literature. It emerges from the Balzan project, and is a personal view of where the learning curve of that experience might lead. I have for the most part preferred not to engage in the sometimes heated controversies that have already arisen within the field at large, on the grounds that they are often irrelevant to the fine grain of literary analysis and liable to distract readers from pragmatic encounters with works of literature as such. For the same reason, arguments and hypotheses derived from other disciplines are only sketched in: awkward complications have often been elided, possible objections passed over.

In all this, I have followed a pragmatic principle which I developed when coming to terms with some of the more complex aspects of literary theory in the later twentieth century. Instead of attempting to preserve complete fidelity to particular theories or articulations of theory, I read in each case for the insight, the fundamental principle or perspective offered by the theory in question which was capable of renewing the understanding of a given work or (better) corpus. One also needs to bear in mind that cognitive science is still in an early phase of development and that many of its hypotheses remain conjectural.

For these reasons, too, and not only for reasons of personal preference, I have been selective in my choice of cognitively informed sources.[1] Among the perspectives omitted here, or only referred to in passing, are the cognitive linguistics of George Lakoff and Mark Johnson, together with the notion of 'conceptual blending' developed by Gilles Fauconnier and Mark Turner; some forms of cognitive narratology and poetics; theories of 'affect' and the emotions; and above all the comprehensively phenomenological approach that is associated primarily with Shaun Gallagher and his colleague Dan Zahavi. This latter omission will surprise some, since I talk a good deal about 'embodied' approaches. But I believe that, although the phenomenological tradition plays a crucial role in the prehistory of modern cognitive science, its historical status doesn't accord it any priority in relation to the field as a whole (except no doubt for philosophers committed to phenomenology in the first place). Everything I wanted to do in this book could be done, it seemed to me, without investing in a neo-phenomenology of that kind (or indeed any kind of systematic philosophy), which comes with a lot of complicated baggage of its own. That said, the project of neo-phenomenology is a powerful player in the current cognitive arena, and I have included some references at relevant points, together with key titles in the bibliography.

Finally, it's not my intention to present a 'new' cognitive *theory* of literature, to be added incrementally to existing literary theories. Others may want to propose that move, but I think it risks all kinds of confusions. What the current interdisciplinary conversation on cognition offers is not a theory, or set of theories, custom-built for literary study. It offers a wide range of interesting hypotheses and conjectures about the way human cognition works—its capacities, its constraints, its deficits—together with a good deal of solid experimental work which is beginning to give substance to some of the hypotheses (and exclude others). Since literature is a product of human cognition and illustrates its functioning at an especially complex level, one might expect that particularly intensive range of reflections to be at least relevant to literary study and to draw attention to things we hadn't seen before, or hadn't seen clearly enough. It offers insights, perspectives, possible new avenues of approach. Even where those disparate moves come together to form a theory (of perception, mental imaging, communication, motor resonance, and so on), however, the theories that emerge are—again—self-evidently not *literary* theories that can be 'applied' to literary materials, and it would be misleading to present them as such.

Thinking with Literature is designed for anyone interested in English and foreign literatures, including the Greek and Latin canon. Although it is not a teaching manual, the cognitive themes and arguments explored here are mostly of the kind that can easily be communicated to students—many of them are already in the media, or available in high-quality 'popular' publications such as Daniel Kahneman's *Thinking, Fast and Slow* and Chris Frith's *Making Up the Mind*.[2] Philosophers, psychologists, and linguists might be interested in some of the arguments and examples, but I didn't set out to respect the agendas, conventions, and logics of other disciplines. This is a book where literature itself provides the primary energies.

Its structure is therefore not self-evident, and requires a preliminary user's manual. The opening chapter is an introduction, but not in the formal sense: it provides a series of preliminary, non-technical glimpses of central issues. Chapter 2 sets the scene more methodically, and might therefore be read as a second introductory chapter. Chapter 3, by contrast, moves directly into the register of literary analysis, with a close reading of a four-line poem, followed by a brief narrative example. These are pragmatic examples of cognitively inflected reading. Chapters 4 and 5 are more 'discursive' chapters, introducing major cognitive topics at the broader level.

Chapter 5 ends at a point where two paths can be followed. One leads directly into the exploration of 'cognitive mimesis' in two specific textual examples, one dramatic, the other narrative; the narrative thread is then picked up in the subsequent chapter, which offers a cognitively inflected reading of a single novel. The other path follows the discussion of literary imagination into the domain of 'images' (figures), focusing on micro-examples drawn in the main from poetry. After considerable hesitation, I decided that the bifurcation could best be dealt with by placing the chapter on 'cognitive figures' immediately after Chapter 5. Although this sequence breaks the link between the discussion of simulation and mimesis in Chapters 5 and 7, the reader will have no difficulty in restoring the link, and it makes sense to present Chapters 7 and 8 as a connected pair which in turn leads via the theme of reading, its skills and its benefits, to the final chapter on literary values. The sequence also allows a rough grouping of chapters in which lyric poetry is central (3, 5, 6), followed by a group where narrative predominates. In short: those who want to follow the 'mimesis' pathway into narrative should read 5, 7, and 8 (and perhaps also 9) in sequence, adding 6 later (but not forgetting *its* connection to 5).

Regardless of the bifurcation, the later chapters move progressively deeper into the mode of close attention to literary texts rather than the exposition of cognitive arguments and hypotheses. However, the distinction between the 'discursive' mode and the close-reading mode is not at all clear-cut. On the contrary: they constantly overlap, creating an effect (I hope) of mutual dependence. For the same reason, I have avoided confining particular topics within the space of particular chapters and have deliberately allowed key points to recur in different contexts. Finally, as in most of my longer studies, I have aimed to create effects of continuity, if not coherence, by using metaphorical and literary leitmotifs such as the tiger from Henry V's famous Agincourt speech. I hope that, by the time readers reach the end of the book, they will have become familiar with a connected cluster of cognitive themes and be in a position to judge whether or not they enhance the reading of literature across the genres.

A 'virtual manifesto for cognitive literary studies' is offered instead of a conclusion or epilogue. The manifesto is 'virtual' for the obvious reason that the crowd support for this kind of approach is still emergent. Thinking with literature is in any case, by definition, work in progress: the 'towards' in my subtitle is meant to be taken at face value.

Unless otherwise indicated, all translations are my own.

I chose the second epigraph for this book for several reasons. Rebecca Elson (1960–99) was an astrophysicist and a poet who, at her death, left a wealth of notes and fragments of unfinished poems.[3] This one was apparently to be called 'Explaining dark matter', and would have been one of a group which also contains the completed 'Explaining relativity'. Her position between poetry and science is clearly relevant to the project of a cognitive approach to literary studies. So is the conditional 'as if', which borders on a counterfactual. So is the implied theme of underspecification and the inference it provokes. And so, more particularly, is the notion of an obscure unmapped terrain that has to be inferred from tiny points of living light (like poetic images, perhaps). I am grateful to Carcanet Press and to the 'Oxford Poets' series for permission to use this quotation as a motif for the dust jacket of this book.

Acknowledgements

These acknowledgements will be lengthy, but with good reason. My thanks go first to the International Balzan Foundation. Their decision to award me the 2009 Balzan Prize for literature since 1500 literally changed my life. It enabled me to turn a few tentative ideas about how a cognitive approach might be fruitful for literary study into a full-scale exploration that continues to this day. It gave me the resources to establish a team of scholars, especially younger ones, committed to the project, and a wider network of interdisciplinary contacts which has given me access to all kinds of unforeseen perspectives. My conversations with Guillemette Bolens, Robyn Carston, Gregory Currie, Paul Harris, and Deirdre Wilson, together of course with my readings of their own scholarly work and their regular participation in our project workshops, provided the momentum out of which this book developed. I learnt a great deal, too, from the opportunity to talk to project visitors, including especially Warren Boutcher, Mary Crane, Marie-Luce Demonet, Monika Fludernik, Chris Frith, Shaun Gallagher, Philip Gerrans, David Herman, Stephen Mottram, Alan Palmer, Andrew Parker, and Marina Warner. And of course none of this would have been possible without the cognitive energies, the imagination, the efficiency, and the sheer hard work of the core members of the project itself: Karin Kukkonen, Olivia Smith, Kathryn Banks, Tim Chesters, James Helgeson, Raphael Lyne, Ita Mac Carthy, and Wes Williams. Thanks to her twin resources as specialist in world literature and as a remarkably inventive writer of fictions, Elleke Boehmer played a highly creative role, as well as an energetically supportive one, in the evolution of the project. Special thanks are due to the group of Associated Researchers—Miranda Anderson, Jennifer Gosetti-Ferencei, Patricia Kolaiti, Sabine Müller, Kirsti Sellevold, Emily Troscianko—, who enormously enriched the dialogue in their different ways. Invaluable contributions came also from Felix Budelmann, Patrick Hayes, Laurie Maguire, Ben Morgan, Sowon Park, Ritchie Robertson, and many others. It was a particular pleasure for me that Marian Hobson and Michel Jeanneret, my oldest friends in the academic world, were discreetly but actively present throughout the project. Jim Reed, another old friend and sharer of conversations, offered immensely positive insights and gave me excellent practical advice, especially in the earlier stages of the project.

Lecture audiences at the Zaharoff Lecture in Oxford, the George Steiner Lecture at Queen Mary University of London, and the Malcolm Bowie Memorial Lecture, sponsored by the British Comparative Literature Association and presented at SOAS, also at lectures given at the universities of Geneva, Edinburgh, and Paris–Sorbonne, posed challenging and stimulating questions that helped me to develop my reflections on the cognitive project as a whole.

I owe an enormous debt of gratitude to the Governing Body and Officers of my own college, St John's College, Oxford, who responded to the Balzan award with astonishing generosity. They provided matching funds that enabled me to appoint two Postdoctoral Fellows instead of one and an additional Research Lecturer; they made available offices and seminar rooms in the Research Centre and elsewhere; and they offered the services of unfailingly efficient and patient support staff in the College Office and Bursary. Conversations in the Senior Common Room enriched my knowledge of other fields and enabled me to try out my ideas on anthropologists, neuroscientists, psychologists, philosophers, and linguists. I have been fortunate to be able to draw on this remarkable cognitive environment ever since I arrived in the college in 1972, but I never expected it to make the crucial difference that it has made to my life and work in the past five or six years.

Various readings of my drafts for this book have enabled me to erase at least some glaring errors, improve arguments and phrasings, and work my way through to a sense of the book as a coherent whole. Raphael Lyne read the entire manuscript with his customary generosity and finesse; Deirdre Wilson likewise read a complete draft and gave it her unqualified approval, which was enormously reassuring to me, given the importance of relevance theory for my approach; and Kirsti Sellevold's careful and detailed readings have accompanied me through the whole period of composition. Guillemette Bolens's lucid understanding of my project was coupled with the honesty to tell me with no mincing of words that one section was a disaster and had to be dropped (she was of course right). Kathryn Banks, Robyn Carston,

Tim Chesters, Jakob Lothe, and Jim Reed offered perceptive readings of individual chapters and saved me from many local errors and infelicities. I want especially here to thank the anonymous readers appointed by Oxford University Press, whose detailed commentaries on the manuscript were invaluable to me in the later stages. The officers of the Press, especially Jacqueline Baker and Rachel Platt, have been wonderfully supportive and efficient from the moment I first raised with them the possibility of offering them this book. I am proud to have been able, over the last thirty-five years or so, to associate my work with the unequalled reputation of this great publishing house.

Kirsti Sellevold's name has already appeared twice in these acknowledgements, but that won't suffice to indicate how much she has contributed to the book. Without her, indeed, it would never have existed, since she it was who first convinced me that relevance theory and other cognitive approaches offered the possibility of a fresh approach to literary studies. She has shared with me the sheer excitement of the Balzan project, its conversations, its new encounters, its constant opening of unexpected perspectives. She has propped up my flagging morale when difficulties arose, imagined and then helped to make real a place of refuge and recreation on a beautiful Norwegian island, and always believed without hesitation that all this cognitive stuff was worth doing. Her voice is audible from the wings throughout the book, which in that very real sense is hers as well as mine.

Terence Cave
15 February 2015

Contents

Books are not absolutely dead things
(John Milton, *Areopagitica*)

As if, from fireflies, one could infer the field
(Rebecca Elson, 'Explaining dark matter')

1
Openings

Changing the cognitive environment

Cognition—whether animal or human—is alert, attentive, responsive. It has to be. Small lapses may be fatal, or at least extremely uncomfortable. There are times when the cognitive system is resting or idling, but even then the merest hint of an unexpected smell or sound, a flicker on the edge of vision, a shift in the perceived direction of the breeze, will trigger an immediate response. In humans, the range of available responses is potentially enormous, since it includes the capacity for reflection and imagination; in addition, we have learnt to introduce into our environment an ever-expanding repertory of cognitive artefacts, instruments capable of eliciting the most exquisitely fine-tuned responses. Literature, in the broadest sense of the word, is among the richest of those cognitive artefacts. Communicative language of all kinds has the function of changing the cognitive environment of the listener; literature extends that function with a power that is in inverse relation to its immediate use-value in the everyday world. It makes things happen, gives a local habitation and a name to unfamiliar feelings and events, or makes familiar ones strange. Correspondingly, literary criticism needs to be as alert and attentive as any other cognitive activity we perform—arguably more so than most.

The idea for this book began with the desire to make something happen in literary studies. Not some dramatic upheaval or conflict, like the rise of literary theory in the later twentieth century, but rather a shift of perspective that might turn out to be critical. I want to suggest that, since the currently available intellectual environment in which we all operate is changing perceptibly, there will inevitably, sooner or later, be a corresponding change in the terms in which we approach our own subject. I for one certainly read differently now, notice different things, look for different things, bring to bear on my reading a new reflective context. The aim here is simply to pass on something of that change in the weather, offer some models of cognitively informed and inflected reading accompanied by a sketch of the various disciplinary 'frames' that encourage them to emerge. I shall also use certain recurrent terms, metaphors, and conceptions that, for me, embody crucial shifts in perspective. A whole chapter (Chapter 4) is devoted to showing how a single word ('affordance') can make surprising things happen when it intervenes in one's critical discourse. The balloon of the mind, together with Yeats's poem of that name, affords imaginations of flight, imaginative transcendence, and the rigorous constraints under which those possibilities operate. Underspecification and inference are constantly present as the fundamental conditions of human cognition itself. The familiar topic of literary mimesis and the 'immersion' it entails re-enter the scene as an especially acute and sophisticated form of attention (take Joseph Conrad's word for it, not mine). And the body, incessantly exposed to the ecologies that shape it, is in this account always continuous with the 'mind' and *its* ecologies: thoughts and ideas are functions of a biological substratum, not of a computer-like logic.

Conversation

The remainder of this chapter will offer a set of brief 'openings' (imaginative perspectives) which may be regarded as trailers for what follows. The first takes up the image of a vigorous, mind-changing conversation, and thus anticipates the 'cognitive conversation' that will be explored in Chapter 2. In his final essay, Shakespeare's French contemporary Michel de Montaigne imagines conversational exchange as a tennis game:[1]

> Speech belongs half to the speaker, half to the listener, who must prepare himself to receive it according to its trajectory. As in a game of tennis, the defender takes up position and gets ready in response to his perception of the striker's movements and the way she strikes the ball.[2]

Why is this analogy so pertinent, so perfectly adapted to conversational exchange? In the first place, it catches very precisely the mirror effect of conversation, the way speaker and interlocutor use the same instrument (language) and the same skills to read one another's intended meaning. It catches the dynamic aspect of successful conversation, the rapid to-and-fro that requires constant anticipation of what is to come. Although the exchange of language is less overtly physical than a sport requiring trained players, it too draws on skills that are grounded in sensorimotor awareness: the reading of glances, gestures, body movements, together of course with the acoustic material of language itself. Both kinds of skill seem 'natural', intuitive, yet have to be learned: small children find it difficult to throw a ball, let alone catch or strike one correctly. And both, once thoroughly learnt, unfold in the absence of any reflection on the complex cognitive processes that must underpin such an exchange. In this sense, despite the use of simile ('As in a game of tennis'), one could claim that the two activities belong to the same characteristically human suite of behaviours. They are different ways of interacting, but interaction is in both cases key.

In an anthropological perspective, literature is a collective activity, an enduring feature of the way humans share their cognitive environment. Story-telling, poetry, song, dance are not solitary activities, although modern cultures have provided the means for them to be carried out individually and in private. Most people still prize live performance, whether of theatre or song, and the watching of film or video, even at home or on one's smart phone, is embedded in social practices. Conversation (dialogue) is central to most forms of narrative and drama: we love watching the tennis-game of pertinent conversation. Literary uses of language, furthermore, are continuous with everyday uses, literary ways of thinking are continuous with everyday ways of thinking; the world as represented in literature—even in science fiction and fantasy—has essentially the same physical properties and sensorimotor laws as the world we live in.[3] Literature, as a product of the mind, can perform remarkable feats, but it does not occupy a space of its own, demarcated with glass walls, where people walk down dimly-lit corridors, getting a thrill out of seeing jellyfish and sharks at close quarters, but without incurring any risk to their persons. This book is written, in part, against the post-Kantian view of literature as belonging to a special (and consequently marginal) aesthetic domain.

Literature, in short, is part of the human conversation, and literary criticism prolongs that conversation in its own mode. After watching a play, movie, or TV series, people love to talk about it; they enjoy book clubs, poetry readings. As we shall see in Chapters 7 and 8, the ancient conversation of story-tellers and listeners that is preserved in collections like Chaucer's *Canterbury Tales* and Boccaccio's *The Decameron* is echoed in more modern fictions. The so-called *mise en abysme*, much discussed in late twentieth-century literary theory, is a trace of the same interpenetration of literature and conversation. Literature promotes its own downstream conversation, where it becomes mingled with the everyday, the social, the ethical, the political.

In another late essay entitled 'On conversation', Montaigne explores in some detail the cognitive interaction between attentive participants in dialogue or conversation. He says that he is often able to finish his interlocutor's sentences for her:

> I enjoy anticipating her conclusions, I relieve her of the trouble of interpreting herself. I try to grasp her thought as it comes into being, while it is still incomplete: the order and relevance of her thinking warns me and threatens me far in advance...[4]

Language here is not a static, quantifiable material; it is fluid, constantly shifting, like the moves and shots in a tennis game. It depends on a sustained inferential process on both sides, each speaker seeking to infer the other's meaning, supplying it. One can say also that language in such a conversation is offered as *evidence* of what the speaker is thinking: once the evidence is sufficiently clear, any relevant form of words (or none) will do. The thought is grasped on the wing, although just when you think you've grasped it, it's liable to move on. You can only guess, on the basis of the direction, or, better, the *directedness* of your interlocutor's utterances, where her thought is going; the process is open to error, cognitive divergence, even failure, but that doesn't mean that it is invalid or 'undecidable'. The same is true of how we read poems and novels and how they conscript our cognitive capacity for inference:[5] the ultimate meaning they embody is in one sense always open, always future, but nonetheless tightly constrained by an 'order and relevance' that was there from the start (or we wouldn't be reading them now).

As I said a moment ago, what happens in conversations, the worst as well as the best, is that speakers seek to alter each other's cognitive environment, to make some difference, however small, to the way they perceive and conceive the world. That is surely why Montaigne enjoyed conversation, and his *Essais* are arguably among the most powerful and comprehensive of written instruments for inflecting the cognitive environment of the reader.[6] In that sense, his book is a paradigm of literature itself: literary works make you think differently. Admittedly, they may sometimes return you to comfortably familiar or reassuring thought-worlds; they may dangerously simplify the problems that, in the real world, you sooner or later have to face. But that is true of human inventions of all kinds, including language itself; they require what has been called 'epistemic vigilance', the capacity to calibrate their truth value, their use-value, or their outcomes in real-world contexts. The downstream conversation we call literary criticism has emerged as a special mediating language, and eventually as an academic 'discipline', because of the perceived capacity of literary works to alter the cognitive environment of the reader in ways that are powerful, potentially disturbing, and not at all self-evident.

Vigilance, however, doesn't demand the constraints of a formal logic.[7] The view of language, and thus of literature, that I want to promote here perceives it as an open medium, the very opposite of a prison-house. Hence my recurrent use of metaphors and examples featuring balloons, flight, things that happen on the wing and the hoof. In accordance with that principle, I shall also avail myself of vocabulary used by linguists who speak of 'ad hoc concepts' or by cognitive psychologists who study the ways in which we actually perceive and think about the world—words like 'salience', 'emergence', 'affordance' that reflect the constantly shifting engagement between cognition and environment as things loom into focus, demand attention, fade, or are discarded as irrelevant. In fact, even the word 'between' in that last sentence can be misleading, since cognition is itself a feature of the environment. Humans live in a cognitive ecology.

Ecologies of the imagination

Speaking of human ecologies, here is another way of thinking about what literature does:

> There was an old man with a beard,
> Who said, 'It is just as I feared!—
> Two Owls and a Hen,
> Four Larks and a Wren,
> Have all built their nests in my beard.'[8]

This is a 'nonsense' rhyme in the sense that, if you ask what its propositional content is, you will draw a blank. There may have been an old man with a beard, but if so, Edward Lear isn't referring to him. No variety of bird is likely to be so bold as to attempt to make a nest in an old man's beard, and if one of them did try and succeed, it isn't possible, given the limits on the size and density of a human beard, that eight birds (some of them quite large) could do it at the same time. Yet the limerick is perfectly readable and imaginable (Lear illustrated some of his own limericks, including this one). One of the reasons for this is that it is recognizable, to readers who belong to a certain cultural community, as a limerick, a poetic instrument that affords witty or outlandish counterfactuals.[9] But other limericks might be a lot less readable. Here is one:

> There was an old man with a beard
> Who said, 'It is just as I feared.
> A mechanical swallow
> And the spaceship Apollo
> Have just lifted off from my beard.'

Lear's counterfactual scenario works because we immediately infer the ecological possibilities of a beard via the analogy of a bush, which is often applied to beards. The beard *lends itself* to bush-like uses, and once that cognitive bridge ('affordance') is available, one can easily cross it and begin to imagine what such an old man might be like, what his habits might be, what his bedroom or kitchen or garden shed might look like, for example, or the other things he might be liable to say. My alternative version doesn't work because there is no such bridge. One could say that this is an instance of invalid collocation, as when someone ignorant of standard usage in a given language uses a phrasing which is grammatically well formed but not in use: 'members of the communist party are not very thick on the floor in Kent'; 'that's an enormously sheer cliff'. This phenomenon will be discussed further in Chapters 4 and 6, but we can already put forward the suggestion that the whole literary archipelago[10] works in this way. It explores the outer reaches of plausible collocation and counterfactual conception, but what counts as 'plausible' is not (at least not always) decided by reference to a rigorous logic. It is decided by the biological functioning of evolved human cognition.

Lear's world of birds in a beard is also emblematic of literature as an imaginary ecology, an extended environment for readers, listeners, audiences, and passers-by (momentary perchers to inhabit). Later I shall speak of it as a multiple, nested ecology, more (perhaps) like a coral reef than a beard or an archipelago, combining intricate constraints with burgeoning freedoms and new possibilities. The philosopher J. L. Austin famously introduced into philosophy, and into the pragmatic study of language more generally, the notion of 'how to do things with words'. Lear's limerick shows one how to do things with imaginary things, shadowed by a strongly implied sense of how not to do them.

Recognizing life

> Books are not absolutely dead things, but doe contain a potencie of life in them to be as active as that soule was whose progeny they are; nay they do preserve as in a violl the purest efficacie and extraction of that living intellect that bred them.[11]

Let's paraphrase Milton's famous remark from the *Areopagitica*, adjusting it a little to suit the perspective of someone interested in the value and function of literature. Literature, one might say, is an instrument of human cognition, continuous with spoken language yet with a longer life-span and more sustainedly reflective. The agency of individual human thought acting through this instrument it has invented has a peculiar power: we recognize it as the product of a living creature. The old analogy between books and offspring ('my book is my baby') as reformulated by Milton still delivers the intuition of deep biological relation between thought and the body that makes it much more than a metaphor. Such statements, memorably encapsulated in

Milton's style, are capable of profoundly changing the cognitive environment of the reader: a conserved cultural insight comes alive again for a new generation, the work of culture mimicking at a vastly increased speed the work of phylogeny.

One of the reasons why Milton's formulation is so powerful is that 'not absolutely dead' is quite different from '(a)live', which sounds like a trite, worn-out metaphor. The concepts 'alive' and 'dead' have lost the compelling cognitive relevance of distinguishing between a live thing and a lifeless thing. Milton's phrase inhabits the disquieting zone between deadness and life, the zone that belongs to things that are uncanny or, to use Freud's telling word, *unheimlich*.

Something of that feeling leaps on you out of the undergrowth like a small but scary beast as you watch the puppeteer Stephen Mottram manipulate a handful of ping-pong balls. When there are only three, or four, nothing much happens, but when a fifth is added, coordinated just so with the others, a figure 'comes alive' as it crosses the threshold for the minimum number of features required to produce the effect of a live thing.[12] Cognitive psychologists talk about this threshold, too;[13] it seems to be deeply embedded in our response to the perceived world. Movement is clearly of the essence: there is a schematic outline, of course, but what really allows a particular feature of the environment to be identified as a living creature is the way its movement is articulated.

The problem is that recognition of life, despite its cognitive complexity, comes too naturally for us to be able to analyse it. It is an essential skill that organisms have acquired over billions of years, and are therefore extremely good at; it involves high-speed processing of large quantities of convergent data, matched against models that are partly acquired through experience from the earliest days of life, but must also be in part inherent in cognitive structure (birds do it, bees do it, even crustaceans in the seas do it). We know what it looks like, what it feels like, to make such and such a movement (to keep one's balance, for example); and because the world we share with birds and fish imposes the same constraints, and our bodies have a lot in common with their bodies, give or take a few feathers, fins, and gills, we can recognize the swooping, three-dimensional moves made by a bird or a bat, and the fluid movements (again in three dimensions) that fish make in order to engage with their environment. Essentially, I would suggest, it is that kind of skill of recognition that we use when we judge that a particular collocation 'works' in our native language, whereas another collocation, no less grammatical, sounds wrong or awkward; and of course, at the far end of that scale, it leads us (perhaps) to judge that Jane Austen's *Pride and Prejudice* 'comes to life', whereas P. D. James's would-be sequel *Death Comes to Pemberley* spectacularly doesn't. It's not a mysterious skill, just one that is very difficult to unpack.

One thing that it certainly relies on is the assumption of *agency*. The behaviour of a living creature, whether in motion or at rest, has a peculiar kind of directedness: its movements are the expression of an intention which may be more or less overt. Perceiving the intended movement or action of another living being is exactly what makes one see that it *is* a living being in the first place.[14]

This insight can be explored in a number of different directions. It justifies the reading of literature not as neutral text but as an animated affordance, an exquisite puppet show in which underspecification invites the spectator's cognitive faculties to supply what it takes to make the storyworld come alive. It justifies the whole set of critical moves that are opened up by the notion of kinesis, the mutual perception and interpretation of bodily posture and gesture. And it takes one—imperfectly, unreliably, but irresistibly—into the labyrinth of other people's minds, their beliefs, their feelings, their intentions, their promises, and their deceits, since we can't perceive others as being alive unless we can imagine that they have thought-worlds.

I return finally to Montaigne, who, like Milton, understood the life that resides in books. He wrote prolifically, but I need only quote a single phrase. Montaigne (again like Milton) was bilingual, having been brought up to speak, read, and write Latin as a native language,[15] and this phrase is written in Latin: 'Et versus digitos habet' ('A line of verse, too, has fingers').[16] It is borrowed in part from the Roman poet Juvenal, who wrote verse satires of contemporary life. In this poem, Juvenal is mocking the way Roman concubines use Greek terms of endearment to excite their ageing clients. The word I have translated as 'terms of endearment' here is simply 'vox' ('utterance, voice'), and it becomes the antecedent for a terse two-word sentence which uses a metaphor to make the sexual reference explicit: 'Digitos habet' ('it has fingers'): the effect flips from the auditory (Greek murmurings) to the haptic (fingers caressing). Montaigne inserts the phrase, broken off from the surrounding text of his essay, as if it were a straightforward quotation. But he has silently added a new subject, 'Et versus' ('a line of verse, too, [has fingers]'). It is now poetry's fingers that touch the reader erotically: Montaigne is conducting in this essay a close reading of sexual encounters in the poetry of Virgil and Lucretius.

The substitution is brilliantly imagined and calculated, not least because the analogy between fingers and lines of verse is cognitively grounded in both shape and function. It's not by accident that one of the metrical units of Greek and Latin poetry is the 'dactylic' or finger-shaped metre (one longer syllable or segment followed by two shorter ones). Fingers have been tapping out rhythms since before the beginning of recorded time; the sensorimotor conjunction of touch, rhythm, and sound (in drumming, for example) is also interactive, designed for transmission to other humans via their own motor perceptions and the neurological pathways that connect them to their cognitive apparatus as a whole. If you know Latin, and especially if, as most of Montaigne's readers were, you're familiar with Latin verse, you know in your fingerbones what Montaigne's reinvented line means, how it connects with the extraordinary lines of erotic Latin verse that Montaigne is exploring in his own haptic way.

Montaigne's sleight-of-hand is integral to the much-studied manoeuvre by means of which he links his intimate, first-hand knowledge of ancient poetry to a quasi-confessional account of his own sexuality and thence to a powerfully transmitted sense of the trajectory of his inwardly felt life from youthful arousal to reflective old age. You can speak of all this in thematic terms, or as an instance of Renaissance *imitatio* (imitation of the writers of Greek and Roman antiquity), but however you do it, your reading will be fed by the cognitive-somatic infrastructure, the sense in which Montaigne's essays as a whole are an act of extended cognition that is still astonishingly available for us to explore. Why do people continue to read them more than four hundred years after they were written (they seem especially popular in our own day)? Not because they contain certain kinds of knowledge, or philosophical wisdom, although there is no doubt a lot of that too, but because we infer from them the continually remade presence of a living, embodied mind.

In Chapter 3, we shall be looking at another poem where hands play a key role as a metaphor of extended cognition, where the haptic sense is foregrounded, and where the drum-taps of versified syllables make themselves communicatively felt. Meanwhile, it is enough to have shown by means of a single micro-example how literature, and writing about literature, can recognizably 'come to life'. Montaigne's Latin line offers us the enactive model of a critical intelligence rooted in our bodily experience of the world. Paraphrasing it somewhat, one is tempted to say that cognitively inflected criticism, too, might have fingers of its own.

2

Cognitive Conversations

Literary studies: a cognitive discipline

It's time now to set the agenda at a broader level. What, first of all, is implied by the phrase 'thinking with literature'? At its core is the anthropological assumption that 'literature' (in the broadest sense) is neither a sideshow nor a side-issue in human cultures. Whether one thinks of it as a practice or as an archive, literature is highly pervasive, robust, enduring, and pregnant with values. That is the case even if one believes that it is often trivial and at times pernicious. Most— perhaps all—of the tools devised by human cognition are fallible and susceptible to misuse, and that qualification is, notoriously, as valid for the natural and social sciences as for the arts. I suggest that, however one looks at it, literature is both an instrument and a vehicle of thought. The kind of thinking it affords may in some cases be close to philosophical, ethical, or political thought, but it is never reducible to those modes. Literature, characteristically, thinks in its own ways, and it follows that literary reading, together with the professionalized forms of literary study, should programmatically avoid any such reduction. Literature is a special *object* of thought and hence of knowledge.

Arguments of this kind have been made before,[1] of course, but they have been given a new force and a new turn in our own time by what I have called 'the cognitive conversation', that is to say the intermittently acrimonious but more often constructive and convergent dialogue that has gradually been established across a whole range of disciplines on the nature, functioning, and evolution of human cognition. In neuroscience, advances in research on brain function have been made possible by sophisticated new scanning techniques; cognitive psychologists are conducting experiments designed to clarify the ways in which we actually think (as opposed to the way we think we think), and reassessing the development of the imagination in childhood. Linguists are working with psychologists and philosophers on how to infer mental processes from human uses of language; philosophers in both the analytic and the continental traditions of philosophy are focusing on the problems posed by human cognition; and evolutionary anthropologists are addressing the question of how our cognitive capacities may have evolved from those of our primate ancestors. From these cross-disciplinary dialogues, a number of key strands are emerging: new ways of thinking about language as a cognitive instrument, a significantly different understanding of the relations between perception, affect, imagination, and the so-called higher-order rational functioning of the mind, and (thence) fresh approaches to the understanding of the mind–body problem.

The conversation has also spilled over into the public domain, attracting enormous attention and interest: hardly a day passes without some aspect of cognitive research being reported in the media. Many of these reports are no doubt superficial, inaccurate, over-hastily enthusiastic by academic standards, but it could hardly be otherwise: popular accounts of painstaking long-term research will always look flimsy to experts. The point is that they catch the public imagination, especially perhaps where they have medical implications. Cognitive deficits and their treatment have always played a role in the way human cognition has been understood, but in modern times they have become especially salient, whether one is thinking of autism spectrum disorders, dementia and Alzheimer's disease, or the investigation of accidental cases where a specific region of the brain has become compromised or disabled.

It's symptomatic of the complexity of this broad interdisciplinary field that the sense attributed to the words 'cognition' and 'cognitive' varies quite widely according to disciplinary context and even within methodologies specific to particular disciplines. In everyday parlance, they are associated above all with understanding and knowledge, in contradistinction not only to perception but also to affect and volition (desire), and this 'folk' sense is also common in philosophy and linguistics. After all, knowing, understanding, and believing, as mental states, appear to be qualitatively different from perceiving and feeling. More specifically, they are subject to evaluation as true: you can't

claim to know something unless you think it is true. No such test is
available for the feeling of anger or the pleasure (or otherwise) of
eating an oyster. However, most cognitivists nowadays give the word
'cognition' a much broader sense, embracing mental functioning and
mental processes as a whole. Those processes include abstract
and rational thought, imagination, emotion, and somatic reflexes
and responses. These are assumed to be connected and mutually
interactive processes. In other words, it is increasingly clear that
pure thought, as conceived of in logic and mathematics, is an abstraction from anything we experience in daily life, saturated as such
experience is with feeling, imagination, and deeply rooted physio-
logical resonances. The point here is not that there is no difference
between believing and feeling, or between understanding and pre-
conceptual apprehension of the world, but that any viable model of
human cognition will have to regard these domains as mutually
porous to a significant—often a critical—degree.

In that perspective, the study of literature appears as an essentially
cognitive discipline. Literature offers a virtually limitless archive of the
ways in which human beings think, how they imagine themselves and
their world. The documents in this archive are neither static nor
passive; they thrive on mutation. They are a product of the
powerful—though sometimes inscrutable—pressures of cultural evolution, while at the same time they are communicative, or, as we say
nowadays, interactive. They invite participation and provoke reciprocal acts of imaginative thought. They are also thoroughly
embodied, in ways that I shall be looking at more closely in the course
of this book. All language is grounded in the ecological context from
which our species emerged and which it has itself refashioned, but
whereas some forms of language strive to bootstrap themselves 'up'
towards abstraction, literary language and literary storyworlds are
saturated with somatic responses of all kinds, from rhyme and assonance and onomatopoeia via kinesic verbs to full-scale counterfactual
simulations such as 3D versions of science fiction and fantasy movies.

We return here to the claim that literature in the broad sense is the
most far-reaching and enduring vehicle and instrument of human
thought, the most revealing *product* and *symptom* of human cognition,
an outgrowth of one of the most fundamental of human cognitive
instruments, namely language itself. Such a claim entitles literary

specialists to join the cognitive conversation not only as learners, but as fully-fledged contributors. Philosophers and experimental psychologists might find the sheer irreducible tangle of the literary world hard to cope with, but, with the help of specialists who are thoroughly familiar with its topography, they might find that it offers a remarkable source of evidence for the ways in which we think. Meanwhile, within literary studies as an autonomous discipline, a cognitive approach should be capable of offering both a general explanatory framework for the phenomenon we call 'literature' and a set of tools for close reading of individual texts. This book seeks to show how those two perspectives might work together.

Bridging the cultures: literature and science

Given the potential richness of the cognitive conversation across disciplines, why is it that mainstream literary specialists are still reluctant to draw sustenance from it, still less contribute to it? The first wave of cognitive psychology and linguistics certainly made an impact in the later twentieth century on film studies and on media studies more generally, and literary studies have, with some delay, begun to follow suit: there are already many specialists in cognitive narratology, 'theory of mind' studies, conceptual blending studies, evolutionary criticism, simulation and embodiment studies, and the like, and their work is being increasingly noticed.[2] But cognitive methodologies and explanatory frameworks have not yet begun to inflect the common language of literary study; indeed, they often meet with resistance both from those who remain attached to traditional modes of literary history and criticism and from those who pursue variants of the literary theory that characterized the late twentieth-century scene.

One reason is that, in the last fifty years or so, literary study, and notably literary theory, has had a different interdisciplinary agenda, one that has drawn variously on Saussurean linguistics, Lévi-Strauss's structural anthropology, post-Freudian psychoanalysis, post-Marxist theory, post-Hegelian phenomenology, and related cultural strands. It has also become engaged in manifestly crucial concerns of our own day: the politics and ethics of gender and of the postcolonial era, for example. The emphasis has of course shifted, often dramatically, during this period, but many of the underlying habits of thought and points of reference have remained constant. Under those circumstances, anything approaching a reorientation of perspective, let alone a paradigm shift, is likely to be a slow process.

A more fundamental and widespread objection to cognitive methodologies for literary study arises from the belief that cognitive science can never account for the distinctive character of literary works, their unique ability to crystallize particular modes of thought, feeling, and experience; science is (as the saying goes) always already reductive.

A preliminary answer to this kind of objection has already been sketched out above: literary study is a mixed discipline; it lends itself very well to dialogue with other disciplines because its language and methodologies are for the most part not impenetrably technical. The current dialogue on questions of cognition that so vigorously flourishes across the interdisciplinary spectrum can already be thought of as a bridge linking what has notoriously been referred to as 'the two cultures': neuroscientists talk to experimental psychologists, who themselves talk to philosophers and linguists; all of them, from their different viewpoints, are capable of throwing light on the immensely complex object of study that we call human thought or human cognition and its products. It seems unreasonable to claim as a matter of principle that literary study has nothing to learn from or contribute to those discussions and debates.

No one, however, should think that the exercise is an easy one. One kind of difficulty is methodological. Experimentation in the sciences conforms to rigorous protocols of exact measurement, repeatability, verifiability, and statistical probability which require years of training, and which in any case may seem unsuitable for most kinds of literary research, where other protocols (historical, editorial, etc.) are in place. Yet some literary colleagues, with the help of colleagues in the relevant science, are now beginning to devise controlled experiments to investigate (for example) the way in which people read, or perceive dramatic action on the stage. The results of those experiments, as of all scientific experiments, need to be treated with caution, but they may eventually lead to unexpected insights that could make a significant impact on mainstream criticism. Let's wait and see: the jury is out, and it might be a while before they come back in.

Meanwhile, those looking for new openings for literary study are more likely to borrow broad innovative concepts or insights from the physical and experimental sciences, especially perhaps those that cross over into the public domain. It is in part the sustained media interest in cognitive science, whether neurological or psychological, that has created a climate in which 'breakthroughs' look temptingly available for transference to other contexts. In essence, that is the approach that I adopt in this book. But one can only adopt it if one acknowledges that this less 'technical' mode of transfer risks becoming a kind of pirate raid in which one grabs some interesting-sounding ideas and carries them off for consumption on home territory.

One of the most widely discussed of these ideas is the notion of 'mirror neurons' or motor resonance. Another is what is variously called 'theory of mind' or 'mind-reading', the attribution of mental states to others. The two are indeed connected: the ability to read other 'minds' certainly passes through the body (gesture, eye contact or gaze direction, and of course oral utterance), and the fact that our bodies resonate *physically* with other bodies, real or imagined, may well be one of the phylogenetic precursors for the more complex interpersonal dealings from which human culture arises. Although both these areas remain highly controversial, no one doubts that recent neuroscience has made such cognitive processes salient: one may argue over terminology and its conceptual consequences, but the phenomena remain there to be explained. Their importance for the fine grain of literary expression is already beginning to be demonstrated by informed literary critics. In this way, new perspectives may be opened up, or new ways of handling old problems; the phrase 'making salient', which itself implies a cognitive perspective, affords a way, precisely, of thinking about such things. Equally, scientific experiment can exclude some possibilities, or at least undermine common beliefs, for example about the reliability of our reasoning or decision-making processes.

More broadly, the concern with cultural particularity that literary specialists profess needs to make allowance for the neurological, biological, and ecological constraints within which culture operates. We come here to a fundamental issue. There is a sense in which science attempts to establish, or at least strains towards, truths that are permanent, atemporal, universal. In cognitive neuroscience and psychology, the aim is to uncover the architecture and functioning of the brain and thus show how the mind works, how humans think, how animals, babies, and children think, and so on. Literary specialists worry about the essentialism or 'innatism' those aims seem to imply; most of the materials we work with belong to a cultural order, and culture is conspicuously relative to particular groups and societies. We are, with good reason, wary of universalist claims, which are readily translated in our field into the currency of cultural hierarchies and elites, gender bias or ethnic prejudice. So a more robust argument is needed if we are to construct a firm grounding for moves across and along those interdisciplinary frontiers. Let's now try to see what such an argument would look like.

The first move is, from the outset, to stop thinking in terms of frontiers, dividing lines, oppositions. 'Nature' and 'culture' are only in a very limited (although certainly at times useful) sense opposites. If life on this planet is 'only', in the end, a rather peculiar and transitory chemical froth generated by the long-term physics of the universe, then 'culture' is merely a secondary, although admittedly exuberant, froth produced by one in particular of the planet's temporary life-forms. Culture is a function of nature; birds' nests and beehives and the social habits of primates are what those creatures do, extensions of their 'nature'. In that sense, a bird's nest is not very different from the shell of a mollusc. When humans began to make clothing for them-selves, they took the model of skin and body hair and made it more flexible, so that it became possible for them to move across sharp temperature gradients; their quaintly complex language is an exotic avatar of birdsong and the calls of primates, extended and multiplied with a breathtaking improvisatory freedom. The evolved architecture of the human brain is no doubt impressive, but it is impressive as much in what it lends itself to as in what it is or does. It lends itself, among other things, to intensive development in the extended years of human childhood and to further development thereafter. 'Development' here means structural development—changes in the brain itself—as well as in the materials it stores and recycles (the 'storing' of materials just is a change in the material brain). There is an important distinction, of course, between that which can be transmitted to the next generation genetically and that which relies on lifetime learning processes. Even there, however, creatures can only learn what they are genetically equipped to learn, and there are certainly long-term feedback pro-cesses at work that erode that apparently simple opposition: the learning of language and its relation to the inherited brain architectures that make it possible is still a highly problematic question, but no one thinks that language is either *wholly* innate or *wholly* acquired.

This perspective, which stresses the mutual porosity of the concepts nature and culture, may usefully be supplemented by another, designed to take account of the cultural and historical uniqueness of literary artefacts. An anthropological view of literature as a product of human cognition would need to work on a series of different time-scales. The longest is that of human evolution itself (say two or three million years at least), the slow incrementation of changes that took place in the hominin body structure and brain architecture. Much shorter in comparison with this evolution, but still very long in comparison with the time-scales that literary specialists normally deal in, is the period that began with the rise of complex cultural practices and syntactical language, and thus, one may assume, early forms of story-telling and 'poetry' (probably in the form of sung or chanted language). The date-range for those developments is still very uncertain: it might be as early as 200,000 years ago, but many people think that something like 120,000 years is probably a better guess. Subsequently, changes continued to be slow by our standards, perhaps because of environmental constraints. Human cognition only began seriously to flex its muscles after the last Ice Age, that is to say around 10,000 years ago, with the emergence of agriculture, making possible the development of cities and other large-scale forms of social organization.

That familiar story is the story of an evolution enormously accelerated by the intervention of culture. The word 'culture' is meant here in the broadest sense, including all kinds of implements and artefacts conceived and constructed by humans. Cultural improvisation and innovation in that sense enabled modern humans better to exploit their environment, to thrive in larger and larger communities, and thus not only to survive but also to sweep across the habitable earth, adapting themselves and their environment as they went. Even after the ice retreated, however, many thousands of years passed before writing systems developed to the point where recorded history began, bringing with it the first 'literary' texts which were able to survive without relying on human memory. The recording, archiving, and amassing of cultural capital that becomes possible at that stage inaugurates the era we recognize as ours, with its accelerated cultural mutation and diversification, its new technologies of conservation (memory) and circulation.

The point of evoking these different time-scales is to show that a simple opposition between 'universal' cognitive resources and 'local', highly differentiated cultural resources is liable to foreshorten and falsify the picture. What we are dealing with here is more like a single set of overlapping processes. The hominin brain has certainly evolved through feedback from techno-cultural activities (tool-making, for example), and, conversely, culturally acquired skills draw on the evolved flexibility of the human brain, its cognitive fluidity.

In methodological terms, this perspective would encourage on the one hand an 'upstream' approach, positing plausible 'prototypes' of story-lines, storyworlds, or poetic modes: a good deal of work of this kind is already being done.[3] The 'downstream' approach that is its corollary is more daunting: one would need to show how different speeds of change intersect in a single work, and thus to trace in that work the dynamics of cognition in time. The result, even if provisional, might help to display what one might call the specific cognitive positioning of the work as a unique artefact, its place in a network of historical and cultural coordinates—history and culture being themselves, once again, a function of cognitive capacities and constraints. Cultural improvisation is the evolutionary niche peculiar to humans, and the traces it leaves behind—the very signature of human cognition trying to overreach itself—are nowhere more visible than in the intricate folds and ramifications of literary artefacts.

If literary works are to be read in that perspective as the signature of cognition in action, their hallmark—an intrinsic *connectedness*—needs to be preserved. Their delicate yet wonderfully efficient organization depends on endless transactions between understanding and affect, motor response and conceptualization, large-scale ethical, social, or political vectors, and minute, barely perceptible inflections of sound and sense. In other disciplines, those connections, where they exist, are liable to be undone in the interests of a universal taxonomy or a logic of abstraction; if they are then put together again, it's likely that they will look suspiciously tidy and above all predictable. Literary specialists live with the unpredictable, the one-off, the irreducible tangle, or perhaps rather with that higher-order tangle that we call art. It follows that they should uphold the value of the distinctive ways of reading that literature requires.

Literary study is not an *exact* science, and is not likely to become one in the foreseeable future. Yet it aims at precision, whether in its way of accounting for the detail of literary works, in its procedures for establishing those texts as objects of understanding, or in its recourse to historical and cultural contexts of all kinds. It aims at rigour of argument based on verifiable textual and other evidence, and if its arguments are probabilistic rather than apodeictic, that feature distinguishes it only in relative terms from the procedures of other disciplines. Finally, it has recourse to general explanatory frameworks which may be implicit or highly explicit (literary theory), but which are always situated in a relation to prevailing cultural and academic concerns. It belongs, in other words, to history, and must necessarily be conscious of that history, just as it is conscious of the intrinsically historical character of the artefacts that it examines. In that sense, too, and it is one of the most important, a properly constituted cognitive approach to literature should insist on its histories, from the history of our own times via the longer history of written language to prehistory and the vast, fragmentary narrative of evolution.

Reflective and pre-reflective cognition

Literary criticism (as distinct from literary history and its avatars) has always inhabited a niche between intuitive and reflective response. There are many good readers who are not academics, so academic critics have to argue that their explanatory frameworks, theories, and formal protocols, their poetics and their rhetorics, add value to the individual experience of reading. Which is of course not the same as saying that their specialist tools and skills need to be subordinate to, or even consonant with, that experience. Counter-intuitive reading is as important to literary criticism as counter-intuitive hypotheses are to science.

This question invites a brief excursion into a key aspect of cognitive science which will resurface more than once in the chapters that follow. It is a fundamental assumption of research in this field that cognition is for the most part a high-speed process (the speed is measurable in micro-seconds). It moves so swiftly that the individual agent is unaware of its functioning unless problems are encountered, much as you take your breathing for granted unless you run a marathon or have a chest infection. This mode of thought is adapted above all to the kind of rapid decisions that all living creatures with evolved nervous systems need to make on the hoof: if you stop to think, the creature behind you with sharp teeth and powerful jaws will have your back leg off. Of course errors are made, but provided that there are fewer errors than successes, the species will survive. Humans use the same high-speed mode in most forms of physical activity, in everyday communication, including reading, and in many interpretative and decision-making processes. That language 'works' at all is astonishing when one begins to ask what kind of cognitive processes might make it possible; the virtuoso acrobatics performed by skilled simultaneous interpreters is comparable in many respects to the complex sensorimotor calculations (not to mention mind-reading inferences) that have to be presupposed when two outstanding tennis-players are engaged in combat.

The speed is reduced progressively, however, as obstacles or unforeseen situations are encountered. At a certain point which is hard to locate precisely, cognition moves from unreflective or pre-reflective to reflective.[4] It's easy but false to regard this opposition as an antithesis and to assume that it can be mapped directly onto other oppositions such as mind/body or human brain/animal brain.[5] The human brain evolved from an animal brain and is deeply connected with it. Over evolutionary time, human reflective capacity must have emerged *progressively* from a brain that operated unreflectively (or indeed pre-reflectively): human thinking isn't another completely different type of thinking pasted onto an old, outdated model, but an outgrowth that endows the older model with greater scope and flexibility. All its operations, arguably, are 'mixed', open for permutations of interconnection which are at once limitless and constrained. And there is clearly constant feedback, from earliest infancy, between the pre-reflective and the reflective. Reflective procedures which have been rehearsed sufficiently often become pre-reflective, as in second-language learning, while even cognitive experiences that occur only once (an encounter with a school bully, an embarrassingly disastrous interview for a job) may, if highly salient, become a grounding for future pre-reflective response.

In Chapters 3 and 8 I shall refer to the opening sentence of Joseph Conrad's *Lord Jim*, which brilliantly anticipates Jim's whole story in a single imagined encounter. We can take a first look at it now:

> He was an inch, perhaps two, under six feet, powerfully built, and he advanced straight at you with a slight stoop of the shoulders, head forward, and a fixed-from-under stare which made you think of a charging bull.[6]

Well, think of a charging bull. When you register visually the animal's posture and the direction of its charge, how soon do you make it hotfoot for the nearest bull-proof exit? Pretty soon. By then, an interpretation of sorts must have automatically happened, and one can assume that any non-human animal in a similar situation would have no less effectively 'read' the predator. Humans do more than that, however, and this character is a human, not a bull. Conrad's readers won't stop when they've extracted immediately useful information from the stoop and the stare; they will begin to predict where such a posture might come from, what its implied story is, was, will be (past in the narrative fiction, future in the telling of the story). Yet despite those proliferating supplements, there is a perceivable continuity, an indivisible gradient between bodily response and cognitive analysis. Reflective cognitive response *emerges* visibly in this sentence (and the novel) from an instinctive, unreflective mode of apprehension.

A cognitive reading of literary texts, then, would seek to uncover the hidden work of rapid inferencing and on-the-wing construction of meaning that makes it possible for an experienced reader to make sense of even the elaborate prose of Proust, Henry James, or Thomas Mann without stopping to reflect (although stopping to reflect is also part of the reading process). At times, the result might seem self-evident. We knew that that was what we were thinking, didn't we? That effect is a sign that we're on the right track: good literary criticism is often the art of coming at the self-evident from an unexpected angle. But of course the precise choice of angle is essential here, just as, in the defamiliarization effect that twentieth-century critics so often drew attention to (it was in fact one of the great enduring insights of that period), you have to defamiliarize in exactly the right way if you want the trace of a half-effaced meaning or image to blaze out again like the colours of a restored painting.

Counter-intuitive readings would of course remain central to such a literary agenda: we need to question assumptions, experiment with apparently implausible angles and perspectives, whether they are derived from literary theory or from cognitive science. The aim would be to connect the intuitive and the counter-intuitive modes, as they are connected in our own cognitive processes, rather than to separate them antagonistically.

The reflective calibration of frames that are both consonant with cognitive research and well adjusted to the character of a particular work is no easy matter, however, and if some of the early ventures into cognitive criticism looked reductive, that is because some hypotheses of scientific origin were too swiftly seized on as skeleton keys that will unlock all kinds of doors. The skeleton, in this domain, is just the beginning: think of the fossil record and of the work needed to construct from it a half-way reliable narrative of evolution. The difficulty is at times sufficient to make one despair; yet without the fascination of what's difficult, no enterprise, least of all literary criticism, is worth much.

A model of communication

Literature is made of language, and although literary study doesn't need to be supported by a complete theory of language, it does need a conception of the kind of thing language is, and broadly of how it operates. Of the options currently on offer, the one I regard as clearly the most promising for literary critical practice, although perhaps the least often cited by cognitivists in the literary domain, is relevance theory, also known as cognitive pragmatics. Relevance theory, which drew its initial inspiration from the work of Paul Grice on the 'logic of conversation', was developed by Deirdre Wilson and Dan Sperber (their founding study dates from 1986) and is still being elaborated, extended, and modified by them and their colleagues (notably Robyn Carston).

It is essentially a model of communication, seeking to show how language is offered by a speaker as evidence of intentions, beliefs, imaginings, states of mind and body, sometimes whole thought-worlds, in the expectation that that evidence will evoke analogous forms of thought in the interlocutor and thus modify his[7] cognitive environment.[8] The evidence is always partial, and depends on the assumption of a 'mutually manifest context', where 'context' refers to the cognitive resources (knowledge, cultural habits, etc.) available to both speakers. Those contexts will never match perfectly, but their working adjustment makes it possible for the speaker to assume that the interlocutor will successfully infer an optimally relevant meaning from her utterance.

Sperber and Wilson encapsulate the notion of optimal relevance in the following double principle:[9]

1. The ostensive stimulus is relevant enough for it to be worth the addressee's effort to process it.
2. The ostensive stimulus is the most relevant one compatible with the communicator's abilities and preferences.

The principle of relevance, according to Sperber and Wilson, replaces all of the 'maxims' that, according to Paul Grice, are required to realize the 'cooperative principle' of effective communication.[10]

Seen in this perspective, all uses of language are highly under-specified: speakers rely on a continuous inferential calculus on the part of the interlocutor. Every time we hear or read an utterance, we unconsciously and unhesitatingly[11] draw an enormous number of inferences that allow us to project ourselves into the mind of the speaker, to fill out the sketch she has provided, and to make it into something we can understand and imagine: Robyn Carston speaks of 'the teeming underworld of human cognitive processing'.[12] This is as true of literary works as it is of everyday language, and often even more so. The thought-world of a novel and its characters is never spelt out in full in the text: we are given clues from which we infer a whole series of other characteristics, properties, and implied physical and mental events. The thought-world of a poem has a different dynamic, but in cognitive terms it operates in the same way.

The application of relevance theory to literary texts throws up interesting (and unresolved) questions, for example on what it is that literature may be said to communicate. In principle, however, since literature is composed of utterances, it must operate by the laws that apply across all language use; it might at most be thought to have some special protocols of its own within that domain. What the relevance theory view of language has to offer is, first, that it is capable of providing a model of agency and intention that is viable for acts of literary expression without falling back into naive assumptions about either. Secondly, it insists on the mobility and fluidity of mental processes, the extraordinary rapidity of the inferential calculus that accompanies every utterance and every act of understanding and that renders such activities for the most part invisible and unconscious. Literary reading and literary criticism (indeed, one might say, literature itself) might then take on the task of slowing them down to the point at which they begin to emerge into the domain of conscious knowledge. Thirdly, relevance theory vigorously counters the view that language is *exclusively* a code consisting of fixed conventions. It is of course partly coded, but the coded elements are only a springboard for the limitless possibilities of nuanced expression that may be realized as speaker and interlocutor mutually exploit their respective mental resources and potential imaginings. 'Human conceptual resources', as Robyn Carston (again) puts it, 'far outstrip the meanings encoded in linguistic systems.'[13]

What emerges then is a way of imagining language as both *light*—like an instrument or weapon that is easy to carry and deploy—and *porous*, full of spaces waiting to be filled. It's an ingeniously complex scaffolding that allows one to reach places one otherwise couldn't reach by devising new ad hoc poles or ladders and then, in the end, performing acrobatic leaps, or requiring one's interlocutor to perform them.

Fundamental to this view of language and cognition is 'theory of mind', or mind-reading, which will be further explored later (see especially Chapters 7 and 8) in the context of detailed dramatic and narrative examples. Arising from psychological studies of autistic children and adults, and taken up not only by experimental and developmental psychologists but also by linguists, by anthropologists working on cognition in an evolutionary perspective and by philosophers, mind-reading has become a major topic in the study of narrative fiction, where Lisa Zunshine is its best-known exponent.[14]

For relevance theorists, the concept seeks to capture the way that speakers and interlocutors need in some sense to read each other's mind in order to achieve the high-speed communication you see happening in everyday conversation.[15] It denotes not some elaborate conceptual construction, but a pragmatic assumption that each participant in a dialogue has a mind like the other; that each strives as far as possible to imagine the extent to which the contexts referred to may or may not be common to both; and that each attempts to infer the most plausible or relevant intention of the speaker ('What's she on about?'). It is a way of matching or harmonizing cognitive perspectives, and is certainly involved in complex responses of the kind we refer to as empathy.

Mind-reading may in practice often be imperfect, or dangerously misleading, or comically inappropriate, but that doesn't stop us doing it with a reasonable degree of confidence. It seems that some animals engage in mind-reading of a kind; but only humans are able to handle several levels of embedded intentionality. For example, I can say: 'I know what she's thinking'; 'she believes that I know what she's thinking'; 'I think it's unlikely that she believes that I know what she's thinking'; and so on, although most people lose the plot after the fourth or fifth level.

In literary contexts, mind-reading operates between readers and authors, between readers (or audiences) and characters in fiction, and between the characters themselves. We need to remember here that it is deeply linked to underspecification: the reason that some fictional characters seem 'alive' is that the narrative affords precisely those limited but suggestive indications about the character and his or her behaviour—the five essential ping-pong balls—that would allow us, in the case of a real person, to infer their cognitive profile and anticipate their likely utterances or actions.

The language of literature, and above all of poetry, makes the connection between these perspectives especially salient. Its bold and highly precise modes of underspecification act like a prompt or a trampoline, creating unlimited possibilities for imaginative leaps into the blue—or into the minds of others. To show that, all you have to do is compare a haiku with the large-scale poetic and fictional structure elaborated by Dante, who reads the minds of tormented souls, virtuous pagans, beatified figures from his contemporary world, angels, and God himself. It's important to emphasize once again here that mind-reading is never unproblematic, that at best it's a probabilistic exercise, and that it often goes disastrously wrong. Everyone knows that from their everyday experience of partners, families, friends, and social or business environments. In fiction, the scope of those disasters is commonly expanded, tested to the limit. Many fictions, indeed, and by no means only modernist ones, seem designed to show that knowing other people is tragically impossible. Yet its possibility remains one of the foundations of human communication and society.

Modes of embodied cognition

Relevance theory, however, expressly offers a model of linguistic communication, and it has had little to say hitherto about what in other cognitivist domains, including the literary, is known generally as 'embodiment'. Conceptual content may, for relevance theorists, be accompanied by perlocutionary effects (effects not intended, or not expressly intended, by the speaker, including accidental ones), but these are considered to be side-effects, emotional or sensory 'noise'.[16] Rationalist approaches such as these belong, in the most approximate general sense, to what are known as 'first-generation' cognitivist studies, in which the human mind was assumed to be a thinking machine, on the analogy of a computer. Current 'second-generation' approaches insist, as I have done from the outset in this study, on the continuity between body and mind. This conception of embodied mind takes various forms. Some focus on the relation between reason and emotion.[17] Some emphasize the extension of mind out through the body into the world, the constant interaction and feedback between mind and its bodily instruments, and thence between the embodied mind and the environment (extended or distributed cognition).[18] This dynamic relation is often said to be 'enactive', that is to say that perception and cognition, rather than being defined as independent powers of the mind operating on the world, are entirely defined by their active and constantly updated engagement with the world.[19] Embodied mind, in such a view, is pre-eminently *performance*. It is not hard to see why these terms might be of value in the study of literature, whether narrative or dramatic; I speak of them most explicitly in Chapter 4 via the closely related theme of 'affordances', but they often appear elsewhere.

I prefer to focus here on another key term of reference for this book. Kinesis, or motor resonance, is defined and illustrated at some length in Chapter 3, since it seemed to me appropriate that it should arise from a context in which the imagination of movement is at once brilliantly realized and highly focused in the space of a few words. In Yeats's quatrain, as in Conrad's opening sentence, Stephen Mottram's puppet show, or Montaigne's reading of erotic verse, a miniature scene comes to life. It does so, the kinesic approach argues, because the 'imagination of movement' is not some symbolic or figurative effect, operating reflectively: it is a faint but distinct echo in the reader's own motor response system of what it takes in sensori-motor terms to perform a highly specific gesture. The kinesic effect has been eloquently explained, described, and amply illustrated by Guillemette Bolens in a study which was seminal for my own work, and readers are referred for a more detailed account to that study.[20] For the moment I would simply say that, once one begins to notice such effects in literature and indeed elsewhere, the experience of reading becomes subtly different: kinesic reading brings to the surface something you always already felt when you read the text properly, but somehow ignored for the sake of supposedly 'higher', more intellectual or aesthetic pleasures. Or perhaps one should say that one is here precisely in the realm of the aesthetic as it should be understood: for the Greeks, *aisthesis* just is sensory perception.[21]

It goes without saying, however, that kinesis, even where it is intelligently deployed as an instrument of literary criticism, needs to be integrated into a whole suite of other procedures. It needs to be connected, for example, to different kinds of perceptual representation: much literary mimesis is in fact not saliently kinesic, which doesn't mean that it is ineffectual. Above all, kinesis should be understood as playing a fundamental role in mind-reading, in the broadest sense of that term. It can even be argued that kinesis and mind-reading are different aspects of the same process. Motor resonance is an ancient adaptive breakthrough, allowing vulnerable individual creatures to respond rapidly to critical movements made by others of their kind, or to move faster than potential predators or prey. From the swarming of fish and bees via the flocking of starlings to the behaviour of crowds at sports events, motor resonance has to be presupposed to explain the extraordinary capacity of large groups of living things for entrainment (automatic synchronization).[22] On the platform provided by that profoundly conserved adaptive function, more complex animal brains have evolved a wide range of more flexible skills—the ability to hunt in packs, the formation of familial and social groups, the refinements that become possible with vocal communication. When you try to guess someone's intentions, or their mental habit, or their social attitude, from their posture and gesture, motor resonance will always be there, a slight but distinct sensation that allows you to feel something like what it is to be that person, where they're coming from; their very language may have 'fingers', too, touching you in unexpected places. You put all that together with other information, maybe prolonging the analysis by means of conscious reflection, either silently, on your own, or in dialogue with others. However you do it, you're not in fact reading abstractly remote 'minds': what you read is bodies, together with all of the elusive, often hidden, thinking that human bodies do.

One of the things that thinking human bodies do, if this whole process works, is feel empathy. Empathy can be mutual or unrequited; it can be erroneous or misplaced; it can be deficient as the result of brain damage, inherited dysfunction, or social deprivation. Yet it is always potentially there as part of the 'normal' equipment of human response, from babyhood onwards. And it hardly needs to be said that it is empathy that allows us to engage so deeply in the lives of fictional characters, and indeed to bring them to life in the first place. It is a precondition of immersion in stories and songs and poems, and not least, of course, in the mimesis of drama. If motor resonance and mind-reading, considered as a single suite of responses, are what affords empathy, then we can hardly speak of the way literature works for us without bringing those responses back to the reflective surface.

The twin functioning of kinesis and mind-reading is, as I see it, the best possible evidence for one of the principal arguments I want to propose in this chapter. Any notion of a radical cleavage between unconscious and conscious (pre-reflective and reflective) mental functioning runs counter to the fundamental premise of embodied cognition, namely that all cognitive processes operate on a gradient between sensorimotor perceptions and responses on the one hand and so-called higher-order conceptual activities on the other. This gradient should therefore not be regarded as a mediation between two antithetical poles (mind and body), with some problematic 'mixed' area in between, but as mixed along its whole axis, with no radical breaks. The human mind evolved out of the animal mind, and is not simply a function of specialized brain areas with corresponding mental functions.[23]

Towards a cognitive criticism

This survey of some of the topics of cognitive research and their possible relevance to literary study should give a foretaste of the models one might draw on in these and related areas. The topics I have sketched are designed to exhibit a family resemblance, and above all a mutual compatibility, which allows one to hope that a more comprehensive synthesis might eventually be possible, give or take a few local lines drawn in the sand. An unstable synthesis, of course, not a doxa: this interdisciplinary field is moving fast, and anyone who is not willing to move with it is liable to be left high and dry with a handful of desiccated mirror neurons.

Before embarking on case studies and further cognitive topics, I want to insist on a fundamental principle: the best literary criticism has always been in some sense a pragmatics, and a valid cognitive methodology must draw on the skills that the best literary critics already have. The reason for that is simple. As an object of knowledge, literature—and I again use the word here to include all forms of fiction, story-telling, poetry, song, drama, essay-writing—demands those skills. I return here to a point made earlier: literature is by its nature cognitively mixed. It refuses to separate thought from emotion, bodily responses from ethical reflection, perception from imagination, and logic from desire. And everything suggests that, in that sense, it does what the mind does: as Mark Turner famously put it, the literary mind just is the human mind.[24] At the same time, literature can never be reduced to a phylogenetic archetype. It demonstrates the essential fluidity and mobility of human cognition, its adaptive inventiveness. Literature can therefore provide a prolific and wide-ranging set of test-cases for pragmatic cognitive enquiry. For mainstream literary specialists and readers, however, what is likely to matter most in the end is the openings offered by cognitively inflected reading. That is where the possibilities of thinking with literature will, I believe, have their furthest reach, and it is to a first example of close cognitive reading that I now turn.

3

The Balloon of the Mind

A micro-example: the balloon and the shed

> Hands, do what you're bid:
> Bring the balloon of the mind
> That bellies and drags in the wind
> Into its narrow shed.[1]

W. B. Yeats, *The Balloon of the Mind*

I would guess that an experienced reader would require no more than about thirty seconds to read this tiny poem and arrive at a first view of what it's about (what its 'propositional content' is). Yeats has after all done most of the work for us by making the phrase 'the balloon of the mind' salient in advance as a title. It glosses the principal image of the poem and thus sharply constrains the way it can be read. The consequence is that one will infer an emergent allegorical proposition which in the event remains incomplete (underspecified), since it invites a further inferential move: if the balloon is the mind, what is the shed into which it is to be pulled? The symmetry of the logical form strictly limits the number of possible answers: what kind of a shed might be relevant to, appropriate for, a mind-balloon? It might be reason ('the narrow shed of reason') or some other controlling cognitive instance. But when a poet speaks of 'hands' and directs them to do what they're bid, one is likely to think of the activity of writing a poem, and this will pre-empt ('prime')[2] the way we gloss the 'narrow shed'. Since this poem is a single quatrain, a distinctly cramped space into which to fit the ballooning thoughts that poets are reputed to have, the inferential equation is likely to be completed accordingly. The poem evokes the struggle to contain the imagination within a tight poetic form.

I have of course slipped in some further inferences here, without specifying them, for the sake of economy (I have substituted 'imagination' for 'mind', for example). For the same reason, I have also omitted some possibilities that seem to fail on closer scrutiny. If the shed had been a skull, one would have expected 'brain' instead of 'mind', and the conception of a balloon-like brain being somehow manhandled into a skull is in any case too grotesque for a poem that provides no other evidence for such a reading (if the poet had been a famous brain surgeon, of course, the calculus of inferential probabilities would have been quite different).

In cognitive terms, the interpretative procedures I have used are entirely standard. They exploit the cognitive resources you draw on when someone you are speaking to is slow to find the right word or words to finish a sentence and you finish it for her. Which in turn are the resources you use whenever you hear or read a sentence: you begin immediately to guess where it is going and progressively confirm or drop possibilities as new evidence comes up. In order to do this at all, you have to assume that someone (in this case, 'the poet', who happened to be called William Butler Yeats and was not known to be a neurosurgeon) is communicating with you, directing you with some precision, in his very underspecification, towards a particular conception—what the poem is about. In other words, the inferential calculus you perform is unavoidably dependent on an assumption about the poet's intentions, or the poem's directedness of meaning, which amounts to the same thing.

It's important to emphasize that underspecification is not a local phenomenon, although it may feature more or less prominently (Yeats's poem, like a haiku or an epigram, is strongly or saliently underspecified). It is a universal condition of all language use, except perhaps in telephone directories and the like. It is literally not possible to 'spell everything out' in words,[3] and most language users know better than to try (the risk being of course that their interlocutors will rapidly become bored and stop listening). One can be fairly certain that Yeats doesn't tell us how to gloss the shed, or the hands, because (a) it's easy to find appropriate glosses, (b) it's more interesting and entertaining for the reader, as it stimulates cognitive response, and (c) it generates a richer spectrum of implicatures. This last term belongs to the vocabulary of relevance theory, where it refers to the intended meanings that can be derived inferentially from a given utterance ('implications', by contrast, are not necessarily intended); I shall come back to the term in Chapter 6, but I want to introduce it here, in the context of a close reading, in order to induce a small but crucial shift in interpretative habits from a notion of readerly autonomy towards the more interestingly constrained perspective of an intentional calculus.[4]

That authorial gloss pointing us towards 'the mind' encourages, appropriately enough, a conceptual outcome. Concepts are the speciality of human cognition (the human 'mind'), whether one thinks of them as mental events with a neurological underpinning that is still little understood, as linguistic phenomena (sounds or written signs), or as tools for handling a complex environment. What this poem is 'about' in that perspective is the performance of a cognitively difficult operation.

It might even be plausibly argued that the cognitively 'upward' movement towards abstraction is given further lift by the slightly bizarre character of the central image. When have you ever seen anyone trying to get an inflated balloon into a narrow shed? One of the most ancient strategies of interpretation when faced with an 'obscure' or refractory image is to assume that it is *designed* to elicit a conceptual response (an allegorical reading).[5] Twentieth-century poetics recasts this move as a mode of defamiliarization: something in a poem that blocks what at first looks like a commonplace sequence forces the reader to reread at another level, which is likely to be more rather than less conceptual.[6]

Let's now focus more closely on the word the poem opens with: 'Hands'. One could inferentially say that this word, placed so saliently, makes tangible the *difficulty* of writing poetry (what Yeats elsewhere calls 'the fascination of what's difficult'). Hands are a kind of metaphor (a metonym, perhaps) for the effort of controlling the balloon-like imagination through poetic form. In that sense, the word would point towards the upward-going, conceptual trajectory. Yet it does so in a way that presents poetry-writing as a craft, an artisanal activity: the apostrophe 'Hands, do what you're bid' cannot help reminding you, before you even arrive at the conceptual gloss, of the hands that write and of the hands that perform rougher, more physical tasks.[7] In other words, it makes the difficulty *tangible*.[8]

Once one takes that second path, towards the implicatures of the metaphor itself, a lot of things change. Of course, all competent readers of poetry would in any case speak of the 'imagery' of the poem, of the swollen balloon (carrying strong implicatures of colour) and the dour shed. My experience is that many insist, in fact, that the scene evoked here is primarily visual. Perceptual processing varies a good deal from one person to another: we all know that some people 'visualize' more strongly than others, while others have a finer acoustic or olfactory sense. But the visual, for humans, always has priority: sight has traditionally been thought of as the noblest sense, because it provides rich, panoramic information about the environment, and therefore lends itself most readily to conceptual activities such as the grasping (or recognizing) of categories. Smell and touch, by contrast, are widely thought of as 'animal' senses, better developed in non-human animals because their interface with the world is more directly localized.

If we start again, however, and suppress the habit of thinking of images as 'pictures in the mind', what emerges above all is the haptic character of the scene that Yeats stages for us: the feel of the balloon, the pull on the ropes, the sheer implied awkwardness or friction of the encounter. Take the apparently neutral word 'bring' with which the encounter begins. It belongs to a category of verbs that deliver the sense of a directed movement as perceived from a particular angle (point of arrival or departure):

> When you come to visit, bring a pair of warm shoes.
> Take the shoes with you when you go to visit Aunt Rose.

Such verbs often use prepositions (or prepositional inflections, or verbal aspect in some languages) to further define the direction: English phrasal verbs provide some striking examples. In Yeats's poem, the dynamic trajectory of the encounter is determined by 'bring ... into', which thereby also excludes a whole series of possible readings. 'Bring into' implies that the shed is in some sense the balloon's proper destination, and this implicature is confirmed by the possessive 'its'. If, at one level (the conceptual), the balloon belongs to the mind, at another the shed belongs to, is the right receptacle for, the balloon. Only a particular kind of balloon can be *brought into* a shed: this cannot be a party balloon, for example. The shed emerges as something like a hangar for aircraft rather than a place to keep garden equipment. Other implicatures here have to do, again, with artisanal work: think of examples such as 'bring the two surfaces into line with one another'.

As I've already suggested, however, the sensorimotor directedness of this trajectory is of course disturbed by the intervening reference to the way the balloon itself resists the effort to bring it in. The haptic character of the encounter resides specifically in the tension between the effort to get the damn balloon into the shed and its wilful resistance, its 'drag'. Let's note in passing that the drag is a function of air pressure: captured air, like the air pressure we call wind, is a truculent, often unmanageable force. The scene, at all events, is felt within the muscles of the body and across its skin surfaces, not least because the balloon too has a body (it 'bellies') and a strongly implied skin surface.

For the reader, these somatic notations are *kinesic*. Kinesis is the transmission (usually from one body to another) of motor activation which the observer of some salient action or physical sensation feels as a neural readiness to perform the same action.[9] If I see you hammering a nail into the wall, I am likely to *feel* myself upright, wielding a hammer horizontally (with what that implies in terms of the position of my arm, the effort required to resist gravity). If I see you hammering a nail into the floor, the muscular responses will be configured differently: the head and the arm are turned downward, the falling (gravity-assisted) movement of the hammer needs a different form of muscular control. I can feel all that instantly, without reflection. Even where the movements in question are communicated in language, as I have done here, the same responses are triggered. Of course such responses—like the expressions of direction we looked at a moment ago—are 'ghost' feelings that are usually fleeting, but they are the result of activity in the neuronal area associated with the action in question.[10]

Kinesis may pass via the visual field, but it may also pass via language. In first-generation cognitive science, which used the computer as a model for brain function, it was widely assumed that language production was located in a specific area of the brain, supported by a memory store which was something like a combined dictionary and encyclopedia.[11] The current consensus is that conceptual language (i.e. lexical items, as opposed to syntax) is distributed widely across the architecture of the brain, and more specifically that it is closely connected to centres of motor response. This would help to explain the way such kinesic effects can be triggered by language. Since Aristotle, it has been commonly assumed that the lexical meanings of words are purely conventional except in a few marginal cases, but it is now beginning to look as if their extrinsic conventionality is overridden, especially for native speakers of a language, by the way words are learnt and used. The view of Barsalou and others is that they are acquired in specific situations, and carry with them those situational or 'ecological' associations.[12] As we have seen, the verbs 'bring' and 'take' carry with them a ghost echo of movement perceived from an individual viewpoint; think too of the series skid–slip–slither–slide–glide, which elicits instant calibrations of the dynamics of a body moving across a smooth surface.[13] They may be reinforced by onomatopoeia, or by alliteration, but the phenomenon as such doesn't require these effects. Poets, and writers of literary prose, are liable to make more intensive use of motor resonance than do everyday speakers, perhaps because they have a strong 'feel' for language, as we say (that expression may be more literal and more physical than we are inclined to suppose). It isn't difficult to think of strong cases, from Seamus Heaney back to the poet of *Beowulf* or *Sir Gawain*, from Proust back to Rabelais and Shakespeare. And readers who have a 'feel' for language will predictably respond to instances that might leave others cold (have I left you cold, reader? can you feel the chill in your bones?).

These heightened sensitivities have been referred to as 'kinesic intelligence':[14] the neurally grounded ability to respond to such triggers and potentially to build them into a wider set of connecting frames (here, for example, the conceptual frame evoked earlier). Kinesic intelligence, as I read the phrase, carries with it the presumption that it is a set of skills available to humans by virtue of their ability to reflect on experience, analyse it, and of course to speak about it; everyone can do this, but some are better at it than others. However, I would want to insist here as elsewhere that there is no sharp cut-off point between the way animals 'read' each other's movements and the more elaborate performances that humans have developed out of that evolutionary adaptation.[15] Let's recall here the first sentence of *Lord Jim* (see Chapters 2 and 8). It is telling that Jim is said to remind one of a charging bull: his posture and movement, *mutatis mutandis*, are of the kind that animals too can interpret (otherwise they would be easy prey, or toothless predators). The reader of Conrad's novel feels them first, perhaps, in her body, but her body already 'knows' in advance the other things the human mind would want to say about them, and already expects (since this is a novel) that there will be a good deal more along those lines in the several hundred pages devoted to Jim's story. She knows it because the embodied kinesic understanding she shares with animals has become saturated with instances of the reflective kinesic intelligence she has acquired since her earliest childhood through cognitive communication with other humans.[16]

Everyone who is willing to attend to Yeats's poem, to use their kinesic intelligence, will see that the tiny but explosive group of words at the centre of the poem ('balloon', 'bellies', 'drags') operate together to produce a kinesic response. They will also grasp intuitively that the nature of that response in turn depends on the whole sensorimotor context, from the hands to the shed—the task that has been laid on the hands in the first line. And they will draw on a wide range of contextual factors that relevantly enrich these same perceptions— places they have encountered them before (have you tried windsurfing? putting up a tent or hanging out washing in a high wind?), items from a common cognitive archive of cultural–historical information about balloons, knowledge about Yeats and anything else he may have said about balloons, and so on.[17]

We're not done yet. What the hands do, in the sensorimotor frame of reference, is pull an inflated balloon into a shed. But in the conceptual frame, the balloon is the mind: on the basis of my earlier argument, let's take an inferential short cut and call it the poetic imagination. If we then conceptualize the hands as writing hands and if the shed is a poem, or more specifically this poem, something else happens. The implicatures of 'shed' are readjusted, or better reappraised, in order to accommodate the concept of poetic form. Yet they are still highly artisanal: one thinks of writing in terms of tools, instruments, building skills, and the like. A poem, in that perspective, is not a rarefied conceptual thing, a creature of the transcendental imagination. It's an ingenious gadget, or a small, compact box that delivers, when one opens it, an explosive cocktail of responses.[18]

This poem in particular offers itself as in one sense a humble, rather crude box, a shed put up by an amateur who has not bothered to line up the base properly. Quatrains are usually isometric; even if all four lines are not the same length, there will be two pairs of isometric lines. That's how one recognizes them as quatrains: they have a clear pattern. No two lines in this one have the same number of syllables;

instead, we have the idiosyncratic sequence 5–7–8–6. A competent reader of poetry will easily see the correlation between the dilation of the two middle lines as the balloon 'bellies and drags in the wind' and the contraction of the final line as the balloon is confined. She might, however, also read the sequence as an unresolved tension that warps the expected symmetry of the most fundamental unit of the modern Western lyric poem, the four-line stanza. The tension is visible on the page, but one might well want to insist that poems are not visible objects, still less static objects. They move in time, according to a rhythm of speech that includes breathing; they co-opt the body and its proprioceptive sensations. This poem markedly offers itself as somatic in that sense, precisely because its conceptual implicatures are from the first word haptic, embodied.

Another line of argument opens up from the conception of the poem as an invented thing, a tool or instrument. This argument would replace the notion of 'form' and 'genre', which have implications of neutrality and conventionality, with the notion of an agent-directed, designed artefact that takes its place in the history of cultural evolution. Yeats's poem can be classified as an epigram: a short poem encompassing a witty 'conceit' (poetic composition is like getting a balloon into a shed). It uses conventions of form that are widely used in modern Western European poetry (the isometric rhymed quatrain). But it is not so much the classification that counts here as what these formal constituents afford. They are the cultural equivalent of what a given ecological environment affords for the creatures that live there. I shall speak at greater length of 'affordances' in Chapter 4, but I want here already to make the essential move from a formalistic type of analysis to a dynamic, agent-driven, purpose-directed perspective, where 'genre', for example, is considered as a pool of resources accumulated over centuries and constantly renewed, adapted, manipulated, transformed by skilful instrument-makers. The successful innovations survive, others fall away; success may depend on cultures so local that other cultures wouldn't see the point, but it's obvious that the most successful (and some of the others) are fully capable of crossing the most unexpected borders. What literature affords, indeed, is cognitive and cultural fluidity. It licenses all kinds of inventive moves precisely because, unlike practical technologies, it isn't tied to concrete outcomes in the real world (although it may make things happen there, too). It changes the cognitive environment of readers and thereby progressively changes its own ecology as new affordances emerge or drop away.

In a cognitive reading, 'style' is inseparable from the mode of directed thought. It is the shape in which a kinesic sense of captured life and movement emerges, via the linguistic substratum, from its embryonic conception (what the poem was meant to mean, what it was meant to make happen). In Yeats's tiny, extraordinarily under-specified poem, the captured life and movement is realized in the struggle between hands, balloon, and shed: the tension and drama of that struggle reminds one of the opening scene of Ian McEwan's novel *Enduring Love*, which offers itself in exemplary fashion to the kinesic intelligence of its readers. In the poem, however, the 'captured life' resides not only in the scene as such but also in the implicatures that stream out from the perceptual simulation. The balloon is a body, a semi-living thing imbued with purposes of its own, responding to the vicissitudes of the air both inside and outside its 'skin'. The poem—the little cramped shed—is full of air, of space, of the blowing of the wind that is also *breath*, the prototypical metaphor of thought, spirit, life itself.[19] As in McEwan's balloon scene again, there is also danger: movement upwards, against gravity, goes against all the sensorimotor responses that humans become conditioned to through their experience of the world. Humans would love to fly, but can't; the very idea makes them imagine falling headlong from the balloon, the plane, the cliff-edge. What Yeats's poem affords above all, one might say, beyond even the conception of poetry and its difficulty, is a sense of the heady but also risky space that fills the poem, of the thought that is beyond language. Underspecification becomes then not just the general condition of all human expression, but the particular way in which this poem imagines its own airy substance.

Close reading the cognitive way

This slow-motion analysis is something like a classic 'close reading', except that it uses a different perspective and a critically different vocabulary. The difference lies partly in the explanatory framework ('what is going on when we read a poem like this one?'), but partly also in the way that the framework brings into focus details that might otherwise have remained peripheral and draws attention to responses that are usually taken for granted. Cognitive analysis, in fact, is often directed at showing what is at stake in the supposedly 'self-evident', although sometimes self-evident responses and effects turn out, when one looks at them closely, to be surprisingly counter-intuitive.

The key point here is that, when we perform a cognitive activity like reading a poem, a great deal has happened before the outcome of the reading comes into full consciousness.[20] The brain has evolved to handle sensorimotor response at maximal speed, and the brain–body development of individuals from childhood on continuously streamlines that process into adulthood. The kinesic is therefore a high-speed response and needs to be 'slowed down' reflectively if one is to analyse it at all. Conceptual analysis appears rapid because it takes short cuts (look how quickly we produced a reasonably stable assessment of what the Yeats poem is about), but the reflective mode that it entails is in fact, by comparison with sensorimotor response, in the slow lane. So we have here a distinction that is not unlike the classic opposition of 'intuition' and 'reason' or 'conscious thought', except that the two modes are no longer purely mentalistic. They operate within the overarching frame of embodied cognition, where thought and bodily response are constantly interpenetrating, communicating with each other, not least in complex multitasks like reading poems. The interpenetration is guaranteed by the evolution of the human brain out of an already advanced and highly complex animal brain, but its capacities are exponentially increased by constant feedback. Consciously learned knowledge can be produced reflectively, but also becomes at least partly 'internalized', as we say: you don't, for the most part, think about what you're doing when you ride a bike or even clean your teeth. Such motor actions, and their conceptual counterparts, become embedded in what is often called 'procedural memory', which is now known to be distinct from other kinds of memory (short-term working memory on the one hand and episodic memory on the other).[21]

So when you sit down to read the Yeats poem on your own, or when you discuss it with a group of first-year students, some of whom have never tried to think consciously about a poem, you will necessarily be setting in motion a dynamic interaction between reflective and pre-reflective which goes back to early childhood. The formal notation of metre, rhythm, poetic 'form', the canonic repertory of poetic figures, the sorts of things that modern poets in English or other languages have done with poems, all this may to a greater or lesser extent be already acquired by the reader, but the fundamental affordances that poets (and others) draw on were there from very early on. They were there in the songs a carer sings to her baby, in the rhymes and rhythms the baby hears before it can speak, and also in the sensorimotor responses that living creatures have developed over aeons in order to prepare them for engagement with their environment. In that sense, children are born into a poetic ecology, or more broadly a 'literary' ecology.[22]

Thinking with Pooh: the balloon and the bees

I shall return in Chapter 5, at least in passing, to the question of how children think. Meanwhile, I want to move the focus from these abstract explanatory comments to a classic of children's literature which also features a balloon. The very first story in *Winnie-the-Pooh* comprises an elementary but astonishingly sophisticated ABC of the cognitive moves that humans make and that, as children, they learn to extend pre-reflectively and then to understand reflectively, often through stories.[23]

The story proper opens with an act of teddy-bear cognition. Hearing a loud buzzing noise from the top of a tree, Winnie-the-Pooh 'sat down at the foot of the tree, put his head between his paws, and began to think.'[24] Putting one's head between one's paws is a gesture of withdrawal from active engagement with the environment in order to promote reflective activity. Pooh uses it to construct a chain of inferences: buzzing means bees, bees mean honey, and 'the only reason for making honey is so as *I* can eat it.' The logic of this last inference is a biologic, motivated by the creature's own needs; it may appear naive, but the inferences humans make are routinely inflected in this way. Similarly, the inferential chain as a whole is basic, the kind of thing one would expect of a 'bear of very little brain', as Pooh will often be called (Christopher Robin, after this story, will even say that he has *no* brain). Yet they are reflective rather than pre-reflective: real bears on the lookout for honey wouldn't sit down and put their head between their paws. Pooh, of course, has language as a medium for reflective cognition; or at least the author supposes that his thoughts can be mapped onto syntactic language.

Pooh now plans his assault on the honey, using the prime instrument of evolved human cognition, namely cognitive fluidity, the ability to conceive of alternative scenarios and predict which is most likely to succeed. He envisages successively two possibilities. The more obvious is to climb the tree: the tree affords nesting for bees, but also climbing for small bears. On the way up, Pooh sings a song as a kind of commentary. His song sets up an analogy between trees and stairs as a climbing affordance: 'If Bears were Bees, | They'd build their nests at the bottom of trees', so that they wouldn't have to climb up all those stairs. The analogy is based, moreover, on a *counterfactual* imagining ('a very funny thought'): 'if Bears were Bees ...' (and its converse 'if Bees were Bears ...'). Counterfactual thinking is indispensable to complex acts of planning and prediction, and it's a good thing to have if you want to write fiction.

The first plan fails, however: the upper branches are more fragile, and one breaks, sending Pooh back to earth. The second option is more sophisticated, requiring a set of inferences that the story leaves implicit. In order to reach the nest, Pooh needs to overcome gravity without a mediate affordance (a tree or staircase). Think Christopher Robin, who thinks at a higher level and has a wider range of affordances at his command. Think balloons. Eureka! Christopher Robin has two party balloons, one green, one blue. Nicely ecological: Pooh deliberates on their relative advantage as camouflage (leaves or sky): which will outwit the thinking of the bees ('they might think ... they might think.... Which is most likely?')? Christopher Robin points out a planning problem: Pooh has forgotten that he needs a disguise as well. So he chooses the blue balloon and rolls in the mud in order to simulate a cloud.

Pooh, as a developmental psychologist might say, has in these ways stipulated his pretence (let the balloon mean sky, let the mud signify a grey cloud).[25] Most of this pretend logic, within the storyworld Milne constructs, is adequately plausible, but what about the balloon as an affordance for countering gravity? One could refer here to the historical moment, the period of the airship to which Yeats's poem also belongs, and to the somewhat longer period during which hot-air balloons, then helium balloons, achieved the lighter-than-air flight that was the precondition for Milne's fantasy of bearish levitation.[26]

Yet the counterfactual assumption that you can make a balloon ascent using an ordinary party balloon is plausible as the realization of the child's desire to fly like a bird or a fairy or an aeroplane.[27] For the reader, it's not difficult to see what it would be like to inhabit a world where teddy bears could do such things. We would regard it as implausible if Pooh had chosen to float upwards using a jar of honey on a string (perhaps as bait for the bees), because what a honeypot affords for upward movement is not apparent. Similarly, we unreflectingly set aside certain aspects of the physics of balloon ascent: we don't, for example, ask why Pooh's balloon stops rising at just that point. In other words, the counterfactual assumption operates like an ad hoc metaphor: it works if the fictional event resembles a real-world event *in relevant respects.*[28]

Pooh's effort to mind-read the bees, which began with his camouflage plans, continues now that he's aloft: he thinks they're *suspicious*. He then imagines a new way of making it plausible that the bees would think he's a cloud, and this provokes an authorial intervention attributed to the reader-as-character (Christopher Robin): 'Silly old Bear!' But the reader indulgently continues to accept the storyworld as it is, and eventually its plausibility is adjusted to conform more closely to the real world: the bees remain suspicious, and indeed initiate what looks suspiciously like an attack.

There is a nicely judged illustration by E. H. Shepard at this point in the text. The angle of Pooh's gaze leads one to infer that he's thinking about the bees; more specifically, he's thinking about what the bees might be thinking about (namely that he isn't a cloud, and that the threat to their air-space must be removed). But there is something else here that the picture takes up from the story, where we hear later that Pooh's arms 'were so stiff from holding on to the string of the balloon all that time that they stayed up straight in the air for more than a week'. You're not only reading Pooh's *mind* here: you're also feeling what he feels physically. His upstretched left arm clings grimly on to the balloon, and you can feel the strain in his shoulder and in his neck, as he anxiously turns his head sideways and upwards to track the bees. These motor responses are inferred simultaneously, I would suggest, with the mental ones: in the end, it makes little sense to separate them. Kinesis and mind-reading occupy the same gradient.

Finally, the extensive framing of this first story makes it ostensively explicit that the Winnie-the-Pooh stories are an extended game of *shared pretence* played by an adult (the author) and a child (his son).[29] They build on one of the most common games of shared pretence between parents and small children, which is itself already a form of fiction: the attribution to toy animals (and bees) of mind-states and other human forms of behaviour.[30] In Milne's stories, mind-reading activities are often brought into focus by explicit references to the mental capacities of the characters, both in the stories themselves and in the extra-diegetic frame. These effects run through the whole collection, forming a constant thread of empathy that emerges, for example, in Christopher Robin's anxiety at the end that he might have hurt Pooh when he accidentally shot him with his (toy) gun.

I would suggest that the enormous success of the Winnie-the-Pooh stories may be due in part at least to the skill with which Milne does what parents try to do—teach their children about thinking, about belief and imagination, but also about the cognitive skills the children themselves have already acquired in relation to the less well-equipped imaginary minds of their toy animals (or of their younger brothers and sisters). Teddy bears with some brain (but very little) afford many pertinent openings for this activity. As for belief in the storyworld, this too is invoked in the final dialogue between the narrating father and his listening son. When Christopher Robin asks about the outcome of a future story, the narrator refuses to offer a spoiler, but Christopher Robin nods, claiming that he 'remembers' it—after all, he is a character in the story, and the action is supposed to have happened already. But he uses a subterfuge:

> 'I do remember,' he said, 'only Pooh doesn't very well, so that's why he likes having it told to him again. Because then it's a real story and not just a remembering.'

As a comment on the cognitive mode of fiction, this is pretty good going for a child of Christopher Robin's age, even if he is himself a fictional character.

4

Literary Affordances

How to sit on a chaise longue

In Jonathan Franzen's novel *The Corrections*, Chip's father Alfred, who is suffering from Parkinson's disease and other associated disorders, tries to sit down on a chaise longue in his son's apartment:

> In the living room, Alfred was summoning the courage to sit down on Chip's chaise longue. Not ten minutes ago, he'd sat down on it without incident. But now, instead of simply doing it again, he'd stopped to think. He'd realized only recently that at the center of the act of sitting down was a loss of control, a blind backwards free fall. His excellent blue chair in St. Jude was like a first baseman's glove that gently gathered in whatever body was flung its way, at whatever glancing angle, with whatever violence; it had big helpful ursine arms to support him while he performed the crucial blind pivot. But Chip's chaise was a low-riding, impractical antique. Alfred stood facing away from it and hesitated, his knees bent to the rather small degree that his neuropathic lower legs permitted, his hands scooping and groping in the air behind him. He was afraid to take the plunge. And yet there was something obscene about standing half-crouched and quaking, some association with the men's room, some essential vulnerability which felt to him at once so poignant and degraded that, simply to put an end to it, he shut his eyes and let go. He landed heavily on his bottom and continued on over backwards, coming to rest with his knees in the air above him.[1]

The attempt makes him painfully and startlingly aware of how much of our sensorimotor experience we take for granted. Sitting down is just something you do—the how-to of the operation is dealt with by procedural memory and needs no reflection or discussion.[2] Yet it relies on an exact and complex fit between the shape and mechanics of the human body and the design of the seat in question, whether it be a stool, an upright chair, a capaciously upholstered armchair, a sofa, or a chaise longue. Or possibly a stone wall of the right height, or the lap of a person whose size is suitably related to the sitter's. Note that Franzen not only makes this self-evident activity salient; he also devises fungible images of it ('it had big helpful ursine arms to support him while he performed the crucial blind pivot').

This is a stunning example of the literary use of motor response (kinesis). However, I want to focus here on what one might call the ecological relation between human body and seat that forms the grounding for this kinesic effect. Dogs, birds, and spiders would use the same object in other ways, if at all, and the different kinds of seat referred to above have been devised by humans to serve a broad spectrum of sitting habits or requirements, from upright attentive postures suitable for eating from the surface of a table or for using a computer, to soft sofas for lounging on, rocking chairs for rocking (and dozing) on, and lovers' seats for kissing on. These different kinds of chairs, or more precisely the range of uses to which they can be put, are known as affordances, and in this chapter I shall look at ways in which the notion of 'affordances' might provide a different perspective on the things that literature can make happen—the ways in which it can change our cognitive environment.

What is an affordance?

The term 'affordance' was coined by James J. Gibson, an American psychologist best known for his cognitive theory of perception (his paper 'Theory of affordances' first appeared in 1977).[3] He invented the noun on the basis of the verb 'to afford', in the sense of 'to provide', as in 'the trees afford a pleasant shade'. It has since been used, and its sense has been extended or modified, in a number of disciplinary contexts, notably philosophy, IT studies, and design studies.[4]

Gibson defines the word as 'what the environment offers the animal, what it provides or furnishes, either for good or ill'.[5] This vision of the environment as a site of potentialities for behaviour and adaptation has important antecedents, not least in the notion of *Umwelt* (the environment as perceived by the creatures that inhabit it) proposed by the German-Estonian ecologist Jakob von Uexküll; Maurice Merleau-Ponty's phenomenological thought focuses on the ways in which human cognition is moulded by the physics and dynamics of the empirical world (not least the human body); and all of these thinkers were undoubtedly familiar with earlier, broadly Darwinian conceptions of the reciprocal shaping power of the environment and its inhabitants.

According to Gibson's definition, affordances are thus the potential *uses* an object or feature of the environment offers to a living creature. The affordances of a tree are, among other things, perching, nesting, and nourishment for birds, a (relatively) secure and nutritious habitat for certain insects, above-ground locomotion and fruit-gathering for squirrels and primates, construction materials or a pleasant shade for humans. However, I want from the outset to broaden the definition to include not only the uses of an object but also the object itself viewed in the light of those uses: the tree is in that sense a multiple affordance; the wheel is an affordance for transportation, for pulleys and gears, for clockwork, and so forth. This broadening is not likely, I think, to cause any confusion, since the context will immediately make it clear which sense is the relevant one in any particular case. A similar plurality is available in the everyday use of the word 'imagination', which can denote not only the faculty, but also the process of imagining and indeed its object: Henry James famously claimed that he had 'the imagination of disaster' (letter to A. C. Benson, 1896). This last use is now somewhat archaic, but a few hundred years ago it was standard—Montaigne, for example, often speaks of his 'imaginations', meaning the objects of his reflection.

The advantage of the widened sense will be obvious: it enables one to signal more consistently the shift of perspective the word carries with it. If one says that a tree offers affordances for nesting, feeding, perching, climbing, shade, and so on, the tree remains an indifferent entity in the material world, with the affordances added on as it were, whereas if we think of the tree as an open-ended affordance (affordances are by definition open-ended, since someone or something may always come up with a new use for the most unlikely object), we regard it as already part of an ecology in which individual things collectively form a complex network of reciprocal relations.

It follows that affordances in this extended sense are not a particular class of objects or artefacts: the word refers to a thing in its instrumental aspect. In principle, anything can become an affordance if it is considered in the light of a particular use. The emergence of human cognition transforms the landscape, of course, bringing with it the possibility of reflective instrumentalization, intentional design, but one needs to say at the outset that human intention is itself a natural phenomenon, that culture extends nature and is continuous with it. Once again, we're on a gradient here, not caught in an antithesis. Some animals are indeed capable of turning natural features of their environment into what one might call constructed affordances: birds gather materials for their nests, primates use sticks to prise termites out of tree-trunks. Such behaviours seem to be largely the outcome of very long-term evolutionary adaptation, and are thus subject to rigorous constraints. Birds and wasps always perform a specific set of activities in their nests and never improvise new uses for them. In other words, the room available for individual agency (choice of nesting materials and the like) is vanishingly small.

The affordances invented by humans, at least from the later stone age onwards, are by contrast improvised according to local needs and local materials, and embed themselves culturally rather than phylogenetically. Adaptations and innovations can now be made exponentially not only from generation to generation, but also from one skilled user to the next. Such human-made affordances comprise tools, instruments, devices of all kinds. Some are single-use inventions (like surgical tools or tin-openers), but more often they are multi-purpose or incremental (the wheel is used initially for transportation, but then as part of a pulley system to draw water from a well). Balloons too are adaptable affordances: they can afford flight for humans, decoration or fun at parties, or imaginative reflection.

As Gibson points out, affordances can be built on other affordances, creating distinctively complex ecosystems. They can harbour those other affordances hierarchically within their own structure, or act as platforms for further affordances. Imagine again a tree (or a beard if you like[6]), full of nests and insects burrowing and woodpeckers pecking and children climbing and apple-pickers picking and foresters pruning and people cutting off a branch to make a cricket bat or a bow or a boat or a table. One might well speak here of 'nests' of affordances, like nests of tables.

In the natural world, the coral reef is a multiply interdependent, outward-branching entity of this kind. Human cultures, thanks to the power of improvisation, are in this sense like ever-expanding, ever-changing coral reefs. The line of adaptation from floating tree-trunk to raft to hydrodynamic boat to sailing ship to steamship to ocean liner, battleship or nuclear submarine describes an affordance cluster that at each point is itself a critical affordance for local cultures (shore-living, sea-going, war, trading, colonizing, leisure pursuits, etc.). The internet is similarly an embedded affordance cluster, whether it is viewed synchronically or diachronically.

In such ways, humans create their own adaptive ecologies, imagining potential affordances (use-values) not available in nature and then improvising the instruments or devices that could supply them. That reversal of the order of affordance is of course critical, and it has become obsessive in modern times: industrial societies invent new needs, and then the means to supply those needs, in an ever-accelerating cycle fuelled by powerful rhetorics of publicity.[7] The mirage of infinitely nuanced individual identity is largely driven by the same dynamic. The range of possibilities offered by a consumer society affords the very idea that we can choose to be individual in the way we have our hair cut, the colour we paint our houses, the kind of underwear we choose, the books we read, the online conversations we nurture, and these choices of course inflect actual behaviours. The affordance culture encourages us to think and act as if we were different from those around us, even if the others select their personal styles from the same range of offered potentialities.

The interrelation of invariance and variance is indeed critical to the concept itself. Gibson describes an affordance as 'an invariant combination of variables ... one might guess that it is easier to perceive such an invariant unit than it is to perceive all the variables separately.... Perception is economical.'[8] According to that account—and I think this is the key to the value of the word for literary study—the successful affordances are the ones that enable us to grasp multiple phenomena as packages, or as integrated wholes. Note that they work because, while affording that single conspectus, they don't efface or suppress the seething mass of particular things that inhabit them. All those birds nesting in the beard of the old man of Dundee presumably have their individual lives, their eggs, their worms, their recreational flights, their mating sessions, and we apprehend all that in the tangle of the beard itself as a single *Umwelt* or ecology. The concept of 'self', or of 'mind' itself, or indeed of cognition, is best seen as an affordance package in this sense, rather than as a metaphysical essence or an empty abstraction.

Gibson also emphasizes that the notion of affordance cuts across the subjective–objective antithesis (p. 129). The invariant thing in itself is, we assume, just out there, being its neutral self. But from the point of view of the creature that sees its potential as an affordance, it's an object with a purpose: for the owls, the hen, and the rest, the beard is 'our home', a safe place, a comfortable place, a place where it's easy to find strands of stuff to make a nest out of. Any object conceived as an affordance is thus conceived at once objectively (invariance) and subjectively (open to creative use and variation). Another way of saying this—perhaps a better way for our purposes, since the subjective–objective opposition has been tediously overworked in literary studies—is to say that an affordance necessarily implies agency, intention, purpose, but (initially at least) as a potential to be realized. A conical piece of stiffened fabric with the apex cut off is potentially a lampshade; but it might also potentially be a hat, or a collar to prevent a dog from scratching a wound. Who knows what other uses someone else might come up with? An affordance is thus, in a sense which is highly relevant to other strands in my argument, *underspecified*, and its specification depends on relevance. It's a thing that adumbrates a purpose or indefinite set of purposes; only a particular use and a particular context can select the *relevant* purpose.

The extraordinarily intricate and ever-expanding set of human cultures is always, of course, constrained by the physical properties of materials and their availability (although an empirical constraint, it should be remembered, is precisely that which offers possibilities of use). Accident is also a critical enabling factor, opening up unthought-of possibilities: a tree that happens to fall down across a river creates a new pathway that can be imitated elsewhere thanks to tree-felling affordances invented for other purposes; the concept of a bridge begins to take place. However, as the use of words such as 'improvisation', 'invention', 'thought', 'purpose' shows, human affordance-building is largely driven by cognition. And that means in turn that it presupposes an apparatus of mental or cognitive affordances. The relation between what is phylogenetic here (the evolution of cerebral architecture) and what is 'cultural' (that which is not genetically inherited) is especially complex, but it is not difficult to see once again that they lie along a shared gradient that exhibits no neurological or ontological break. The hominin brain has certainly evolved through feedback from affordance-related activities (tool-making, for example), and culturally acquired skills draw on the evolved flexibility of the human brain, its cognitive fluidity; that is precisely the sense in which human culture is a phenomenon in nature.

As a way of recapitulating the argument so far, it will be useful here to consider a terminological point. The effects afforded by human cultural evolution can be viewed as the expression of 'extended mind'.[9] Essentially, the notion of extended mind proposes that where external media (books, notebooks, computers, etc.) display sufficient functional similarity to cognitive processes (memory, calculation, etc.), they should be regarded as part of the cognitive process itself, thus extending it into the material world.

The problems associated with the use of the word 'mind' have led philosophers working in this area to adopt in its place a range of expressions such as 'extended cognition' and 'distributed cognition' which don't run into those difficulties, although there is still controversy over what exactly is meant by ascribing cognition to phenomena beyond the confines of the body (or indeed of the brain).[10] However, one might safely think of the complete set of both inherited and cultural cognitive equipment that humans can bring to bear at a particular time and in a particular context as 'cognitive affordances'. The set would, together with physical instruments (tools, devices, etc.), include concepts of all kinds, from 'dog', 'house', and 'year' to 'love', 'mind', 'affordance', 'literature', and (of course) 'language'. Language itself is for humans the key empowering affordance, allowing the development of secondary language-based affordances, artefacts or instruments made out of language, such as metaphors, literary genres, poetic and narrative forms, and individual literary works. Here the coral reef is developed to its most exotic, ever-changing, ever-proliferating extreme.[11]

Language as affordance

Before moving to the question of what purchase the word might give us on literary study, I need to add two remarks on language as a cognitive affordance. As I indicated in Chapter 3, some recent work on the cognitive processes involved in language use have suggested that language, as it is learnt by native speakers, is not stored as a dictionary with an accompanying syntax; it is connected with, or embedded in, sensorimotor responses and decision-making functions.[12] This 'situational' view of language acquisition would help to explain the theories of language as somehow bonded to reality that have recurred throughout Western culture from Plato to Mallarmé. It's been fashionable to treat such theories as a naive illusion, but it's beginning to look as if language is mapped onto the way we perceive the world at a quite fundamental level, constraining the ways you can talk about things. One example proposed by Glenberg and his colleagues is that if you imagine someone saying 'Hang your coat on the vacuum cleaner', you might hesitate, but then you'd picture a vertical hoover (rather than one of those little beetle-shaped ones) and perhaps feel a ghost movement in your arm as if to perform the action. However, if they said 'Hang your coat on the teacup', you'd be at a loss—the movement is simply not performable. What is especially relevant in the present context is that Glenberg and Kaschak regard this view of language as an extension of the Gibsonian theory of affordance. Coat-hooks and coathangers are affordances designed specifically for the shape of that particular human artefact, but if one lacks a designed facility, it is always possible to improvise one. You can use the back of a chair, for example, or a banister post on a staircase, or (if you're out in the country) a suitably shaped branch or twig. Anything affording a sufficient vertical drop will do: at a pinch, an upright vacuum cleaner but not a horizontal one. And certainly not a teacup. These relations are intrinsic to our way of perceiving the world; since they constrain our possibilities of action, they become cognitively embedded so that we scarcely notice them except in unusual cases, such as devising a ladder or platform that can be used on a curving staircase to access high shelves above the staircase. Affordances structure our perceptions of sensorimotor experience and constrain our ways of reimagining those perceptions, whether through concepts, language, or other media.

Secondly, if you accept that language is an instrument, a multi-purpose affordance, you need to think of it as being end-directed—as having an intentional dynamic. And that in turn implies the activity of agents—the agent who offers the language, the interlocutor or reader who receives it. Even more importantly, if language is an affordance, it can't be regarded as in any sense an end in itself: it offers itself for improvised use in particular *contexts*. A dominant literary-philosophical perspective in the last fifty years has asserted the priority of language over thought: on this view, thought is always already language. This conception is both powerful, even self-evident, and inadequate. It is self-evident because the cultural explosion is unthinkable without language; most of our conceptual thinking is certainly carried out on a day-to-day basis via the mediation of language, and the particular conceptual possibilities afforded by a given natural language, equally certainly, can determine whole tranches of one's cognitive experience. Having the word 'affordance' in one's active vocabulary, for example, changes things radically, a change which becomes awkwardly salient when one wants to translate the word into French or German. Yet such a view of language is inadequate because it is always possible to translate concepts, recontextualize them, and as one performs those routine if complex tasks, it becomes evident that language is intrinsically instrumental, not ontologically prior. It is, in the end, another of the affordances improvised by humans from materials in the natural world that began with the shaping of stone tools, and perhaps, at the same time, with emergent vocalizations: 'Hands, do what you're bid …'

Literary affordances: conventions, genres

The direct representation of affordances, not surprisingly, is endemic in literature. The Franzen example offered at the beginning of this chapter stands out only by the quality of attention to the 'ecological' relations that define an affordance as such, and by the author's evident consciousness of what he is doing. One can imagine all kinds of ways in which one could explore this route further. One could, for example, revisit fictional representation across a wide chronological range and in different national traditions of writing to determine whether this perspective yields interesting results for the history of mimesis. At the most ambitious end of the scale, one might indeed envisage a rewriting of Auerbach's monumental study. One could explore connections between affordance representation and other features of narrative fiction, not least psychological and social features, since the ecological or environmental relation is fundamental to the way any social or psychological interaction, whether actual or fictional, functions and develops over time. Or one could seek to characterize the aesthetics of affordance in particular writers.

Ambitious as such a project might sound, it would only be an accessory to the wider study of literary affordance and affordances, since what is at stake here is nothing less than the instrumentality of literature, its uses as an instrument of thought. In the longer run, this question becomes that of literature itself as a human invention, the question 'What is literature *for*?' with all its cultural, social, and ethical reverberations.

For the time being, let's develop an idea proposed in Chapter 3 and concentrate on the more modest task of considering what happens when we redescribe literary *conventions* as affordances, whether they be generic conventions, formal conventions (rhyme, metre, etc.), or conventional thematic elements, from standard plot-lines to literary commonplaces and formulaic phrasings. In the last fifty years or so, thanks largely to the model provided by Ernst Robert Curtius, an enormous amount of work has been done to map out the formal conventions and commonplaces of Western literature, especially in the Middle Ages and the Renaissance. At the same time, post-Saussurean linguistics has emphasized the extent to which language is based on convention, while modern poetics and rhetoric also have a lot to say about conventions. Structuralist and poststructuralist narratology, in particular, established a poetics where the recurrence of formal elements, thematic tropes, and story models were treated predominantly as conventional, having value only in their diacritical relation with other elements.

One of the results of these lines of research has been to call into question the agency of individual speakers and writers. During the last few decades, a powerful theoretical doxa has insisted that individuation is imposed on us from 'outside', and in particular by the conventions we unconsciously assimilate from infancy onwards; in other words, the individual is always already entrapped within the prison-house of convention. Now, the concept of convention cannot of course be dispensed with. Particular cultures and languages can only function because they rest on collectively agreed and relatively stable points of reference; cultural and literary traditions are likewise dependent on the recurrence of recognizable elements. However, the word carries with it a powerfully conservative connotation, and also a negative one: that which is conventional is unoriginal, boring, or even sinister (as in the notion of language as a prison-house[13]). If you redescribe convention as 'affordance', the picture is immediately transformed. What was static and merely constraining affords all kinds of unexpected possibilities, ways of breaking out into new territory.

In this perspective, then, it becomes possible to redescribe the relationship between form and its particular instantiation not as a relation between vehicle and content, but as an ecological, adaptive, and ultimately innovative interaction. Take the sonnet form, for example. The sonnet was first used in the thirteenth century, at a time when poets were experimenting with all kinds of new forms. The first poet who used it cannot possibly have guessed how productively its shape would lend itself to colonization by logical and rhetorical procedures. That only became clear when it was developed by the fourteenth-century poet Petrarch, and much later by French and English poets (including of course Shakespeare). One of the procedures that became salient, and then definitive of the sonnet as a form, is the so-called 'turn', which occurs typically after the quatrains: a point of articulation after which the argument or state of feeling elaborated in the quatrains is resolved, often in a witty or aphoristic formula. The semi-invariant structure of the sonnet affords that possibility of a turn. So, for example, the quatrains may be subordinate clauses, with a main clause completed in the final tercet or couplet; the beginnings of each metrical subdivision may be marked by anaphora; the binary division lends itself to simile ('Just as … So …'), and to antithesis ('Spring has come, but I am melancholy').[14] And then in each case the whole singular utterance as articulated by an individual poet becomes itself a new affordance, making things happen elsewhere— in the minds of readers, in other poems, perhaps even in the world (a sonnet sent to a potential lover on 14 February affords the possibility of actual sexual relations).[15]

When we speak of the sonnet as a category of poems, we assign it to a genre. Like other categories, genre is a short-cut affordance allowing particular items to be described or evoked as one of a group that share a number of characteristics. As in Wittgenstein's famous example of the category 'game', it is pointless to expect that genre characterizations will afford precise definitions. A category always has borderline members, some of which may share few features with mainline members while at the same time sharing features with members of other categories. The epigrams of the Latin poet Martial, those of Oscar Wilde, and Yeats's 'The Balloon of the Mind' are culturally and formally very different, even though they share qualities of concision and pointedness ('wit').

To regard genre as an affordance invites one to consider it within the perspective of cultural evolution.[16] Stories, representations, poetic utterances, and the like vie in their various cultural contexts for use-value and audience preference. When a use-value begins to assert itself, it attracts other makers, who reinforce and also vary the model. In this way, a degree of invariance (or repeatability) provides an accepted platform that affords new potentialities. The epic poems of Homer, Virgil, Apollonius of Rhodes, Dante, Tasso, Du Bartas, Milton, and others demonstrate the unexpectedly wide reach of those potentialities while remaining recognizably within a common template; or perhaps it would be better to say that each of them both reinforces and revises the template. The novel and its antecedents and avatars follow an analogous trajectory: hence the difficulty of defining the novel, of deciding when it 'starts', what 'counts' as a novel (*Don Quijote*, *La Princesse de Clèves*, *Tom Jones*, *Great Expectations*, *The Waves*). At each point, there are only unexpectedly productive mutations of existing templates, new affordances (in both the nominal and the verbal sense of the word). In this trajectory, there are of course moments when a collective consciousness of the category emerges; new generic categories are designated, or existing ones may shift, relocating the affordance template across a significantly different set of generic characteristics.

The English word 'novel' is an example of the former, the French word *roman* an example of the latter; the word 'elegy' has also changed its generic sense since antiquity. Even more strikingly, Montaigne inaugurated a whole genre by unwittingly baptizing it. The title of his famous book, *Essais*, was clearly not intended by the author to be a genre title: there was no such genre in his day, only a number of relatively informal modes of writing that might be called 'miscellanies' (*mélanges*) or present themselves under some ad hoc title. The word *essais* and its cognates is used within Montaigne's book to mean 'attempts', 'trials'; it draws attention to the cognitive mode the writer adopts (thinking experimentally). Within a few years, and particularly in England,[17] 'essay' became the name of a genre of which Montaigne's *Essais* was recognized as the foundational text. The point of retelling the story here is that it reveals the *emergence* of a highly complex literary affordance, a 'new' way of writing that is also a way of thinking. The emergence is completed downstream, a posteriori, by the recognition of this new phenomenon as a distinct affordance-cluster, a new ecology for writers to inhabit, reshape, and build on. Through the act of recognition, furthermore, a concept (the 'essay') reveals its character as a cognitive affordance.

A good deal of discussion around genre seems predicated on the idea of a distinct beginning, or at least a decisive turn; it looks back down the series of individual works towards an archetype or proto-type, as in the work of Vladimir Propp or Northrop Frye. Yet, as Montaigne's case shows in exemplary fashion, literary instruments are often defined and recognized retrospectively. Thinking of genres as affordance-structures helpfully reorients attention *forwards*, towards the restless reworking of existing templates. The evolution of literary artefacts, like that of other kinds of artefact, is a dynamic process, ruthlessly shaped by prevailing cultural forces (which, according to the theory of extended cognition, are culturally adapted cognitive forces). The great pastoral novels of the seventeenth century were enormously popular in their day but almost unreadable now. Even the best of modern soap operas will no doubt go the same way. Conversely, the essay had an afterlife that Montaigne could not possibly have imagined.

The basic generic templates, as has been pointed out by those who seek to describe literary phenomena in terms of evolutionary con-straints, are so enduring that they are virtually invariant: stories ending in marriage or death, narratives of journeys and homecom-ings, of decisive battles or of clever characters who survive because they are good at manipulating people and circumstances ('tricksters'), songs of love and loss, recognition plots. These allow listeners and readers rapidly to enter the storyworld, or the mood of a song, by fulfilling expectations. A certain logic is imposed which reduces the world's complexities to a simplexity.[18] Innovation can come through the 'noise' created by cultural transmission, from individual to individual, generation to generation, or language to language. But innovations that don't bring viable affordances with them will soon die away. The ones that remain are precisely and paradoxically those that are most pliable, lending themselves to new uses and new secondary affordance platforms: the coral reef again. Listeners, spectators, and readers want their expectations fulfilled, but only so far. They also want variety: they are stimulated by defamiliarization. And that often comes where two or more generic affordances 'interbreed', disturbing established patterns and creating an effect, precisely, of disturbance.

This phenomenon is well known to historians of literature and poetics. It emerges, for example, in early modern discussions over tragi-comedy, which is sometimes understood as a tragedy with a happy ending, but also as a tragedy with generic imports (from romance, for example), or again as a tragedy with comic or burlesque interludes, as in Shakespearian tragedy. Both Shakespeare and Molière wrote so-called problem comedies, which are only problematic if one starts with a reductive view of what comedy as a genre (and as a way of communicating) affords. Mozart's *Così fan tutte* maintains a knife-edge balance between its overtly burlesque plot and the high emotional stakes that are expressed through the music.[19] Ibsen, too, developed the affordances of the bourgeois *drame* as conceived in the eighteenth century in such a way as to create new possibilities of resonance that can be missed if one overemphasizes the stereotype. And the endless debate about where modernism begins in drama, the novel, and poetry could perhaps better be approached by thinking of the new works that arose as the product of a critically accelerated refashioning of currently available instruments of expression, fuelled above all by emerging economic and technological affordances at a hitherto undreamt-of level of complexity.

Form as affordance

Let's recall here our reading of Yeats's 'The Balloon of the Mind' and redescribe it briefly in terms of the affordance structures that operate at every level of this tiny poem.

To say that it is an epigram assigns it at once, as I have already suggested, to a genre that includes short, witty, and often satirical poems by Latin writers such as Martial and their avatars in the Renaissance. The compression of the form, emerging in a punch-line or conceit, gives it a 'pointedness', as if it were a pointed weapon, or at least a nail designed to pin its object down; and it often works, as here, to connect two notions (balloon and shed, together with their implicatures) that are in some sense dissonant with one another. It would be hard to find a better example of a poetic affordance designed to penetrate and alter the cognitive environment of the reader.

The single four-line stanza operates in this instance as a platform for the nest or package of affordances constituted by the poem. However, we need to infer an anterior 'ghost' affordance, namely an isometric four-line stanza with full rhymes. This presupposed stanza is one of the basic units of Western poetry since the Middle Ages; it is fundamental to stanzaic poems generally, and also to the sonnet, which features two or sometimes three isometric rhymed quatrains. It is a unit that can be used for all kinds of poetic themes and purposes, like a small square or rectangular box (something you might buy in the storage section of IKEA, for example). If you haven't got that ghost affordance in your mental furniture store, your reading of the Yeats poem will be seriously deficient, although of course you'll still be able to read it at other levels—the mind is a flexible instrument that compensates brilliantly for its own lacunae.

The specific formal affordance used in this case varies from the template in ways that we are likely to associate with incipient modernism: it is not isometric (5–7–8–6) and it features half-rhymes (bid–shed, mind–wind). The box, in other words, is warped, or distorted, but that effect will only become salient if the ghost affordance is presupposed. It is then that you hear the tapping fingers of metre shift to off-beat rhythms.

On this warped platform are displayed the perceptual (predomin-antly tangible) affordances of the poem: the hands, the balloon, and the shed. Hands are the most fundamental of human affordances: manual or manipulative skills are essential to the exponential devel-opment by homo sapiens of designed affordances. The balloon, as I say elsewhere, corresponds to the ancient dream of being free of the weight that holds us down, or hurls us down if we step over the edge of a cliff: the dream of rising rather than falling. But it can also be threatening, like McEwan's runaway balloon. It has to be contained, and the shed is the all-purpose IKEA box, another fundamental type of affordance: it affords storage, and crucially also imposes a constraint.

So what's going on in this miniature scene? One could say that Yeats engineers a new affordance-cluster out of existing ones, setting them against one another not simply conceptually or even imaginatively, but also, as we saw, kinesically (recall the effort involved in trying to pull the bellying balloon into its narrow box). The tangible awkwardness and friction of that encounter produces a tiny but distinct explosion of which the energy continues to reverberate long after in the body and mind of the reader in the form of implicatures. That is what the best poems do, and that is why they are such wonderful and powerful affordances.

Cultural improvisation: agency and purpose

I return in conclusion to a fundamental question: is the notion of an 'affordance' as applied to literature too universal to be of any value? Is it a jack-of-all-trades concept that affords mastery over none of the particular things that really matter in literary studies? What's the use of a word that applies both to the stick a monkey uses to get termites out of a tree-trunk and a poem or a novel?

Affordance theory is of course a weak theory in the philosophical sense of the word 'weak': the breadth, the inclusiveness, of its explanatory power is purchased at the expense of depth. Yet it is also a bridge concept, linking the broad-brush picture with the most particular refinements of individual texts. What it bridges, rather successfully, is the critical gap—often seen to be a problem in cognitive literary studies—between the respective time-scales of human evolution and of cultural history. In Chapter 2, I spoke of the different speeds at which phylogenetic and cultural evolution have moved (and are still moving). The ecological backdrop of affordance theory is valid for the entire evolutionary picture, not just of humans but of life itself.

With human ecology, however, it makes a decisive shift in the form of imagined, invented, and improvised affordances. Human affordances just are the instruments of cultural evolution. We would like to know a great deal more about the pigment pots at Blombos or the early cave-paintings of Chauvet, since those specific improvisations, when connected to other features of their contemporary culture, would deliver powerful insights. When we study the Epic of Gilgamesh, the Norse sagas, Shakespeare's plays, Virginia Woolf's novels, or *The Tale of Genji*, we have more to go on, so much more in the case of modern works that the cultural-historical detail fills the whole screen. But there is always a relation between the small local ingenuities and the continuing long-term reinvention of culture as an adaptation to changing conditions and as a way of reaching out towards probable, possible and even impossible futures.

The word 'affordance' *presupposes* that relation. It also reminds us at every moment that the processes we study are dynamic, targeted, agent-driven (although accident of course constantly intervenes). Formalistic theories will never render that restless sea-change adequately. And crucially, this is a word that, while referring to a generality, has no meaning without the particularity of the relations that it installs. There's no point in calling a beard an affordance unless you refer (for example) to the nesting opportunities or possibilities of disguise that it affords; and there is no point in referring to recognition plots as affordances unless you say what particular thought-processes they promote and explore. Affordances are Janus-faced: they point both back towards the vast expanses of evolutionary time and forward along time's arrow towards the present and future outgrowths of human cultural improvisation. They are at once immanent dynamic form and *emergence*, the phenomenon as it takes shape in the moment.

Finally—and I return here to a key leitmotif of this study—the word affordance has a heuristic value in that it is capable of promoting a *redescription* of familiar aspects of, or issues in, literary analysis. You may say in particular cases, 'I knew that already', or 'there are other theories for that'; I would reply: 'Yes, but you haven't seen them from this angle before.' In some cases, the shift of angle may be relatively slight, but it's nevertheless critical: it reconfigures the whole field. A new set of ideas cannot be assimilated by methodical or methodological accumulation alone. You need eureka moments, or, more modestly, an instrument that makes a difference, a vehicle that can take you *further*.[20] In other words, you need an affordance.

5

Literary Imaginations

Imitate the action

What does it feel like to be a tiger? It's unlikely that the first audiences of *Henry V*, or indeed Shakespeare himself, had observed a tiger leaping to seize its prey. So how could he have dreamt up the line 'Imitate the action of the tiger' as a key item in a rousing speech whose rhetorical force has echoed down the ages? Here is the rationalizing reply: because we know (Elizabethans knew) that tigers are powerful creatures, famous for springing on their prey; carnivorous; male-gendered; violent yet beautiful. The audience infers these qualities and believes that Henry's army will infer them too, and know that the King wants them to behave like that, wants them to think of themselves as powerful and beautiful beasts of prey. Here is what you might call the imaginative reply: neither the fictional soldiers nor the audience infer those qualities as abstractions, as general knowledge. Instead, they mentally simulate the action of the tiger. The word 'mentally' here refers only to the fact that they don't actually leap up and make as if they were tigers. In all other respects, what they imagine is physical. They catch an echo of that powerful leaping movement in their bones, as we say, or in their muscles, triggering the exhilaration that accompanies the enactment of a supremely efficient and goal-directed movement, the exhilaration of *potential* victory (like the aria 'Nessun dorma' from *Turandot* used for the 1990 World Cup). This chapter will explore the cognitive underpinnings for the imaginative simulations that literature affords.

Flights of the imagination

Let's begin by recalling once more Yeats's 'The Balloon of the Mind'. The central metaphor is likely to trigger in the reader a wide-ranging series of inferences. In an era when lighter-than-air balloons had become a common spectacle and indeed a common form of transportation, the principal connotation of the metaphor is flight, upward movement, escape from the downward pull of gravity. When that connotation is blended with the concept of mind, we're liable to think of the kind of mental flight we commonly refer to as imagination, with 'inspiration' as a special sub-category of imagination (note that the word 'inspiration' carries etymologically the notion of a supernatural breath or wind).

The analogy works at several different levels: one is the lightness, the upward movement against gravity; another is no doubt the shape, which is vaguely reminiscent of the head or the eye (one thinks, for example, of the famous 1878 Odilon Redon image of the eye-balloon); another again is its apparent emptiness: it's filled, as people have been saying since those days, with hot air. Smaller balloons (from party balloons to the kind with baskets that are used for individual ascent) are usually brightly coloured, and this corresponds to the way we think about the imagination as a 'colourful' faculty.

The association of the imagination with a lighter-than-air balloon is in fact quite common in the nineteenth and early twentieth centuries. The French Romantic writer Alfred de Vigny's drama *Chatterton*, about a poet who died young, was published with a preface dated June 1834. The preface distinguishes three types of writer; the third of these is the oversensitive, vulnerable, and tormented Romantic poet, who is a creature of the emotions and the imagination:

> When emotion was born in [the poet], it was already such a deep and intimate part of his nature that, from infancy, it cast him into states of involuntary ecstasy, endless dreaming, untrammelled inventiveness. It is above all the imagination that governs him. His powerfully constructed mind [soul][1] retains and judges everything by means of a capacious memory and an unerring, incisive intuition; but the imagination carries his faculties up towards the heavens as irresistibly as the balloon lifts its basket.[2]

It's remarkable that the imagination is associated here with a wide range of cognitive states and skills. Placed under the sign of the non-rational (emotion), it combines heightened states of mind with a capacity for entertaining mental representations decoupled from the everyday world (dreaming), with the ability to invent and improvise, and with a richly furnished memory. All of these will appear again later in this chapter as aspects of human cognition.

Vigny's notion of the imagination is of course the Romantic one, full of unconfined energy: the balloon pulls upward irresistibly and is blown away into uncharted territory. Famously, the suspicion of the imagination which was endemic in medieval and early modern thought, up to and including the Enlightenment, was countered in the earlier nineteenth century by the notion that the imagination has a creative power, and more specifically a *cognitive* power, that gave it ascendancy over 'scientific' reason, materialized as the latter was in the technological innovations of the industrial revolution. Variants of this view have persisted into the twentieth century, contributing to the increasingly sharp divide between the 'two cultures' of which we are still, palpably, the inheritors.[3]

In earlier periods, before the lighter-than-air balloon was invented in Europe (the Chinese were well ahead in this field), the ascent of the imagination could be represented figuratively in a wide range of different ways. Marina Warner's book *Stranger Magic* brilliantly charts some of the manifestations of imaginative flight, on magic carpets and various other improbable affordances, from the world of the *Arabian Nights* and its afterlives.[4] I shall offer only a single pair of examples, taken from the sixteenth-century French Catholic poet Pierre de Ronsard and the seventeenth-century English Puritan poet John Milton, who use strikingly similar expressions to speak of imaginative inspiration as upward flight. Milton evokes 'our high-raised phantasy' in his poem 'At a Solemn Music', probably written around 1633–4;[5] Ronsard's phrasing in his 1554 *Hymn to Bacchus* is 'We raise up to heaven the human fantasy'.[6] In Milton's case, the motor for the ascent is the power of music; Ronsard's imaginative flight is ascribed to Bacchus, a god known not only for his powers of intoxication but also for his wild chariot-rides and his skills as a cosmonaut (having found Ariadne on the beach at Naxos, he carries her up to the heavens in his chariot and turns her into a star). What both imply is that the poetic imagination can gain access to essential truths that are not available to rational thought. Shakespeare's soliloquies on the imagination in *A Midsummer Night's Dream* and other plays also exploit images of flight, lightness, and mobility, and thus provide a further set of early modern examples of this imaginative calculus.

What I mean by 'imaginative calculus' here is the delicate balance these poets achieve between the release of imaginative powers on the one hand and a religious or ethical framework that licenses what would otherwise be a dangerous deviation into illusion and unreality. Putting it historically, what was once regarded literally as supernatural inspiration (having a god inside you, filling you with divine breath) begins to be read in a secular, material sense as a function of the human ability to reach beyond, to think counterfactually. The most compelling image for that ability is, once again, the fantasy of defying gravity, rising into the air. So the lighter-than-air balloon materializes the possibility of going beyond immediate constraints, with all the excitements and risks that that entails.

The awkward wrestling match that Yeats's poem stages between the hands and the balloon, on the other hand, points to a fundamental incompatibility between balloon-like imaginings and the rigorous structure of conceptual thought or its equivalent in poetic form (the discipline of the quatrain as a narrow shed). We all know about the conflict between the rational and the imaginative. It recurs in many different forms: Plato's exclusion of the poet from the ideal Republic; the iconoclasm or asceticism of certain religions; the suspicion of fiction that runs as a theme even through fiction itself (think of Catherine Morland in *Northanger Abbey*, think of Emma Bovary, both avid readers of imaginative fictions); or the suspicion of mimesis and immersion in recent literary theory. It is a matter of common observation that some people are addicted to fiction, poetry, imaginative writing; some people are allergic to it and want to hold on tight to the empirical, the commonsense, the rational.

The history of philosophy, theology, and literature, from Plato onwards, is in fact littered with dire warnings about the capacity of fiction to mislead, confuse, or seduce vulnerable readers. The ubiquity of censorship, whether light-touch and liberal as in Western countries, or tightly controlled by political and religious authorities, is also a tribute to the potentially subversive power of the imagination. Against Vigny's Romantic image of the untrammelled flight of the balloon one can set a late Enlightenment use of the same image by none other than Goethe. It occurs in a letter written in the year after the first manned ascent in a tethered balloon took place in 1783. Goethe is as usual fired up with enthusiasm for Enlightenment values, and, paradoxically enough, he uses the earliest experiments with hot-air balloons to bring the spiritualizing imagination down to earth:

> Just as, in the old days, when human beings were tied to the earth, it was a benefit to direct their gaze to the heavens and make them aware of the spiritual domain, it is an even greater benefit nowadays to bring them back to earth and to reduce somewhat the elasticity of their tethered balloons.[7]

Around a hundred years later, Henry James—who was especially fond of balloon metaphors—also provided checks and balances for the mind-balloon in the preface to his novel *The American*:

> The balloon of experience is in fact of course tied to the earth, and under that necessity we swing, thanks to a rope of remarkable length, in the more or less commodious car of the imagination; but it is by the rope we know where we are, and from the moment that cable is cut we are at large and unrelated: we only swing apart from the globe— though remaining as exhilarated, naturally, as we like, especially when all goes well.[8]

These various instances allow us to trace the persistence of an imaginative anxiety, and an anxiety about the imagination, which has ancient origins. The tricky duality of imagination as at once creative alternative thinking and deceptive illusion, 'mere' fantasy, is endemic in human reflection on the nature of thought and has reappeared regularly at the centre of debates on the value of literature and of art more generally.[9]

Learning to imagine

Psychologists have recently explored this question from another angle by studying the way children think. In the opening chapter of his remarkable book *The Work of the Imagination*, published in 2000, the developmental psychologist Paul Harris evokes the work of the two most influential twentieth-century theorists of development in infancy and early childhood, Freud and Piaget. Both, he points out, promote a view in which infants begin by being self-absorbed in a world of fantasy and wish-fulfilment; as they grow older, they acquire the capacity to reason and adapt themselves, more or less successfully, to what Freud calls the Reality Principle. In this scenario, the imaginary domain is illusory and (if it continues uncontrolled into adulthood) potentially pathological. Harris claims that the evidence of his work with children suggests something very different: 'reality-directed thinking comes first';[10] pretend play and absorption in imaginary worlds only begins when the child has already established a working relation with the real world:

> The capacity for pretence is an important foundation for lifelong normality.... I shall argue that when pretend play does emerge, children draw to a remarkable extent on the causal understanding of the physical and mental world that they have already built up during infancy.... To the extent that absorption in fiction is not a short-lived phenomenon of childhood but a capacity that endures a lifetime, it is appropriate to ask what it is about the cognitive and emotional make-up of human beings that disposes them toward such sustained involvement in other people's lives—including the lives of fictional characters.... For example, children's ability to entertain counterfactual alternatives to an actual outcome is critical for making causal and moral judgements about that outcome.[11]

There are two key points here. In the first place, Harris seeks not only to reduce the opposition between rationality and imagination, but actually to make them interdependent. Secondly, he connects fiction both with the imagination of counterfactual alternatives and with everyday situations where judgement is required. In other words, fiction is conceived here explicitly as a (potentially) useful and effective instrument of thought.

If Harris's account is correct, we should avoid constructing a narrative in which either 'reason' or 'imagination' must come first, and think in terms of their mutual interdependence from the outset. I would argue, in fact, that the distinctively human ability to entertain mental representations and deploy them beyond the bounds of immediate perception and precipitate action is not conceivable as purely rational-logical or purely imaginative-mythical. Rational projections of what might happen in the future, or rational analyses of what has already happened in the recent or more distant past, all depend on a capacity for moving away from momentary sense-experience and immediate needs—a capacity for creating an alternative thought-world. As soon as you have that capacity for thinking counterfactually, for thought-experiments, the horizon of what it is possible to think opens up indefinitely. On the other hand, if those alternative scenarios proliferated without control, the individual would become confused and unfit for survival in the real world, where there are unarguable physical needs. So the balloon of imaginative experience does need to be tethered to the real world, and vice versa. Reason and imagination are not just mutually dependent: they're mutually constitutive.

Cognitive fluidity and epistemic vigilance

Paul Harris isn't the only cognitive psychologist to propose this view, which is enthusiastically defended also, in a different perspective, by Alison Gopnik.[12] One doesn't have to accept all of her hypotheses, or of Harris's for that matter, in order to see the point, the sheer imaginative vision, of this perspective on the way we learn to think. It's crucial to the view of literature presented in this book, so I shall briefly elaborate it here, picking up the themes of cognitive fluidity and cultural improvisation which have already been referred to in earlier chapters.

Cognitive fluidity—the ability to shift between different mental representations, imagine alternative possibilities, predict possible outcomes—is in most recent accounts of human evolution the distinctive feature that gave hominins their ability to adapt, survive in different environments, and spread in successive waves to virtually every part of the world. A key benefit of this enhanced mode of cognition is the capacity to improvise on the basis of locally available materials instead of relying on phylogenetically fixed behaviour routines:[13] the human culture of invented and improvised affordances that we looked at in Chapter 4 just is the expression of cognitive fluidity.

In order to operate freely, cognitive fluidity depends on two further capacities. The first is the exploitation of resting or leisure time, when the mind is not under immediate pressure for executive action. When your cat is sitting in the garden, it may be on the alert for hunting opportunities (or sudden attack from your pit bull terrier), or it may just be recouping its energies, but it is presumably not planning its activities for the next few days or rehearsing options for catching a particularly elusive mouse. Cognitive psychologists sometimes speak of the capacity for 'offline' thinking as central to human cognition, and the metaphor is useful, provided that it is recognized as a metaphor. As I've said elsewhere, antitheses are usually misleading as a way of talking about the way the mind works. When Winnie-the-Pooh sits thinking with his head in his hands (see Chapter 3, last section), he's not engaging directly and physically with the world (eating honey, visiting Piglet, looking for heffalumps, etc.); his sensorimotor activity is reduced to a minimum, and to that extent he could be said to be doing 'offline' thinking. However, cognitive fluidity becomes for humans an alternative form of engagement with the world: think of what happens when a group of people sit round a table to discuss business opportunities or academic research (or fictionally to listen to Marlow in Conrad's novels). Cognition is in that sense always enactive, environmentally engaged.

The second cognitive process that has to be presupposed if the ability to entertain alternative imaginings is not to lead to mental chaos is the constant monitoring of what one might call the epistemic status of a particular representation. When you have a dream, you may be a little confused as you wake up, but you will soon tag it (or 'frame' it) as a dream. When I had a particularly unpleasant dose of influenza in the pandemic of 1957, I had an aural hallucination which I can still vividly recall nearly sixty years later. I also remember my relief when I realized that it was 'only' a hallucination brought on by high temperature and an ear infection. You know, as you read this, that what I am writing is neither a novel nor a poem, but a set of conjectural arguments that are meant to have a certain relation to pragmatic experience of the world (literature being a phenomenon, an object of knowledge, in that world). The kind of thought-experiments proposed by philosophers and the counterfactual versions of the past imagined by historians or novelists are each assigned a place on a spectrum of relations to the real that extends from representations mapped directly onto the real (surveyors' reports, instructions for assembling a shed, and the like) via counterfactuals, thought-experiments, and fictions to dream, delusion, and fantasy. At the latter end of this scale, it becomes especially important to distinguish between imaginings which are not in the individual's control (hallucinations, dreams, illusions, certain kinds of delusion) and those that are voluntary and communicated as such. The distinction may not always be clear-cut, but there is no doubt at all that we need such categories and that we constantly try to assess their relative truth value.

The tagging procedures that appear to be implied by human cognitive flexibility have been specified in some detail by Leda Cosmides and John Tooby,[14] and their model seems to me still to be relatively robust. We might note in particular that they see this cognitive tagging as a hierarchical procedure, not as a single activity of surveillance. In a literary context, one might, for example, take the category 'literature' as implying a preliminary overall assessment; within that field, 'fiction' assigns a particular status that can be further refined by the sub-categories 'realist', 'fantasy', 'science fiction', etc. Those commonplace labels are, however, only the beginning of the story. As one reads a novel, calculations of plausibility will be constantly maintained, intrusions of 'historical' characters or events will lead to reassessments, and the question of ultimate value (What is the work telling us? Where is it going?) will be at least intermittently entertained.[15] Once tagged, whole sets of features can remain in their place while the attention shifts elsewhere (for example, in cases of authorial intrusion, or even real-world intrusion: your spouse comes in and asks you whether the dinner is ready yet). We don't usually have any difficulty in manipulating this quite complex set of cognitive variables and 'knowing where we are'.

In *Why fiction?*, a brilliant study of cognitive aesthetics, Jean-Marie Schaeffer uses the metaphor of 'braking' or 'decoupling' to characterize the cognitive mechanism that allows us to become immersed in fiction without responding as if the fictional scenario was real (one might think of this as analogous with the spontaneous and involuntary uncoupling of our motor responses during dreaming).[16] For Schaeffer, this decoupling function arises specifically from the need to defend oneself against *deception*, itself an evolved response that affords evolutionary advantage, but enormously expanded in humans by the availability of language as a mode of (true or false) communication. Fiction is a pretence, and thus potentially a lie or deception; however, if it declares itself as such, whether externally or internally, the potential for deception is defused. Pretence is a weapon; shared pretence is a game.[17]

The one drawback of this argument, it seems to me, is that it focuses too exclusively on fiction. As I have suggested, 'decoupling' or 'tagging' (in various modes and degrees) has to be presupposed for the whole range of cognitive activities that we designate collectively under the rubric of the imagination; fiction (literary or otherwise) is only one of these, or perhaps rather one set. Without such filtering mechanisms, we don't just risk being deceived; we are liable to lose contact with reality and enter into a delusory world from which we cannot voluntarily escape.

Another way of approaching this phenomenon is provided by Dan Sperber and his colleagues, who have proposed the term 'epistemic vigilance' to designate the cognitive mode of self-protection that results in what Schaeffer refers to as 'decoupling': once your epistemic mechanisms have tagged a set of utterances as 'fiction', or 'pretend play', to use Kendall Walton's term, those utterances become 'decoupled' and their lack of direct truth value is no longer threatening. Sperber is especially preoccupied with the kind of pretence that arises from communication: the danger that others may for their own benefit subvert the ideal goal of using language to convey true information and seek to deceive you. In other words, like Schaeffer, he proposes an essential association between pretence and deception. In that view, communication is contaminated by a kind of arms race. I would argue here again that such a powerful cognitive mechanism cannot be limited, whether in its origin or its use, to a single domain, even such a crucial one as communication. Epistemic vigilance is constitutive of human cognition as such. It allows us to keep our bearings amid the proliferation of mental representations that we are capable of generating, and is in that sense the equivalent of the innate mechanisms that allow small children to learn how to handle their bodies in relation to the empirical physics of the world they live in.

It's true that epistemic vigilance, when deployed in relation to fiction, or more broadly to literature, will be expressed by means of a wide range of specialized protocols (paratexts, authorial or narratorial interventions, etc.) that provide coordinates for its epistemic status. But I think it is enlightening to think of these as special cases of the modes of vigilance that traverse human culture as a whole. They may become reified as a means of collective political or ideological control (censorship, surveillance, the 'thought police') for institutions that have an interest in inhibiting deviation and innovation. More pervasively still, they are at work in all the crevices of everyday language, where they feature as concessive or conditional constructions, modalizing expressions and the seething undergrowth of procedurals.[18] It is thanks to these half-hidden cognitive resources that language can actualize the past, give embodiment to possible futures, and even delineate the shape of things that never existed: the possibility that humans might fly, for example, or become invisible, or find the 'lost chord', or a single equation that expresses all the physical forces of the cosmos and their mutual relations.

Finally, it's essential to remember that, although these epistemic filtering processes self-evidently operate as a constraint on how we think, they are also the precondition for the very possibility of imaginative thought. Without them, predictive and counterfactual thinking would be impossible, as would logical and analogical modelling, calculations of plausibility, and a fortiori what we broadly call imaginative literature. If fiction demands a specially acute epistemic vigilance, that is because it claims the right to imagine unconstrainedly, and vice versa. Epistemic vigilance is thus a permit, an authorization, a passport to other ways of thinking the world. The system is of course imperfect and approximate, riddled with systemic inadequacies, easily disabled, or even itself a source of error. That's what one would expect of a set of processes that have evolved biologically. But it is also why we need as many resources as we can generate to refine and adjust its functioning, and one of these is the imaginative thinking we call literature, together with its reflective counterpart, literary criticism.[19] The interaction of imagination and epistemic vigilance is absolutely central to one's view of what literature is and does, and where its value lies.[20]

Imagination and memory

In the earlier tradition of reflection on the relation between the imagination and reason I've referred to, both were taken to be 'faculties', represented in diagrams of the brain as distinct regions.[21] The imagination had the role of conveying the sensible appearances of everything perceived by the senses to the reason, which (ideally) had the power to penetrate beyond appearance to essence. This process also entailed the participation of the memory, which stored the images of things so that they could be recovered as appropriate by the reason.

Nowadays, this interaction between imagination, memory, and reason would be conceived in more fluid, less hierarchical terms; it would indeed be seen as essential to the fluidity that is the signature of human cognition. Recent work demonstrates that human memory is not a storehouse or a fixed record of things experienced in the past. It is a product of the constant connection and reconnection of neural pathways that occurs in individual human brains throughout their lifetimes; it is highly selective, goal-directed, and above all malleable. We remember the past in ways that are useful to us, or suit our current affective needs; our memories are ceaselessly being reshaped without our being aware of it. Like all our cognitive and physical powers, memory is inevitably fallible and approximate. This slightly alarming phenomenon is, it seems, a consequence of a decisive evolutionary advantage. Memory is of course used enactively (unreflectively, automatically) by all living creatures whose behaviour is adaptively modified during their lifetime; it isn't a luxury for them, and it doesn't, one presumes, afford episodic memories such as a pleasant reminiscence of a particularly successful hunting or mating encounter. Humans have the same capacity for 'procedural' memory, as it is often called: that's how we learn to walk, swim, play tennis or the piano. But we also have the cognitive capacity to use our memories 'offline' as a source of materials that afford planning for the future, whether one envisages such planning in terms of a predictive calculus or as a creative expansion of the options available to us. In other words, memory and imagination are not, as earlier faculty psychologists believed, separate domains, but different aspects of the same set of cognitive processes. Counterfactual thinking ('imagination') is not possible without an expanded and malleable memory, and vice versa.[22]

No wonder, then, that one of the principal resources of modern thinking is the extended and shared (collective) memory made possible by writing, print, wireless telegraphy, and modern computing. No wonder that the concept of an empirically corrected 'history' has been devised in the last five hundred years as a resource for collective attempts to understand and adapt to a rapidly changing world. No wonder, too, that some of the greatest masterpieces of literature, from Homeric epic via *The Divine Comedy* to Shakespeare's history plays and the novels of George Eliot or Thomas Mann, have a memorial function that is inseparable from their imaginative reach. I am

thinking here of collective activities and goods, rather than of individual ('subjective') perceptions of the world, but the phenomenology of what we now call the self is clearly the alternative face
of the same cognitive interactions. That the *feeling* of authenticity
in episodic memory is existentially more important than its empirical
truth value is what drives Proust's master-novel of memory and
imagination.

Competing hemispheres

I've argued at various points in this study against the reduction of
cognitive functions to dichotomies and antitheses: the opposition
between imagination and reason, 'fast and slow' thinking (Kahneman), reflective and pre-reflective cognition, kinesis and mind-
reading, and other apparent dichotomies, must be qualified by a
presupposition of constant feedback, overlaps, and cross-connections.
One further duality needs to be mentioned here. Ever since people
first began to pay close attention to what the insides of human heads
looked like, they have noticed that the brain is divided into two
hemispheres joined by a bundle of nerve fibres (referred to in traditional anatomy as the *corpus callosum*). They are known to be function-
ally asymmetrical: in particular, language functions seem to be
handled primarily by the left hemisphere. A good deal of work has
been done on this structural feature of the brain on the basis of deficits
and brain damage (not only to left or right hemispheres themselves,
but also to the traffic crossing the left–right divide), but it is by no
means clear that, as is popularly believed, it maps onto some broader
cognitive opposition between imaginative, creative thought and
logical processing. Most neuroscientists, whether specialists in the
anatomy of the brain or psychologists drawing inferences from that
anatomy in relation to observed behaviour, have therefore in recent
times been cautious if not sceptical about the conclusions that can be
drawn from the left–right dichotomy. The one exception, and it is a
remarkable one, is Iain McGilchrist's monumental study *The Master
and his Emissary*.[23] McGilchrist adopts a boldly holistic view of the
functioning of the human brain and mind in their environment, and
breathes new life into the opposition between the imaginative and the
logical aspects of human cognition while allowing for continuous

crossovers between them. His account is not only descriptive but also diagnostic. He argues that the logical function of the left hemisphere, together with its crucial linguistic capacity, evolved to serve the otherwise 'silent' right hemisphere, but that the servant (or 'emissary') has taken over in human thought, leading to a warped reliance on ostensibly logical and utilitarian concerns at the expense of creative thought. The prognosis is dire: unless we can somehow re-establish the proper relation between these cognitive powers, the human species is likely to destroy itself. I cite this argument not because I believe it to be 'scientifically' true, but because it is plausible enough to support my own underlying argument that literature is a cognitive resource which is irreducible to logical truth values or what philosophers and some linguists call propositional content. However one looks at it, there is trouble in store if we continue to worship 'science', technology, and logic at the expense of other ways of thinking.

McGilchrist's thesis also projects onto the largest possible canvas the potentiality for more local forms of cognitive dissonance in human behaviour. Arguments like those of Kahneman and Ainslie,[24] according to which humans irrationally prefer relatively trivial short-term benefits to much more substantial long-term ones, or hold 'higher-order' ethical beliefs which their bodies more or less surreptitiously evade, similarly point towards deep-seated possibilities for maladjustment or even malfunction in human cognition. We shall be looking at examples of cognitive dissonance in Chapters 7 and (especially) 8, and it is perhaps as well to bear in mind, as we move away from those brightly coloured and optimistically airborne balloons, to remember that Christopher Robin found it expedient in the end to shoot Pooh and his balloon out of the sky.

Images, pale and vivid

What I have tried to do so far in this chapter is to provide a general cognitive frame of reference for what is commonly called 'the literary imagination'. We need now to address a set of specific questions that arise within that frame. The first of these arises from the range of phenomena and experiences covered by folk uses of the English word 'imagination'. In the course of a detailed inventory of these senses, the philosopher Peter Hacker emphasizes in particular the difference between the counterfactual and the perceptual imagination.[25] I have so far spoken of counterfactual imagining, that is to say the capacity to entertain an indefinite series of alternative outcomes, whether pertaining to the past (counterfactual histories) or the future: the difference between these is embedded in the uses of the conditional mood in English and some other languages: 'if Albertine had not missed her plane, Albert would never have met her'; 'if my aunt leaves me her house in Scotland, I shall move there and start an ostrich farm.' This capacity, which is essential for planning, for scientific and technological innovation, and of course for the fictional imagination, is sometimes known broadly as 'imagining that …', although it may not always take that syntactic form, as these examples show. Perceptual imagining, on the other hand, consists of the ability to call up perceptual representations or simulations—in short, 'images'. This is what people are inclined to think of first when the imagination is spoken of, not least because in the English language that sense is present in the word itself.[26]

It can be argued that the two senses are deeply linked, not because 'imagining that' always entails perceptual simulations, but precisely because both are aspects of the human ability to think beyond the immediate demands of their environment. Besides, all our conceptions, however 'abstract', are grounded in perceptual and sensorimotor experience: even a geometric or numerical projection is only imaginable insofar as it can be related to the world as we know it.[27] But even if one admitted the possibility of pure abstractions (nonperceptual imaginings), they would hardly be relevant to the kinds of imaginative representation explored and exploited by literature.

There is a terminological issue here which I have touched on before and which I propose by and large to evade. Powerful philosophical objections have been made to the use of words like 'representation', 'simulation', 'mimesis'; yet none of them, it seems to me, evacuate the need to suppose what is intuitively evident, namely that human cognition is capable of representing, modelling, or simulating objects of perception by neurological processes that are as yet poorly understood, and that it can entertain those simulations—or something recognizably like them—in the absence of corresponding perceptual experiences.[28] In what follows, I shall adopt a pragmatic line. I shall at all times concede that our perceptual systems, memory systems (recovery of perceived experience), and mental representations are approximate, defective, indeed sometimes illusory, and that the ways we talk about them are often crude and inadequate; but I shall assume that these defects are properties of a biological instrumentation which was not evolved under laboratory conditions but through an incalculably large number of real-world encounters and their outcomes. The system we have is not like a machine, a computer, or a mathematical model; it is eccentric, often unreliable, fragile and vulnerable when under extreme pressure, yet at the same time robust. It has got us where we, the denizens of complex human ecologies, are now, and it serves us pretty well. Because the words we use to describe it are also vulnerable to close linguistic analysis (what exactly is a 'simulation' or a 'representation'?), redescription must be a constant task of such discussion, but the phenomena one finds oneself talking about keep offering themselves obstinately to our attention.

Let's look more closely, then, at a particular problem which bears directly on the notion of simulation, and of which literature affords an enormous and exotic range of examples. The problem was already formulated by ancient Greek philosophers, but it has surprisingly been overlooked in many discussions of these effects.[29] As Aristotle puts it in his treatise on rhetoric, 'imagination is a weakened sensation':[30] that is to say that imaginary representations lack the force and clarity of actual perception. We know by introspection that this is true: try to visualize what your kitchen or your garden looks like and think about the quality of the image you construct as compared with actually being in the kitchen or garden. Even the faces of our friends and family are hazy and blurred when we try to visualize them from memory. The imagination isn't a brightly lit theatre of colourful perceptions: it's a dim, ill-focused back room (that too is of course merely a heuristic metaphor). The cognitive psychologist Chris Frith goes so far as to assert that 'imagination is boring', because it seems— surprisingly, perhaps—that we can't adjust and correct imagined representations as fluidly as we can adjust our immediate ('online') modelling of the world.[31]

People of course have different competences in imagined perception. The autistic writer Temple Grandin asserts that she thinks in pictures;[32] people with a strong acoustic imagination believe that they can 'play through' a whole symphony in their minds, attending to the distinctive timbres of the different instruments as well as melodies, harmonies and harmonic shifts, rhythm, dynamics, and overall structure. Even in those extreme cases, however, it remains unclear how close these pictures or sounds are to those that are seen or heard as a consequence of actual perception. The seeming clarity of the offline representation is in any case still limited to that of our cognitive apparatus, the brain activity that models the world, and it has to operate here without the set of stimuli that millions of years of phylogenetic evolution have programmed us to respond to.

And yet we regularly speak of the imagination as vivid, brightly coloured, like the balloon. And the whole of the Western rhetorical tradition has insistently attributed this vividness to literary representations (ekphrasis). So, if the imaginary 'pictures in our head' are dull and blurred, how do imagined scenes deliver that sense of immediacy, intensity? Or to rephrase the question from within a cognitive theory of fiction: how do fictional simulations induce in the reader or spectator a state of immersion, where you are taken over by the imagined scenario to such an extent that you feel frightened, happy, erotically stimulated, angry, disappointed, and so on?[33]

The first move one needs to make here—I anticipated it in my introductory remarks on the imagined tiger of *Henry V*—is to stop thinking of such scenes as 'pictures', a habit that arises in part, perhaps, from the etymology of 'imagination', which seems to presuppose that 'images' (in the pictural not the figurative sense) are central to offline mental representations. A remarkably high proportion of those who talk about such things use predominantly visual points of reference and analogies, whereas it is of course also possible, as I've already mentioned, to imagine sounds and other kinds of sense-experience (the warm sun on your back when you're sunbathing, the refreshing taste of freshly squeezed orange juice straight out of the fridge, the sensation of rubbing your hand across velvet or sandpaper). More generally, it's useful to stop thinking of the mind as an apparatus that can, at will, construct a high-fidelity sensory model of the world as it is. The capacity to imagine is a remarkable phenomenon, but it doesn't have a great deal in common with digital recording techniques. Some of the ways in which it achieves its power arise from the awareness we have of motor processes, in other people's bodies and our own, and this will be relevant throughout what follows. It is a perspective that fits extremely well with the 'affordances' perspective outlined in Chapter 4 and should thus form a central thread, as I see it, in any properly cognitive approach to literature.

Let us then examine some alternative ways of explaining the undoubted sense of intensity that the imagination (or rather imagined representations) can in the right circumstances deliver.

The first experiment reported by Harris in his study of children's imagination concerns an instance of pretend play.[34] An adult carer shows a 2-year-old child a teddy bear and a cardboard shoebox. She makes a twiddling gesture at one end of the shoebox. 'Teddy's going to have a bath,' she says. The child helps her to put the teddy into the box. She then takes a yellow building block and shows it to the child. 'We're going to give teddy a good wash with the soap,' she says. The child rubs the teddy all over with the block. 'There, you see,' the adult says, 'Teddy's nice and clean now. Let's dry him.' She takes a sheet of paper and gives it to the child, who unhesitatingly makes the gestures of 'drying' the bear with it.[35]

Harris points out that the child has no difficulty in participating in the game, in immersing herself in the virtual world the carer has initiated her into with the help of the two or three very ordinary props or affordances used here. What is more, the child is not confused about the relation between pretence and reality. She doesn't really think that the teddy has got wet, for example. If the carer were to fill the sink with water and make as if to plunge the teddy bear into it, the child would no doubt be quite upset and try to stop her. Yet she uses those very basic props as if they really were what they are supposed to represent.

How does this happen? Immersions can be induced in many different ways, but in this case, it looks as if it is the simulation of *actions* that affords the immersion. The objects themselves are only improvised props. Any roughly rectangular receptacle of the appropriate size would have done for a bath; a matchbox could have been used for the soap. Improvisation is key here. Humans have the capacity to come up with props at short notice in order to model a situation: compare the familiar scenario of the old soldier who bores his friends every night in the pub by describing the strategies of the battles he participated in with the help of beer glasses, beermats, pencils, and any other implements that come to hand. In the right circumstances, such props can trigger acts of imagination which are richer than anything that could have been achieved with more realistic means. Children notoriously prefer household equipment over bought toys as features in their game-worlds. The game of chess provides another example: the game itself doesn't require personified pieces (bishops, knights, etc.), but the fact that they are personified lends a kind of virtual reality to the battles the game stages; and if you go to a shop where they specialize in these things, you will be offered a wide range of different sets, each suggesting a different virtual world.[36] Note that the differences are slight, the props are minimal, in relation to the imaginative possibilities they afford.[37]

The next strategy for explaining the power of imaginative representations is to recall the motor resonance theory. When fictional mimesis works, one might conjecture, that's not because it 'paints pictures' for the imagination. It stimulates the neural areas that are involved when we perform a given action or have a perceptual experience: kinesic response is immediate and pre-reflective, rather than cognitively mediated, so it *seems* vivid. Descriptions (ekphrases) that draw on such cognitive effects are likely to be more powerfully immersive for the reader than those that don't. What is more, they don't require extensive mimesis. Miniature kinesic details embedded in a context that is non-descriptive (e.g. a dialogue) can energize that context as a whole: the very economy of the means used (what one might call a micro-mimesis) ensures that the expressive direction of the passage will be communicated to the reader with maximum effect.

Another solution to the problem is brilliantly explored by Elaine Scarry in her study *Dreaming by the Book*, where she argues that the most powerful fictional simulations of sense-experience are those that model the structure of the cognitive process itself, rather than just enumerating sense-data. One simple example would be the zoom effect: the cognitive gaze is led towards a focal centre, just as, when we scan a scene in the real world, we instinctively and swiftly move towards a significant, distinctive, or salient feature. Scarry chooses a complex literary example from the opening volume of Proust's novel *A la recherche du temps perdu*. The child Marcel watches a slide projection of the story of the medieval story-character Golo. When the projector is moved, the transparent images it throws as it passes over the surfaces of walls, curtains, furniture, a doorknob make the solidity of those surfaces salient: they appear real by an effect of contrast.[38] Scarry is drawing here on the theory of perception of James Gibson, the inventor of the term 'affordance', and the relation between the two domains is immediately clear. The mode of 'perceptual modelling' is also thoroughly compatible with the motor resonance theory, in that both are features of what Varela and others have referred to as our 'enactive' engagement with the world.

These different frames of reference are clearly distinct in character and draw on different perceptual and cognitive processes, but their convergence can make for powerful mimetic effects in literature. The first example in Chapter 7 will display this convergence in some detail, and then show how mind-reading operates within the perceptual-kinesic ecology of a brilliantly imagined stage event. The second example, taken from prose fiction, will focus on a shift from kinesic awareness to an instance of asymmetrical three-way mind-reading between characters. Taken together, these two examples propose a flexible model of what one might call 'cognitive mimesis' in prose fiction. By this I mean enactive scenes in which human movement, gesture, or posture in a highly specific environment is continuous with mind-reading. I shall thus draw in that chapter on a number of strands of cognitive methodology, showing how they converge or coincide in complex literary works. Chapter 8 takes this process still further, adding strands such as epistemic vigilance, but absorbing them into a continuous act of critical analysis which is cognitively inflected but never dominated schematically by cognitive methodologies. However, as I have explained in the preface, the link between the present chapter and Chapters 7 and 8 will be suspended in order to address first (Chapter 6) questions of imagination and the image in lyric poetry, while opening up a dialogue with the vision of language as communication proposed by relevance theorists.

6

Cognitive Figures

What counts as a metaphor?

Is the tiger in Henry V's line 'Imitate the action of the tiger' an image? A metaphor? It's hard to decide. As I pointed out earlier, he certainly doesn't expect his troops to go down on all fours and make a tiger-like leap. But the tiger is not properly speaking metaphorical here, as it is in the old but memorable Esso advertisement 'Put a tiger in your tank', or in the (again historic) Chinese claim that the USA is a 'paper tiger'. Perhaps the notion of 'imitation' suggests rather a simile: 'as the tiger leaps to seize its prey, so too you should hurl yourself vigorously into action against the enemy.' In cognitive terms, however, these classifications are not especially helpful. What is striking rather is the invitation to simulate a particular kind of sensorimotor *action*: the simulation is enactive rather than visual. One might form some perception-like image of a big stripy animal, but only fleetingly. Henry's ad hoc tiger motivates a kinesic engagement with the world.

Of course, sensory references, whether in poetry, prose, or everyday language, are often significantly visual, as when Leontes in *The Winter's Tale* says, 'I have drunk and seen the spider' (he is not only, as he supposes, being cheated by his wife, but is also aware of it). But note that even this example, where the notion of seeing is in the text itself, is not purely visual. The reference to drinking triggers a response connected with taste and even tactile sensations (do you want that spider in your mouth, on your tongue, crunched between your teeth?). Other implicatures come in too. In Elizabethan times, for example, spiders were more strongly connected with poison than they are nowadays: it is as if Leontes' cup were literally a poisoned chalice.

So 'images' in literature, as indeed in everyday speech, are not 'pictures', as the word might imply (we return here to a point made in the previous chapter). They are sensory representations (perception-like imaginings) that have what Guillemette Bolens has called an 'expressive direction':[1] they have intended goals and functions, and may often evoke sensorimotor or kinesic responses within a specific context. They are also affordances, vectors of cognitive purpose in which cognition is inextricably suffused with affect. This chapter will focus primarily on small-scale sensory and sensorimotor imaginings in literary texts, and more specifically in poetry.

The cognitive fluidity of the metaphorical spectrum

In a cognitive perspective, 'poetic' language is not intrinsically *sui generis*. There are no features of literary language that don't have a counterpart in everyday speech. The perceived differences are effects of salience and density. We might say that poetry is especially rich in metaphor, for example, or that Donne's metaphor of lovers as a pair of compasses in 'A Valediction Forbidding Mourning' is original, arresting, or idiosyncratic. But it's not abnormal for people engaging in ordinary conversation to use clusters of metaphors, or metaphors that are arresting or idiosyncratic. Similarly, the acoustic patterning that becomes especially salient in verse is also used at a lower level of salience in everyday language to achieve expressive effects (as in the current buzz phrase 'fat cats'). It follows that any theoretical account of language ought to be valid for literary uses of language, although it might need to be elaborated and fine-tuned in order to account for perceived differences.

One might want to say, however, that communicative intention, function, and context have important consequences for the way utterances are processed, and that the *uses* of literary language set it apart from everyday communicative exchange in respect of all these factors. Does this mean that we need a different theory of language use, a different pragmatics, to account for literary works? That question is harder to answer. A theory of language according to which the communication of propositional content has priority is likely to run into difficulty with literary critics who may want to argue that poetry, literary style, perhaps also whole prose fictions, are modes of communication in which propositional content is only one factor, and indeed (at least in some cases) a subordinate one. If Donne's 'A Valediction Forbidding Mourning' or Shakespeare's *The Tempest* or George Eliot's *Middlemarch* is paraphrased, or even translated (translation being a specially confined mode of paraphrase), most people will agree that much of what made the work distinctive will be lost. And it doesn't seem satisfactory to argue that what is lost is only packaging, a residual formal apparatus that is not part of the message; or that it is only the affective and kinesic dimensions of the literary utterance. The hackles of literary readers and critics would instantly rise at the very word 'only' in those last propositions. The manner of delivery is of the essence in the experience mediated by literary communication. That is why 'poetry' in the broadest sense of the word has for three millennia been an exemplary point of reference for the classical tradition of rhetoric, which is itself a theory of communication.

Metaphor, accompanied by its cohort of sister figures, has always been at the centre of Western rhetoric and poetics, but it has emerged as the key figure since the later nineteenth century with the rise of symbolist poetry and the conception of an intense lyrical performance that is close in some sense to the 'content-less' communicative mode of music. That historical question will not feature explicitly in what follows, but some of the examples I have chosen (Verlaine, Éluard) do in some sense take it for granted. It is no doubt one of the reasons why literary critics are inclined to think of metaphor as embodying that which is most essential to the expressive power of lyric poetry (it was not always so). The challenge is perhaps rather to avoid using the word as a token of value and to attempt to identify at close quarters the kinds of cognitive power that it can deliver.

Such issues are in a sense commonplaces of literary criticism, but they need to be addressed again each time a theory of language is put forward. Relevance theory has not yet been much exploited by literary critics,[2] but it offers a way of rethinking a number of fundamental questions concerning the relationship of language to meaning which could potentially be extraordinarily beneficial for literary study. This chapter will therefore take the form of a loose-weave dialogue with recent work that proposes ways in which metaphor might be handled from a relevance theory perspective, and hence touches on questions that are essential to literary forms of expression and communication.[3] The object is to open up a dialogue between the thought-world of relevance theory and the methodological constraints of literary study.

It is a founding principle of the cognitive approach to literature that such an approach, if it is to be both generally valid and useful as an instrument of analytic reading, would need to maintain a working relation between a general explanatory framework and a focus on the infinitely varied particulars of literary texts. Those particulars must not be elided or reduced in the interests of generalities, otherwise their relevance to the work of colleagues in other disciplines (linguistics, psychology, philosophy) will fall away. In literary studies, in other words, the unique detail must always be regarded as a non-negotiable constraint. Nowhere is the importance of detail more salient than in the literary use of figures of speech, and above all of metaphor.

Take for example the deceptively simple everyday word 'of'. It occurs, in figures like Yeats's 'balloon of the mind', as a tiny, flexible instrument for sticking things together or turning one thing into another. Yeats's phrase belongs grammatically to a familiar class of figurative expressions: 'the X of the P' is an underspecified formula that proposes a kind of metaphorical equivalence. It is not unlike metonymy, since the genitive 'of', in literal cases, asserts a property of the thing described, as in 'the colour of the shirt'. But the figurative or poetic version of the expression asserts an approximate identity: 'the mind is a (kind of) balloon'. One might nowadays say in colloquial speech, 'In my dream, I saw this, like, balloon which was my mind and I was trying to pull it into this weird, like, shed thing.' The genitive, in other words, is a minimal procedural tool that slightly eases the shock of metaphorical identification.

What this preliminary example already suggests, I think, is that logically-based distinctions between figural categories have only a heuristic value. Much is made of the so-called opposition between metaphor and simile, but poets in practice turn one into the other whenever it suits them. Here is Baudelaire evoking the prison-house of 'spleen' (one might nowadays call it depression):

> Quand la terre est changée en un cachot humide,
> Où l'Espérance, comme une chauve-souris,
> S'en va battant les murs de son aile timide
> Et se cognant la tête à des plafonds pourris;

Quand la pluie étalant ses immenses traînées
D'une vaste prison imite les barreaux,
Et qu'un peuple muet d'infâmes araignées
Vient tendre ses filets au fond de nos cerveaux, . . . [4]

(When the earth is changed into a damp dungeon, in which Hope like a bat keeps beating the walls with her timid wings and knocking her head against the rotten ceilings; | When the rain, drawing out its endless trails, imitates the bars of a vast prison and a mute population of loathsome spiders come to hang their webs in the depths of our brains, . . .)

What is the function of 'changée' in the first line of this quotation? One could say that metamorphosis in this case acts out the shift into metaphor; but since the word draws attention to the transference itself, it is also close to simile. An explicit simile follows in the next line, providing the key for reading the personification (or batification) of the abstract noun 'Espérance', which continues in densely realized detail throughout the remainder of the stanza: we have here something like a miniature allegory. In the second quoted stanza, a literal evocation of the rain becomes explicitly metaphorical via the verb 'imite': in other words, it again has affinities with simile (and of course with the line from *Henry V* we began with). What one has, then, is a constant blurring of the lines of standard rhetorical or logical categorization. At the height of his powers, Baudelaire is opportunistic, improvising connections in an ever-expanding network. The figurative dimension of the poem (the dungeon scene) infiltrates and saturates its nominally 'literal' or abstract counterpart (a mental experience). I have left out the powerful kinesic effects (the flight of the bat, for example), but even without those, there is a process of embodiment here which can't be reduced to a set of formally defined rhetorical devices. The outcome, one might want to say, is a cognitive tour de force rather than a rhetorical one.

Relevance theorists would, I think, broadly agree with this analysis. They argue that metaphor is not a natural kind but a special variant of processes intrinsic to language use, such as loosening, broadening, and hyperbole.[5] That argument is hard to resist. Despite the prestige attached to the notion of metaphor in literary study, the segmentation and classification of 'figures of speech' that characterizes classical rhetorical theory is indeed in large measure a product of post hoc rational analysis: even the rhetorical tradition itself has always recognized that the contiguity of figures such as metonymy, synecdoche, catachresis, allegory, metalepsis, and metaphor is porous.

A cognitive approach might offer a useful explanation for the recurrent desire to distinguish and classify them. Adopting Dan Sperber's notion of epistemic vigilance, for example, or the 'tagging' approach of Cosmides and Tooby, one might say that the shifting logic of rhetorical figures, which could create epistemic anxiety, needs to be referred to truth values or more generally a relation to the empirical world. Simile is reassuring because it makes explicit the act of comparing two previously unconnected concepts; metonymy, too, is 'tamer' than metaphor because it remains within the domain of the source concept. *Occupatio, concessio, praeteritio,* and other so-called 'figures of thought', for their part, reveal the mechanisms of what might be a deception: that perception might help the speaker to deceive her audience or interlocutor, but it would also allow the knowing listener to recognize the deception. The 'art' of rhetoric might thus be described as an attempt to provide an account of the powers of communicative and persuasive language within a framework of epistemic vigilance.

We return here to an argument that has surfaced more than once in this study: the epistemic calculus, however it is described or characterized, is the indispensable other of the inventive imagination. Always alert, always active in measuring distance from real-world constraints, it thereby also authorizes and liberates counterfactual thinking. Accordingly, poetics should not become a formalistic exercise that assigns each figure to its own separate pigeon-hole. As they are actually used, poetic figures, like other features of language, slide across boundaries, mutate, combine with each other in unexpected configurations. A literary pragmatics, in other words, needs both to recognize and to partake in the cognitive fluidity of the metaphorical spectrum.

An array of implicatures

Let's focus first on one major line of approach proposed by relevance theory that bears on a fundamental issue in literary analysis. The notion of 'implicature(s)' is central to relevance theory's insistence that language is only partially a code; words are offered as evidence of the speaker's thought, which will always be highly context-dependent. The interlocutor derives from the utterance propositional content which is often only implied. Whereas the *implication* of a given utterance may or may not be intended by the speaker, an *implicature* must arise from what the speaker intended to mean, even if it is a somewhat remote derivative of the speech act (a weak implicature). Implicatures are *inferred* by the interlocutor: as we saw in Chapter 2, the work of inference is crucial to relevance theory's conception of language as radically underdetermined. A classic case is the following exchange:

> *Speaker A:* 'Have you read Dan Brown's latest novel?'
> *Speaker B:* 'I don't read rubbish.'

In order to understand speaker B's answer, speaker A will need to draw a two-stage inference: that speaker B regards Dan Brown's novels as rubbish, and therefore that he hasn't read this one and doesn't intend to.[6] The first of these inferentially derived propositions is an implicature; the second, once the first has been derived, becomes an explicature. One could argue that 'rubbish' too requires inferential treatment as a worn-out metaphor meaning something like 'bad novels'; but one could also claim that 'rubbish' in this sense is already lexicalized, in which case no additional inferential work is required.[7] These very basic manoeuvres will be relevant to the more complex instances considered in what follows.

Sperber and Wilson regard poetic effects as a special case of language use where relevance is achieved through a broad range of weak implicatures. This claim is developed through readings of two uncontroversially 'literary' texts, a haiku and Carl Sandburg's poem 'Fog'. The haiku is offered as an example of a 'simple, literal description' giving rise to a 'wide array of implicat[ures] which combine to depict a landscape, a season, a moment of the day, a mood, and so on'.[8] This, too, is at first sight uncontroversial. Here is the haiku:

> On a leafless bough
> A crow is perched—
> The autumn dusk.[9]

We might note that the bird is omitted by Sperber and Wilson from the list of literal details; and that their phrase 'and so on' gestures towards other possibilities that might, for example, include affect. If this is a 'simple, literal description', one might first ask, how does it depict not only 'a landscape, a season, a moment of the day' but also a *mood*? One would surely want to say that, for a mood to be evoked by these words, the reader will need to assign to them something other than their literal sense. Per se, the sight of a bird sitting on a branch on an autumn evening evokes no particular mood. Most readers would, I think, agree that the relevant details for the constitution of a mood are the words 'leafless', 'crow', 'autumn' and 'dusk'. The suffix '-less' is a miniature instance of the rhetorical figure of *praeteritio* (mentioning something while simultaneously saying you're not going to mention it). In relevance theory terms, it could perhaps be regarded as having procedural properties:[10] the adjective as a whole gives us the instruction: 'think of leaves, then subtract them'. As for crows, it's a commonplace of folk knowledge that they're (a) black, (b) solitary birds. 'Autumn' is a season of the year where sunlight diminishes ('less sun', 'sunless'), and 'dusk' similarly denotes the fading of the light: 'autumn dusk' is thus doubly privative. None of these details on their own, or even when presented as a set, would necessarily evoke a mood, as this little story shows:

> That autumn, towards evening, a crow was sitting on a branch. The branch had already lost its leaves, so the crow became an easy target for the farmer, who with her shotgun blasted it into a heap of black feathers and gore.

What ensures that the details will evoke a mood is that they occur in a haiku. Haikus are known to be miniature poetic instruments that afford moods – that is simply what they do. The reader will therefore use any significant clustering of implicatures (leaflessness, black colour, fading of the light, etc.) as mood-affordances. The implicatures of 'leafless' are reinforced by the implicatures of 'crow' and again by those of 'autumn dusk', creating a highly underdetermined yet highly focused effect about which readers are unlikely to disagree to any significant degree, even if they might describe it somewhat differently when asked to do so. Words like 'melancholy' and 'solitude' would be used to characterize this mood, and some might add notions such as the decline of life, bleakness of outlook, and the like, turning the haiku more explicitly into a mini-allegory where the crow would be read anthropomorphically as a *personification* of melancholy, solitude, or a similar affective state.[11]

The object of this extended unpacking of the haiku and its implicatures is to show, first of all, that the word 'literal' has a rather odd status when one talks about poetry. Is this not, pragmatically speaking, a metaphorical crow rather than an item from an ornithological handbook? Is the leafless bough not also a metaphor, rather than an item from a gardening handbook? Admittedly, metaphor is not enacted in the language of the haiku as such. One could imagine a rather bad variant, as follows:

> On the naked arm of a tree
> A coal-black presence broods—
> An autumn crow.

But it's not clear that the processing required to read the metaphors in this version is essentially different from that which is required to read the original version. In both cases, the presence of neutral empirical items can only be explained in terms of a further set of meanings which is obtained by the successive reinforcement of implicatures I've mentioned.

My second main point here is that what Sperber and Wilson call a wide range—or an array—of implicatures is not as permissive and indeed arbitrary as that phrase might lead one to suppose. The operative (salient) details are placed in a precise relation to one another, thus imposing quite rigorous constraints on the range of readings that might be derived. I shall return to this point later, but for the moment I would simply like to assert that poetic language is extremely precise, and that there is therefore a sense in which, instead of using the centrifugal metaphor of an ever-widening *array* of implicatures, one could speak of a web or a cage of implicatures. It's important here to recall that an implicature is an intended implication: the poet knows very well, whether intuitively or reflectively, that her poem will construct such a cage. That's precisely why she writes it.

Finally, the derivation of poetic effects is never exclusively an abstract logical procedure. The logic of derivation I have applied here, and that Sperber and Wilson apply in their analysis of other examples, is not a description of how cognitive processes actually operate but a schematized model of how they might operate, couched in the reassuring language of academic rationality. When I read this haiku, suspending my aim of participating in an interdisciplinary dialogue, 'leafless' emerges not as a rhetorical figure or a privative but as a momentary imagining. It elicits the traces of an experience I have had hundreds of times, the sight of a tree that has just lost its leaves in the autumn, together with the contextual memories that experience brings with it for me, together of course with all the literary occurrences of that same image that are accessible in my personal archive. The word 'dusk' has sounds that are part of its effect, not something added to a literal meaning: a whispering, a rustling, for example. The synonym 'sundown' would not have had the same meaning or produced the same effect (and I do not wish to separate meaning from effect here: the meaning and the effect are mutually dependent). More generally, when I read the haiku, it does in fact communicate to me a 'mood'. I don't just perform cognitive acrobatics, I feel in a certain way that engages my sensory and affective responses. Perhaps it is useful to recall Bolens's phrase and speak of the 'expressive direction' of the haiku. Once again, it makes little sense, I think, to say that my feeling is a by-product: it is precisely what the haiku *means* to communicate.

Ad hoc concepts and emergent properties

I turn now to the interesting question of ad hoc concepts, one of the many useful analytic tools developed by relevance theorists.[12] Here is one of their favourite examples of metaphor as it might arise in everyday speech:

> That surgeon is a butcher.

According to relevance theory, the concept BUTCHER (a tradesman who stocks, cuts, and sells meat) becomes in this sentence the ad hoc concept BUTCHER*.[13] The interlocutor will instantly recognize that the surgeon is not a BUTCHER; he is someone who exhibits some attributes that may be appropriate for a butcher but are not appropriate for a surgeon (cutting through flesh coarsely and without regard for the creature's welfare, for example). The attributes of BUTCHER* would be communicated in such a sentence as implicatures. Furthermore, it is evident that the meaning of BUTCHER* in this sentence is modified in advance, as it were, by the meaning of SURGEON. This is not a butcher in a butcher's shop, but a surgeon-as-butcher. This new and special property of BUTCHER* is known in relevance theory terms as an emergent property.[14]

Ad hoc concepts are not intrinsically metaphorical, but the argument of Sperber and Wilson suggests that all metaphors should be regarded as ad hoc concepts.[15] They involve an on-the-spot readjustment of the listener's standard response to the utterance. We might note here that readjustment is a necessary feature of the listener's understanding of any utterance as it is delivered, since all utterances unfold over time. Potential phonological and syntactical patterns are reinforced or discarded, reference-assignments may be updated, lexical meanings may shift, and ad hoc concepts are formed as new items in the linear auditory flow become available for processing. Such adjustments are made, according to relevance theory, with reference to a mutual mind-reading process between speaker and interlocutor. In speaking about malapropisms and the ease with which interlocutors habitually correct them, Donald Davidson refers to what he calls a 'passing theory', the rapid construction of ad hoc suppositions that may be reinforced or discarded as the utterance proceeds.[16] Projected onto a larger canvas, a 'passing theory' would, I assume, be an equally suitable term for the way that readers of a detective novel (or indeed any plotted narrative) construct provisional interpretations of the action that make enough sense for the reading process to proceed, even though they may sooner or later require considerable adjustment. Red herrings in a fictional plot, one could say, would in that broader context count as something like deliberate malapropisms, although in this case the reader *is* (temporarily) fooled. So we are looking here at a fundamental aspect of communication, not simply of metaphor.

Let's turn for a moment now to the issue of 'dead' or lexicalized metaphors. Suppose I'm driving along a motorway. I enter an area marked out with traffic cones and various kinds of warning notice. One of these says: 'HEAVY PLANT CROSSING'. I'm likely in the context to access the lexicalization of the metaphor 'plant' that signifies 'equipment', 'machinery'. Is this an ad hoc concept? I would be inclined to say that it isn't, since it is lexicalized. The notion of a plant (= a vegetable organism) doesn't come into my head. However, my

8-year-old daughter, ignorant of the sense 'equipment', but familiar with the vegetable sense, might from the back seat be heard to say: 'What a funny notice! How could a heavy plant cross the road?' I would then of course access that other sense of 'plant' and imagine for a moment a heavy vegetable- or flower-like creature, walking (perhaps on its roots) across the road. 'Dead' metaphors of that kind can always be revived: if you know some Latin, you will know that the word 'concept' is derived from a verb meaning 'to grasp' or 'to capture', an etymology that is still active in Germanic languages (*Begriff*, *begrep*, etc.), including English, where one of the lexicalized meanings of 'to grasp' is 'to understand'. There is in other words no clear borderline between 'dead' and 'live' metaphors, only a gradient at one end of which are the dead metaphors that are lost from any conceivable folk memory, while at the other end are new ad hoc concepts which may or may not become lexicalized. What one is looking at here is the process of language formation and development itself, a process known in rhetoric as catachresis: the drafting in of a figurative term when a literal term is absent from the vocabulary of the given language, with the long-term consequence that that word becomes the literal term. When we talk about the 'legs' of a table, we are using what was once a catachresis (an ad hoc concept), but the same is true of a large proportion of the vocabulary of any language, and, arguably, of all of its conceptual vocabulary.

One thing leads to another

Many metaphors in ordinary language, and some metaphors in literary language, are like the surgeon-butcher example in that they have the simple structure 'X is a Y'. Here is one from the opening line of the twelve-line poem 'Clair de lune', by Paul Verlaine:

> Votre âme est un paysage choisi[17]
> (Your soul is a chosen[18] landscape)

Let's assume that an ad hoc concept [CHOSEN][19] LANDSCAPE* is formed by the reader on the wing. She is likely already to have assigned (provisionally at least) a standard referent for 'Your', namely the speaker's (or poet's) beloved. This would enable the reader to form the passing theory that this is a poem attributing to the beloved's nature the qualities of a chosen landscape. These qualities would be described in relevance theory terms as the emergent properties that arise when the concept [CHOSEN] LANDSCAPE is adjusted in relation to the concept YOUR SOUL (it becomes an 'inner' landscape, or perhaps what Eliot famously called an objective correlative for an imagined set of personal qualities).

The remainder of the poem, however, is exclusively devoted to the expansion of the landscape concept. This is a landscape peopled with figures who dance and sing, pretending to be happy, but looking as if they don't believe in their happiness; their song mingles with the moonlight, which makes the birds dream in the trees and makes the fountains in the garden sob in ecstasy. This bald summary of the poem leaves out a number of details, but it will do for my purposes. One could perhaps say here that a secondary series of ad hoc adjustments are made to the ad hoc concept [CHOSEN] LANDSCAPE*. But of course they are not new ad hoc concepts. Once the initial adjustment has been made, the remaining adjustments remain within its scope.

That analysis is perhaps not complete, in that some of the subsequent features of this landscape could themselves be said to be quasi-metaphorical. For example, only metaphorical moonlight can make birds dream and fountains sob. Only metaphorical birds can dream (in the sense implied here, which is a function of human imagination). Only metaphorical fountains can sob in ecstasy. However, a reading of this poem in the frame of reference of traditional poetics and rhetoric would not invoke metaphor here. One would want to say rather that the whole landscape is a personification (of the beloved), a description that makes sense of all the anthropomorphic attributes assigned to the moonlight, the birds, and the fountains. In this respect, if no others, Verlaine's poem is comparable with the haiku, although of course there is no opening 'Your soul is...' in that poem.

One could rephrase that account in relevance theory terms by saying that the ad hoc concept [CHOSEN] LANDSCAPE* initiates a series of emergent properties. Only on arriving at the erotic image of the conclusion will the reader be able to create a single inclusive frame that is compatible with the opening phrase 'Your soul is...'. For a skilled reader (for example, one who has read a good deal of Verlaine's other poetry), the emergence of landscape* properties happens without conscious reflection. In literary analysis, and for readers who may take longer to familiarize themselves with the poetic idiom and materials, it may require sustained reflection, which would necessarily include attention to verse-form, rhyme and other acoustic effects. One could therefore neither say that a sustained metaphor necessarily demands reflective processes of that kind, nor conversely that the initial ad hoc construction of [CHOSEN] LANDSCAPE* is 'normally' carried out intuitively or unconsciously.

We touch here on an issue explored by Robyn Carston.[20] Carston modifies the notion of the ad hoc concept to include a second type of processing that 'metarepresents' the literal component throughout the duration of extended metaphors. She takes issue with Sperber and Wilson's assertion that, in Carl Sandburg's tiny poem 'Fog', the 'fog-cat' metaphor presupposes the formation of an ad hoc concept, which they characterize as LITTLE-CAT-FEET*, whereas in fact the metaphor is sustained over the lines that follow, requiring further reflective work. Here is the poem:

> The fog comes
> on little cat feet.
>
> It sits looking
> over harbor and city
> on silent haunches
> and then moves on.[21]

It will be evident that Carston's approach here is not unlike the one I adopted for the Verlaine poem. In Sandburg's poem, as in Verlaine's, an ad hoc concept is constructed on the wing, but once it is in place, it affords an extension of the emergent properties it suggests which is only complete when the poem ends. Whether an experienced reader will need to draw on a special set of reflective processes in order to make sense of the poem, or to enjoy its effects, is less clear to me, but that is a matter that we may perhaps leave aside here.[22]

There is, however, another question that is difficult to answer but no doubt harder to evade. Does the reflective mode simply unpack what happens in the intuitive, on-the-wing mode? Does it, for example, unpack the rigorously inferential procedures that for Sperber and Wilson characterize the act of understanding? Might one not say that it unpacks the poem according to its own rules for unpacking, whereas the on-the-wing mode has a special kind of logic or processing pathway? That last version of the relation between the two strands looks plausible in so far as reflective literary analysis often overturns the impressions or interpretative intuitions of a first 'naive' reading. First-year students of poetry and other relatively inexperienced readers often say that they find that critical analysis 'spoils' the poem for them, denatures it in some way. Reflective reading, as we saw in Chapters 2 and 3, is often counter-intuitive.

I leave that question too hanging in the air in order to look at another fragment of poetry which may well be an echo of Sandburg's poem. Here are three lines from John Ashbery's poem 'A Call for Papers':

> Meanwhile sleep binds us lightly
> So that we can easily slip away as the season
> Approaches on tortoise feet.[23]

Ashbery's poems are well known for their strange collocations: an apparent theme or topic is established, then another unexpectedly takes over with no obvious connection to what has gone before. Such effects are common in twentieth-century surrealist and dadaist poetry, which explores the outer reaches of defamiliarization. Ashbery, however, has the knack of making his transitions seem in some sense natural, unshocking. This is probably due in large measure to the even, semi-colloquial tone of voice that characterizes his poems. Normal-sounding segments of meaning are established, and the syntactic connectors also look quite innocent until one suddenly finds one has turned a corner into quite different territory. It is almost as if someone were talking away, shifting from one topic to another according to a principle of association that never becomes salient enough to grasp.

The metaphor of the season approaching on tortoise feet is a case in point. That a fog can come in on little cat feet is unpackable according to an implied analogy between the lightness and softness of the fog and the movement of a cat. This one is not so easy. How, one could ask in relevance theory terms, is the ad hoc concept TORTOISE FEET* constructed here? One can try commonsense strategies: tortoises are routinely associated with slow movement coupled with persistence, so perhaps the season approaches slowly but with quiet determination. A well-informed reader may also remember the Sandburg poem and map this metaphor on to the cat–fog analogy (after all, fogs are a variety of weather). And finally, it might be possible to read these lines as referring at some level to death, since analogies between sleep and death are standard. 'Slip away', one would then say, has the same euphemistic quality as 'sleep' and is associated with it by assonance; the four seasons are often used as an analogy for the life-span of an individual; and death, it is commonly believed, approaches slowly but surely. However, there is no contextual support for this conventional reading. The poem as a whole seems to be about a conference of literary specialists or writers, or both. It might simply be that Ashbery intends us to understand that such people sleep lightly so that they can 'slip away' unobtrusively in the morning, missing the boring second day of the conference.

However one analyses it, the TORTOISE FEET* concept is not extended in the way that the fog–cat concept is extended in Sandburg's poem. There is nothing further that has to do with tortoises, or with seasons for that matter, although weather is mentioned elsewhere in this poem, as it is in many other Ashbery poems—it goes, no doubt, with the quasi-everyday idiom and topics he cultivates. TORTOISE FEET* is a singularity, and it is one that is likely to retain some at least of its oddness for the reader, whether she pauses to think about that specific item or reads on in pursuit of an overall sense of what Ashbery is on about. This singularity, it is important to note, is not vague: it tightly constrains whatever interpretative strategy one attempts. It is, one might want to say, a tortoise-feet-like singularity. No weak implicatures ripple away indefinitely from it that are not caught and held in the steady, obstinate treading of those feet.

We might turn here to an argument of Davidson's to which Carston gives a certain prominence in her paper. Davidson puts forward the radical view that there is no such thing as metaphorical meaning. Metaphors have their literal sense and no other. What the literal sense of the metaphor does is to get the reader or hearer to *notice* relevant things, of which there are an indefinite number.[24] The apparent opacity of Ashbery's phrase 'tortoise feet' would not present any problem on this reading. There simply is no 'meaning' of the metaphor as such; its function is to give an instruction to the reader to go on looking for as long as is necessary (or comfortable) for possible tortoise-feet-like items connected with a change of season. And if that is thought to be an adequate argument, one can also apply it to Sandburg's 'little cat feet', to 'Your soul is a chosen landscape', to 'That surgeon is a butcher', and to all other metaphors, with the proviso that in some of these cases (Sandburg, Verlaine) the speaker has given some specimens of the things one might look for when one encounters metaphors such as [fog–]cat or [soul–]landscape.

All this seems at least workable, but a literary specialist (or any experienced reader) is likely to find it unhelpfully abstract. Here is another line of poetry, one that used to be celebrated as a prototypical surrealist line:

> La terre est bleue comme une orange[25]
> (The earth is blue as an orange)

Of course this is technically an example of simile rather than of metaphor. However, as we saw in the case of Baudelaire's 'Spleen', poetry often slides between the two, and in this instance the difference involves only a minor procedural blip in the processing. Let's try reading it on the wing. 'The earth is blue ...' already dislocates expectations, which are formed by archived instances such as 'the earth is green' and 'the sky is blue'. (Some readers might have in their archive the image of earth as seen from outer space, but this reference would be anachronistic, since the poem was first published in 1929, decades before the era of space exploration.) The procedural 'as' promises an analogy that will resolve the difficulty, but the item proposed as analogous, 'an orange', seems to make matters worse: here is an object defined by its characteristic colour (or vice versa— which came first, the fruit or the colour orange?), which is quite distinct from blue on the colour spectrum. In this perspective, the procedural 'as' looks more like a trap set for the reader than an instruction facilitating the recovery of meaning. If we take it out and rephrase the line in the form of a metaphor ('The earth is a blue orange', say, or 'The blue earth is an orange'), this effect becomes very clear: 'as' facilitates not an explanation but another shock. The deceptive reassurance of the simile form sets the reader up for an even more difficult readjustment.[26]

It doesn't help us much to speak of the ad hoc concepts BLUE* and ORANGE*. Equally, to say that the words have their literal meaning here is unexceptionable but unproductive: it doesn't get one any further analytically and it doesn't help the reader to grasp the cognitive impact of the line. Yet the line clearly makes a cognitive impact: it bursts on the imagination, one might say, like a small explosion triggered by 'as'. And what bursts most immediately is incontestably a sense of colour, a clash of blue and orange. One is tempted here to speak of a 'sunburst', and the reasons why that kind of expression emerges here are not too hard to pin down. Among the most straightforward archival links to both 'earth' and 'blue' is 'sky'; once those archival links are activated, the simile 'comme une orange' becomes applicable to 'earth' (rather than 'blue') as a spherical object; but the other spherical object that becomes emergent once the (colour) orange is mentioned is of course the sun. In other words, this line rewrites a very basic, childlike landscape: the earth, blue sky, sun. To this, the noun 'orange', not the colour but the fruit, adds implicatures of ripening (in the sun), sunny climates, and possibly also refreshing drinks, in which case taste or *flavour* intervenes here also. Burst of colour, burst of flavour.

Revising my earlier remark, perhaps we could now after all speak of EARTH*, BLUE*, ORANGE*, and possibly COMME* as ad hoc concepts: whatever cognitive processes are going on in a reader's mind as she encounters this utterance for the first time, they must include a series of provisional conceptual identifications and subsequent adjustments. What I would want to argue here, however, is that these adjustments are not purely abstract-inferential (rapid calculations of the kind 'how could "as" be understood here?', 'which properties of an orange might be optimally relevant in the context of the concepts so far encountered?') but sensory, or rather kinesic. The implicatures set in motion by the line might then be conceived of as an immediately registered sensory resonance, like the unique flavour of the madeleine in Proust's famous scene of sensory recognition, rather than as vague mental inferences continuing diminuendo.

As Robyn Carston argues, emergence has a phenomenal aspect and not exclusively an inferential one.[27] What emerges in metaphor is an imagining of the concept in its literal sense: that, after all, is why we speak of literature, especially poetry, as rich in 'images'. This seems also to be what Davidson has in mind in his 'literal' handling of metaphor. As a student of literature, I find myself agreeing with both Davidson and the relevance theorists, but I would regard their analytic accounts as incomplete if they disconnected the phenomenon of emergence from sensory and motor resonance, or, to put it in another way, if they failed to give due weight to the communicative embodiment that is intrinsic to images, whether for high-art poetry or for everyday discourse.

This type of argument could be developed by invoking the view of language put forward by Barsalou, Glenberg, and others.[28] Their work on embodiment in mind and language has a much wider reference, but in fact the issues arising from the use of metaphor are inextricably linked to that wider perspective.[29] As we saw earlier, they argue that the way linguistic signs are learnt and used is always both situational and connected at some level with motor response. Whether or not this hypothesis is correct, some such process is needed to explain how kinesic effects could be instantly triggered by language, without (it is assumed) passing via an abstract inferential loop.[30] We may focus here in particular on what one might call the 'affordance' approach to concrete reference in language as developed by Glenberg and his colleagues. The claim is that our intuitive (non-reflective) sensori-motor knowledge of material things acts as a tight constraint on our uses of language. Glenberg's example, now well known, could be set out as three sentences:

(1) Imagine hanging your coat on a coat-stand.
(2) Imagine hanging your coat on a vacuum cleaner.
(3) Imagine hanging your coat on a teacup.

(1) is normal, offering no resistance to imaginary action; (2) occasions a hesitation, before the reader selects an upright vacuum cleaner (not one of the horizontal ones) as the relevant object on which the coat may be hung; (3) cannot be interpreted, because teacups have no affordances for hanging items on.

These are not metaphors, but it is not difficult to see how this hypothesis might help us to understand why some metaphors 'work' better than others and more generally why some poems work better than others. The metaphorical utterance 'The fog comes in on little cat feet' is easy to grasp, not because we make a number of abstract inferences about the properties of fogs and cats, but because the emergent image ('concept') of a soft grey cat–fog drifting in on foggy feet is coherent at the sensorimotor level. Here are some variants:

(1) The plane landed on little cat feet.
(2) The car raced down the motorway on little cat feet.
(3) The bird swooped down on little cat feet.
(4) George brushed his teeth on little cat feet.

From these, it is easy to see that there is a gradient of viability which doesn't depend on convention (standard ways of saying things). (1) is unconventional, but it is considerably more viable than (2), since planes (especially small planes) can land delicately. (2) is more viable than (3) because cars and cats are horizontal objects with four supporting items (wheels, legs), and both can move quite fast. (3) is awkward because birds only have two feet; more importantly, their vertical descent is quite unlike anything one can imagine a cat's body performing. But it can still be construed, even if awkwardly, whereas (4) cannot: we might attribute little cat feet to George, but the act of brushing teeth is unrelated to anything that feet might do, whether cat feet or human feet. Similarly with examples such as 'That surgeon is a piano-tuner' which can only be construed with a certain amount of effort. It is true that propositions beginning 'Your soul is . . . ' can be completed with a vast range of different things without breaking sensorimotor constraints, simply because souls don't have many obvious sensorimotor constraints (see variants like 'Your soul is a sewing-machine', 'Your soul is an unmanned spy drone'). Surrealist poetry often draws on permissive concepts in order to make unexpected connections without wholly defying sensorimotor constraints. Éluard's line does precisely that. Colours are permissive concepts, although still within certain limits: the collocation 'The blue is orange earth' is virtually illegible as compared with 'The earth is blue as an orange'. I would suggest that Ashbery's collocations, while unexpected, 'feel normal' not because they conform to a propositional logic but because they offer little resistance to sensorimotor constraints.

The limits of what is communicated

These remarks and examples are designed not so much to offer detailed technical suggestions for extending an existing relevance theory template as to open up a view of the way that the theory might interact with literary studies on some key points.

The first of these concerns the poet (or by extension the literary writer) as speaker and what she wants to communicate. Relevance theory is a theory of communication, and rather rigorously excludes anything other than propositional content from what is or can be communicated. One important exception is Deirdre Wilson's example of a woman ('Mary') who, leaning out of a hotel window, sniffs the air in the presence of her husband ('Peter') with a certain palpable intent. Wilson concedes that Mary's ostensive sniffing may communicate to Peter an array of very weak implicatures, but those implicatures necessarily take the form of implied propositions ('there is a pleasant scent of flowers and freshly cut grass in the air') rather than the sensation or mood she experiences in itself.[31] This is difficult territory, which, if one pursues it in a certain direction, is connected with the question of 'qualia'.[32] I don't propose to go in that direction; I would simply want to say that Mary's gesture has a communicative sense that includes physical sensations and (potentially) affect. It also has an ostensive and contextual precision of its own that is not that of language, whether everyday language or the academic language of philosophers and linguists. One might say, however, that certain kinds of poetry and literary prose enact a similar communicative sense via a special (and again very precise) use of language. And the communicative sense in question is one that, to use Davidson's model, can't strictly be paraphrased.

This is part, although only part, of an argument against using the presence or absence of propositional content as the sole criterion for judging whether a human act is or is not an act of communication. Models that emphasize, in whatever sense, the embodied nature of language would insist that we can, expressly and intentionally, communicate things other than a propositional content. It is not clear to a student of literature why poetic 'effects' should be regarded as in some sense accidental side-effects of the communication of a propositional meaning (in other words, as perlocutionary effects).[33] When Emily Dickinson writes, 'My Life had stood—a Loaded Gun—in Corners', the loaded gun is there in any reading, doing its kinesic and affect-driven work within the cage of imagic coordinates that the poem sets up in its opening lines: the reader is immediately forced into the corner, with the gun loaded, the safety-catch off, imagining a whole life being like that. [34] What Dickinson has done here is to improvise something like a large-scale (but still quite small-scale by some measures) catachresis: she has taken a feeling for which we don't have everyday words and transferred words from elsewhere, loaded words that are ready to fire, to communicate precisely that feeling. And whatever else such utterances do, they certainly change the cognitive environment of the listener, which is one of the tests relevance theory uses for communicative acts. [35]

Poetry is a special case, yes. But we have agreed that the specialness is only an adaptation of everyday procedures within a context which is not that of the everyday. We have agreed that what poetry does, we all do all the time, although less sensationally. Literary language is the sharp end of a gradient that runs all the way back to ordinary language use. The consequence must therefore be that the base model needs to be adjusted somewhat. Despite everything that relevance theorists say about weak implicatures, metaphor, poetic effects, and the like, it seems to me that the standard model they adopt remains that of a practical 'message' where the propositional content can easily be verified and where the utterance itself can be translated into any language without significant loss of meaning. But, as relevance theorists also acknowledge, a great deal of human talk is not of that variety. People spend hours every day, on the bus, in the office, over a cup of coffee, in pillow-talk, communicating meanings, affects, and sensory responses together or separately in language and gesture that is adequately precise.

In order to do so, they improvise, availing themselves of the cognitive fluidity that is distinctive of human thought. They seize on the low-cost linguistic materials they have acquired over a lifetime, the abundant store of their native language as it has been integrated culturally into their contextual, situational, and procedural memories, and they perform gymnastics with it. The gymnastics can sometimes turn into high-level acrobatics, and, on rare (but perhaps not so rare) occasions, into transcendental configurations of gesture and intention that hang shimmering in the memories of those present for a little while and then vanish. That is why the language of James Joyce's *Ulysses* is also a plausible language of the everyday.

It is in this way, too, one must surely believe, that language itself came into being and continues to thrive, changing all the time as it restlessly seeks to go beyond its own limits. Few people doubt that early human language must have been very close to empirical and sensorimotor bodily experience, allowing things to be referred to in their absence, but also allowing improvised transference of those references to other contexts, to broader categories of things, and thus eventually to the conceptual thought that we now take for granted and prioritize.[36] Catachresis and metaphor are not rhetorical flourishes but cognitive instruments for the construction and extension of language.

A cognitive approach to literary studies would agree with relevance theorists—against the doxa of recent literary theory—that language is the instrument of thought, the most flexible, self-generating instrument ever invented by humans. Yet it would also agree that language is not adequate for every purpose, that it is indeed perhaps fundamentally and constitutionally inadequate. Here is Flaubert's famous evocation of that inadequacy at a critical moment in the story of Emma Bovary:

> personne, jamais, ne peut donner l'exacte mesure de ses besoins, ni de ses conceptions, ni de ses douleurs, . . . la parole humaine est comme un chaudron fêlé où nous battons des mélodies à faire danser les ours, quand on voudrait attendrir les étoiles.[37]
>
> (no one, ever, can give the exact measure of her needs, or of her conceptions, or of her griefs, . . . human language is like a cracked cooking-pot on which we beat out melodies for bears to dance to, when we long to move the stars to pity.)

We don't have rich conventional language in which to express emotions, moods, or physical sensations (like the taste of wine). So, once again, we improvise, evoke one thing in order to communicate another, coin words, exploit the abundant (although also rigorously constrained) affordances of metaphor and catachresis. Despite Flaubert's ostensible pessimism about the expressive power of language, he found ways of communicating precisely delineated feelings and sensory responses, ways that have never been surpassed. The relation between language and thought, in that perspective, is rather one of emulation. What we call literature is a privileged testing-ground for and a virtuoso demonstration of that sibling rivalry: it embodies both the leaping forward of language to catch the rapid movement of thought, and the capacity of thought to improvise with language, to go with it where no speaker has ever gone before. In that interplay lies, it might be argued, one of the most powerful motors of human evolution.

7

Cognitive Mimesis

Gloucester's imagined fall

This chapter takes up the discussion of cognitive modes of mimesis or simulation from the later part of Chapter 5. We can therefore begin *in medias res* with the famous scene in Shakespeare's *King Lear* (IV.6) where Edgar leads his blind father the Duke of Gloucester to the imaginary edge of a cliff.[1] What the audience sees is the two characters emerging on to the flat surface of the stage. Edgar insists that they're climbing a hill towards the edge of a cliff, even though the blind man says the ground still seems to him (as it does to the audience) to be level:

GLOUCESTER
When shall I come to the top of that same hill?
EDGAR
You do climb up it now. Look how we labour.
GLOUCESTER
Methinks the ground is even.
EDGAR

Horrible steep.

…

Come on sir, here's the place. Stand still: how fearful
And dizzy 'tis to cast one's eyes so low.
The crows and choughs that wing the midway air
Show scarce so gross as beetles. Half-way down
Hangs one that gathers samphire, dreadful trade;
Methinks he seems no bigger than his head.
The fishermen that walk upon the beach
Appear like mice, and yon tall anchoring barque
Diminished to her cock, her cock a buoy
Almost too small for sight. The murmuring surge

That on th'unnumbered idle pebble chafes,
Cannot be heard so high. I'll look no more,
Lest my brain turn and the deficient sight
Topple down headlong.

GLOUCESTER

Set me where you stand.

EDGAR
Give me your hand. You are now within a foot
Of th'extreme verge. For all beneath the moon
Would I not leap upright.[2]

We are a long way here from the game of giving teddy a bath, but
some things remain constant. The props are minimal, and a kind of
game is played: Edgar says they're climbing a hill when they're not.
Unlike the child in Harris's experiment, Gloucester is deceived,
although with some resistance: he seems to assent in the end to Edgar's
account of what they are doing. On the other hand, the audience knows
perfectly well that this is a game, or a trick (since someone is deceived).[3]

I'm going to return in a moment to the modes of simulation in this
scene, the way immersion is produced. First, however, we need to
acknowledge that what Shakespeare stages here is not just a clever
trick, a device for impressing the audience. It is an episode in a play
that is by common consent one of the most powerful fictional enactments of human values, human error, human despair, and the human
desire for regeneration. The enactment passes through two intertwined
and mutually dependent plot-lines: the story of King Lear and his three
daughters, the story of Gloucester and his two sons. In each case, one of
the children is loyal, the other(s) disloyal; in each case, the father fails to
perceive the true ethical qualities of his children. The Dover Cliff scene
is immediately followed by the entrance of Lear, so that the delusions of
the two old men are brought into direct relation, together with their
parallel experiences of a state of existential despair.

Ultimately, one would want to show in detail how this scene
contributes to the embodiment of the cognitive misprisions and mal-
functions enacted by the play as a whole. For present purposes, we
need only bear in mind that the action it stages is psychologically and
ethically problematic. Why should Edgar trick his father, both by
concealing his own identity and by pretending that he is assisting

him in the suicide he says he wants? This question has been addressed many times by Shakespearian critics, and it is clear that no unequivocal answer can be given, at least as far as Edgar's inferred psychology is concerned. Shakespeare has left this aspect of the action under-specified, without determinate clues that might allow us to resolve it. Primed by the modern dilemma posed by assisted suicide, we might perhaps surmise that he is cognitively torn between the desire to help his father end his misery and the equally potent desire to sustain and care for him in life; he suffers from a recognizable form of cognitive dissonance. It's not difficult, in such ways, to avoid the disquieting assumption that Edgar deliberately, with a kind of Schadenfreude, sets his father up for a comic fall. But even that assumption seems to fit the expressive direction of this play, in which the audience is brought face to face with the most shocking of possibilities.

What we can be sure of is that Shakespeare *meant* to do something powerful and shocking in this scene; in that sense, Edgar is only what Henry James called a *ficelle*, a literary affordance. In another context, Edgar and Gloucester might be thought of as a comic pair in which Gloucester is the stooge, the fall guy: the expression 'fall guy' would in that case take on its most literal motor sense. Tragedies always enact a fall, and this one uses the metaphor at regular intervals. In this scene, the fall becomes quasi-literal. In many productions of the play, Gloucester, as he attempts to throw himself over the supposed cliff-edge, falls flat on his face. And a 'real' headlong fall, leading to certain death, is powerfully simulated in Edgar's speech. What happens here is that the standard tragic plot of a fall that remains heroic (perhaps culminating in a Stoic suicide, an act of ultimate self-mastery) is supplanted by its pathetic inverse: a failed suicide, an old man tricked, a figure that stumbles and falls over. Above all, it is supplanted by a simulated fall. And for the full pathos and shock of that worse-than-tragic fall to resonate in the audience's empathy (and potentially their own moral sense), the simulation at least must be brilliant. Gloucester has to imagine himself on the cliff-edge, and the audience has to as well.

In the game with teddy, language was needed in order to stipulate the pretence, that is to say to reassign meanings to the props: 'Here's his bath', 'This is the soap', and so on. It is needed here, too: the props are even more residual, after all. Only the best will do, otherwise the simulation, at this level of dramatic tension, will simply fall flat. The best is what you get, and it takes your breath away each time as you step up to the edge of that imaginary cliff. But, as we address the language, we should remember that it is designed to be delivered by actors, and imagine, as we read the words, what skilled actors can make of them, beginning with the opening exchange quoted above.

In Edgar's ekphrasis, the perception of the supposed viewer is structured from the outset on a vertical axis ('to cast one's eyes so low'). The sight of birds flying *below* the level of the observer, the top-down view of the samphire-gatherer suspended from a rope (he's reduced to the size of his head, the only thing that is visible), the relative sizing of objects such as the sailing-boat and its dinghy as seen from above: all these model a visual field that is saturated in motor implications, realized variably according to the different agents (birds flying, the samphire-gatherer hanging, the fishermen walking on the distant level ground, the unsettling movement of waves and pebbles).

This analysis of the presentation follows the 'perceptual modelling' perspective proposed by Elaine Scarry. It allows a seamless transition, however, to the kinaesthetic approach of Guillemette Bolens. Motor implications are in fact insistent from the beginning of the scene, with the climb up the imagined hill and then Edgar's instructions ('Come on sir, here's the place'; 'Stand still'), and Gloucester's 'Set me where you stand'. In Edgar's simulation of the cliff, the key kinesic effect is provided by expressions that trigger a response of vertigo. The word 'dizzy' merely introduces the theme; the way the samphire-gatherer 'hangs' picks it up again; but the crucial instances occur in the last two lines of this quotation: 'Lest my brain turn', 'topple down headlong'. What does most of the work here, I think, is the idea of the *brain* turning: people often say that vertigo makes your stomach turn, but that's because nausea usually follows from dizziness. The primary feeling, the trigger, is a feeling inside your head,[4] and that kinesic response, once induced, is then prolonged in the loss of visual control (deficient sight) and the resulting imagination of losing your balance, falling *headlong*: after the mention of the samphire-gatherer's head, that word delivers the full force of a bodily orientation that is terrifyingly wrong. Shakespeare also chooses a precisely kinesic word for the culminating evocation of the fall. 'Topple' is one of those English verbs that capture particular nuances of motor experience. The *Oxford*

English Dictionary gives the meanings 'fall over from a great height or as if top-heavy; fall headlong' and 'lean over unsteadily; totter as if on the point of falling': it belongs to the sequence 'totter', 'tumble', 'stumble', but with the crucial semantic reference of 'top'. Edgar's subsequent remark 'For all beneath the moon | Would I not leap upright' also has a powerful kinesic charge. The word 'upright' might sound odd here, but it implies that Edgar is crouching or cringing back, his body instinctively protecting itself against the danger of falling. 'Leaping' is what Gloucester intends to do, the terrible act of leaping over the edge; Edgar imagines that he can't even bear to jump up into a standing position.

This scene takes its most fundamental force from the dramatic clash between, on the one hand, the taken-for-granted affordance for humans of a flat surface on which to stand and walk (the real stage), and, on the other, the imaginary vertical surface of the cliff. Out of that clash, Shakespeare constructs, at another level, an immersive affordance, a platform from which to launch a complex tangle of physical responses, emotions, thoughts, together with the ethical and existential questions they imply. By the end of this scene, we are ready to face Lear in his madness, and eventually the hanging (we still call it 'topping') of Cordelia, the very mention of which will elicit an ultimately horrific kind of vertigo.[5]

Mind-reading on the edge

There is a further dimension of the Dover Cliff scene that I have so far omitted. It is present in all fictions where the thoughts of characters are represented or implied. This is mind-reading, in the sense I outlined earlier: the attribution of mind-states (particular intentional states) to another person by inference. Let's recall first that this capacity is essential for all forms of intentional communication, since in order to understand a speaker, you have to assume that she is trying to communicate something relevant to you, and therefore that she is reciprocally seeking to infer your mind-set. More broadly, it is essential for human social life and cooperation, and thence for all forms of human culture. If individuals became isolated in their own presumed thought-worlds, the human species would soon become extinct. Of course the process is always incomplete and often dangerously deficient: the very capacity to communicate, which delivers enormous benefits (cooperation, empathy, shared affect), is bought at a high cost when individuals or groups fail to achieve coordination of their mutual mind-reading (for example in diplomacy), or where they deceitfully manipulate the assumptions on which it is based.

Mind-reading is an ever-present aspect of communication in language, but it exploits any information it can, including body-language. If one is thinking strictly of communicative exchange, only intentional gestures and other body-movements are relevant: if you blush when you are telling a lie, and thus give yourself away, the blush is presumably not a part of what you intended to communicate. However, we are constantly appraising one another's language and body-movements and actions in order to determine what their intentional attitude is: we need to predict, in other words, what they are likely to do next. So we read involuntary signs as well as intentional signals; the distinction between those is part of the inferential calculus of mind-reading.[6] Readers of fiction or audiences in the theatre do all this, but they presuppose a further level of intentionality. When an author tells us that a character is blushing, or even scratching her nose, that involuntary response becomes meaningful in relation to the general intentions underlying the fiction (to tell such-and-such a type of story, to represent such and such a character or situation). It may of course also be perceived by another character, for whom it becomes part of their mind-reading activity.

We need to look more closely here at the part that kinesis (motor resonance effects) plays in mind-reading. There are many situations in which motor resonance occurs without any intention to communicate on either side. If I am walking along a cliff path and I come across someone standing on the very edge of the sheer cliff, looking down, I am likely to feel in my body a powerful echo of her assumed physical position (the muscular tension required to ensure perfect verticality, for example), together with the intense vertigo that that position and her downward-directed gaze would induce in me. Those effects occur constantly in spectators of sporting events, and presumably constitute a significant part of the immersive pleasure of watching them. However, we all 'know' instinctively how to use them in communicative situations. When people talk to one another, they enlist their bodies as well as their language to 'get their point across'. Like a bow releasing an arrow, indeed, the body and the gaze in animated conversation are focused on the interlocutor, who adopts a reciprocal stance and gaze. That mutual attention has the function of optimizing the pertinence and directedness of the exchange, but it will also draw into its orbit bodily signs (involuntary) and signals (voluntary) that generate motor resonance. A chopping movement of the hand accompanying an utterance that rebuts an allegation made by the interlocutor may communicate the firmness of the rebuttal, the sense of 'drawing the line', cutting off any possible counter-argument, or any of a number of such implications, depending on the exact context and the relation between speaker and interlocutor. Someone who says 'Bill is a bull-dozer' may accompany the remark with physical movements that suggest a big, tough entity that flattens everything in its path. The point here is not, however, the semantic 'content' of the gesture (even though, retrospectively and reflectively, we can always attribute a semantic content in the specified context): it lies in the way that bodies set up mutual patterns of motor resonance.

It follows that mind-reading and motor resonance are not two separate areas ('mind' and 'body') but twin aspects of the incessant efforts we make to penetrate the intentionality of others and make plain our own. Readers of fiction and theatre audiences are observers of these effects in single or multiple others; they continuously mind-read authors and characters, drawing inferences from what they say and responding to the motor resonances communicated by their words and (especially in visual media) their bodies.[7]

In some fictions, the mind-reading interchanges between characters can be remarkably complex: this is true of Shakespeare's *Othello*, for example, and of quite a number of nineteenth-century novels from Jane Austen to Henry James and beyond. When one adds the mind-reading that is carried out by readers or audiences, the complexity appears to be stepped up a notch. We enter here a terrain that has been explored in recent years both by evolutionary anthropologists and by cognitive literary critics. Ordinary communication demands an embedded intentional reciprocity at three levels. The speaker intends to say X, the interlocutor supposes that the speaker intends to say X, and the speaker expects that the interlocutor will suppose it. Outside the realm of communication, it is possible to imagine a virtually indefinite chain of such intentional suppositions, beliefs, etc., such as 'I believe that my brother thinks that his boss supposes that my partner hopes that I understand that my brother imagines that I am mistaken.' That's a seven-level chain, and most people are likely to find that they lose the thread after about the fourth or fifth level.

The anthropologist Robin Dunbar claims that, in *Othello*, 'with four characters' mind states, plus that of the audience and his own, [Shakespeare] is having to work at sixth order'. He suggests further-more that only great writers like Shakespeare are cognitively capable of operating at that level of embedment, and that, for him, explains why great writers are so rare.[8] Lisa Zunshine seeks to show that, in a given scene in *Mrs Dalloway*, Woolf ' "demands" that we process a string of fifth- and sixth-level intentionalities'.[9] These are fascinating analyses, but I think that they are mistaken in the lengths to which they extend the chain of intentionality. The six-level chain in *Othello* never appears as such: it is constructed progressively and acquired by the audience in manageable segments. We see Desdemona flirting, per-haps innocently, with Cassio; we hear Iago talking to Cassio, setting him up with a particular (erroneous) mind-set; we hear Iago talking to Othello, setting *him* up. There is a striking number of instances of three- and four-level embedments, but we never have to take all six in a single stride. Besides, the intentionality of the author is simply a given: we don't think at any point 'This is Shakespeare telling us that …', nor does Shakespeare need to imagine the audience's mind-state in respect of these specific intentionalities. The audience's participation in the exercise operates in terms of immersion, not in terms of 'thinking that…', 'believing that…'. They don't have to manage any more levels of intentionality than the characters on the stage do. The mind-reading in this play, in other words, is brilliantly complex, but the *level* of complexity never goes beyond what would be possible in gossip between two alert people in a pub. If it did, the audience (who are only averagely gifted) would certainly lose the plot; to put it another way, if you had to be a genius to imagine a six-level embed-ment, you would need to be a genius to understand it. Similarly, in the passage cited by Zunshine, I see no lengthy '*string* of intentionalities', but rather a series of elided shifts between one character's perspective and another's. Of course, the reader has to configure the set as a whole, but I doubt whether any reader would feel the kind of strain that is said to accompany embedded intentionalities at the fifth or sixth level. Although the shifts are disconcerting, it isn't hard to see that Woolf is trying to capture the play of different mind-states, operating separately and simultaneously, across a group of characters present at the same scene.

These reservations in no way invalidate the work of Zunshine and others in exploring the key role played in narrative and dramatic fictions by what one might call cognitive syntax, of which the embedment of intentionality is one salient form. My sense is that, despite the recent burgeoning of work in this area, we are only just beginning to devise and polish the analytic instruments that can be used to display the kinds of thinking that fiction does, and thus to move beyond traditional modes of literary psychology.[10]

Let's return now to the Dover Cliff scene. The most striking aspect of mind-reading in this scene is the way in which Edgar outwits his father's cognitive defence mechanisms (his epistemic vigilance)[11] and manipulates his mental representations. There is a dramatic irony here: his illegitimate brother has already done so illegitimately. But the manipulation can also be seen favourably as a kind of cognitive therapy. By taking him cognitively through the suicide that Gloucester says he wants, and out the other side, he arguably helps to soothe if not heal his trauma, and leads him closer to a final recognition and reconciliation. Something of this kind, at all events, must be what the audience will think as they act as surrogate interlocutors for Edgar's mind-games. No one, in fact, doubts that this scene is designed to create a vertiginous resonance in the audience: like other performances of the imagination in Shakespeare's plays, its virtuoso simulation goes beyond what is strictly necessary for the action. But in so doing, it provides a dramatic demonstration and enactment of empathy. When you stand on the edge of that cliff, feeling Gloucester's vertigo, the pathos and sorrow of being Gloucester become incarnate. We are here at the highest point of what theatre can achieve—not theatre as a trick, a mere illusion, a messing with the audience's mind, but theatre as a place of empathetic resonances and thus a shared world.

How to step over a chair

With Mme de Lafayette's *La Princesse de Clèves*, first published in 1678, we shift to a storyworld that is narrated rather than enacted on a stage, and it famously focuses on what is traditionally called 'psychological' action rather than physical actions and events. I shall focus here, however, on a scene that is highly theatrical, one where a salient physical action is performed on a kind of public stage: the ballroom of the royal court. It's perhaps a good idea to ask oneself whether, in those conditions, the reader's imagination of Nemours's actually performed (but narrated) action is so very different, as a cognitive process, from the spectator's imagination of Gloucester's imagined leap. I leave that question in the air and move, here again, directly to the first encounter between the two central characters, the very young and recently married Princess and the notoriously handsome and socially polished Duc de Nemours.

Although Nemours and the Princess have never met before, they've heard a lot about one another, as any couple of young celebrities in a celebrity-conscious culture could hardly avoid doing. It is a classic case of falling in love at first sight, although we're not told that explicitly. Here is the first segment of the episode:

> As she was dancing with M. de Guise, there was a loud noise over by the door of the ballroom as of people giving way to someone coming in. Mme de Clèves finished dancing, and while she was looking round to find someone she intended to take as a partner, the King called to her to take the person who had just arrived. She turned and saw a man who she felt at once could be no other than M. de Nemours stepping over a seat [qui passoit par-dessus quelque siège] to make his way to where the dancing was....As they began to dance, there arose in the hall a murmur of approval.[12]

Unlike nineteenth-century realist novelists, Lafayette doesn't describe much of the scenery: all we know is that this is a hyperbolically magnificent ballroom in the Louvre, and that the King and the Queens are present, together with the crème de la crème of the court—the note of hyperbolical magnificence is struck by the novel from its opening sentence onward. In this highly underspecified simulation, the furniture as such is not salient: what one inferentially imagines, perhaps, is a blur of sumptuous clothing, a brilliant chiaroscuro created by hundreds of candles, and the surging crowds of elegant figures, polite but also eagerly jostling for position in the limelight (where the Princess already stands). The simulation is not only visual, however: there are sounds, murmurs, voices, some distant, some closer at hand and audible.

This primary contextual level, which relies only on a very general cultural lexicon that anyone who reads the novel is likely to have at their disposal, is structured according to the principle of perceptual and cognitive modelling proposed by Elaine Scarry. At this level, the simulation is dynamic, pointed: it is a *vector* for the physical action of the characters. What motivates it, in both senses of the word, is the trajectory of the bodily presence of Nemours as he crosses the ball-room. We should note here that this trajectory had in fact been set in motion earlier. The narrator tells us that Nemours was in Brussels, where he was preoccupied with his hubristic plan to marry the Queen of England. First, however, he is obliged to come to the French court to be present at a classy marriage. So this is a detour, and he's in a hurry to move on: 'he hastened to come back to court himself' (p. 23).

At the moment when this impatient, highly goal-directed trajectory irrupts into the ballroom, the angle of perception shifts from Nemours to the Princess. She's dancing in that central area; a *noise* is heard over by the door, and the noise is immediately interpreted: someone important appears to be coming in. This sound immediately reorients attention towards that distant spatial point. Even while the Princess is looking round for her next partner, the noise and what it implies remain salient, one infers, in *her* mind.[13] In other words, the explosive energy of Nemours's trajectory is sustained but also unexpectedly hijacked: he is now no longer *going* towards the Queen of England, he is *coming* towards the Princess. The difference is of course funda-mental in motor behaviour and the way it is perceived (the go–come verb pair is central in one form or another in a wide range of languages). Henceforth, in fact, Nemours will allow his English plan to languish and die; Queen Elizabeth has been supplanted by the Princess de Clèves.

Like some kind of smart missile, or a bee that's scented honey, Nemours homes in on the Princess: although he's never seen her before, he makes a *beeline* for her. This way of looking at it is far from trivial: the English expression 'make a beeline for someone' encodes an intuitive knowledge of movement in the natural world, the highly motivated and directed movement of a living creature in its own ecology. Changing the ecology a little, one could also say that

Nemours is perceived to imitate the action of the tiger, clearing an obstacle in his path with an apparently effortless stride.

We have arrived here at the slightly strange detail of the seat that Nemours 'passes over'. One of the inferences the reader is likely to make is that the ballroom is so crowded that Nemours's options for coming through to the dancing area without delay are extremely limited. The milling crowd is solidified, reified, as a compact mass: the seat affords the slender opportunity of a clear path. In this respect, its specification belongs to the cognitive and perceptual modelling of the scene: it communicates in an extremely economical way a whole set of spatial and dynamic relations (poor Alfred in *The Corrections*, trying to cope with a chaise longue, would have understood it all too well).

Within that frame, Nemours's passage over the seat irresistibly triggers a kinesic response. The dynamics of the trajectory as a whole is converted at this point into a bodily gesture that attentive readers will experience as a motor reflex. They will experience it even if they have never themselves stepped over an antique item of French furniture, since our muscles know in advance what it feels like to step over an obstacle. We've seen athletes racing over hurdles and acrobats making light of physical obstacles of various kinds, so we can intuitively imagine how it might feel to step lightly over what is presumably quite a substantial seat (though no doubt one without a back: a sort of upholstered bench).

That primary response carries with it a whole set of further inferences. We know now, if we didn't know it before, that Nemours is supremely athletic: his body is well trained in all the noble sports. He clearly performs this gesture with elegance and aplomb (in the literal sense of that word: one infers that he will retain a vertical posture). If he can risk this gesture, unhesitatingly, despite the extremely decorous behaviour that is *de rigueur* at the court, he must have remarkable self-confidence in his social *standing* as well as his own motor abilities (he can't risk falling over the seat). And his movement, directed as it is towards an exorbitantly attractive young woman, may also be perceived as predatory, tiger-like.

I have spoken here as if the reader registers these things, and of course that is the case. But, because the Princess has become the reflector of this scene, the reader must assume that she knows them too. We know that she knows that Nemours is an alpha male. We also know that she must feel, even if she doesn't know it yet, that he is making this demonstration for her sake. He is coming towards her, coming for her. Because we perceive his powerful, athletic, predatory movement through her gaze, we at once become aware that it has acquired an intensely erotic colouring. We understand that she's turned on, as we would say, by Nemours's trick with the chair. And in a moment, his body and hers, his gaze and hers, will be joined in the dance.

What the novel enacts here, then, is par excellence a 'kinesic' experience, a subjectively perceived bodily movement, coordinating muscles in a perfect fluid sequence. If we ask who is having this experience, we have to say that it is shared: it is in the nature of kinesic actions to be shared. The fictional Nemours feels it in his own body, the fictional Princess feels it in hers, adding a further erotic level, and readers feel it in theirs: if they are reading attentively (and attending to the text rather than to some preconception about the novel), Nemours literally strides right out of the novel into their bodies. Note that it is not possible here to distinguish between body and mind: the motor resonance response is simultaneous with the mind-reading response both within the text and across its border with the world inhabited by the reader. Nor can we represent this instance as a chain of embedded intentionality such as 'The reader believes that the Princess feels that Nemours intends…'. That is not how imagination works. There is a single shared moment of action and perception, perceived differently but compatibly by the participants. The novel constructs that nexus as a single simulation.

One final observation on this segment. In the fictional world, the apparently tiny detail of the seat is a prop both for Nemours's acrobatic gesture and for the fictional participants' presumed interpretations of that gesture. At the level of the narration, however, it is the vector of an expressive direction, to use once again Guillemette Bolens's helpful phrase. It thus becomes an affordance, a trigger for a whole set of cognitive responses that allow us for a fleeting moment, but crucially, to inhabit the mind and body of a fictional character in a seventeenth-century novel.

To complete this example, we need now to look briefly at the dialogue that ensues when the dance is over:

> The King and the Queens… called them as soon as they had finished
> dancing, without giving them time to talk to anyone else, and asked

whether each was not eager to know who the other was and whether they had not already guessed.

'As for me, Madame,' said M. de Nemours, 'I am not in doubt. But, as Mme de Clèves lacks the reasons for guessing who I am that I have for recognizing her, I should be glad if Your Majesty would be so kind as to tell her my name.'

'I am sure', said Mme la Dauphine, 'that she knows it as well as you know hers.'

'I assure you, Madame,' rejoined Mme de Clèves, who appeared rather embarrasssed, 'that I find it harder to guess than you think.'

'You are perfectly capable of guessing,' replied Mme la Dauphine; 'and it is even quite flattering to M. de Nemours that you should not wish to confess that you recognize him without ever having seen him.' (p. 24)

This is a scene of mind-reading, steeped in indications of cognitive activity. Nemours refers explicitly to his own inferential calculus, and claims to be able to differentiate it from the Princess's. But it is the King and the Queens who make most of the running here, drawing highly skilled inferences from what they have just witnessed, on our behalf as it were; they do it with the advantage both of observation at close quarters and of their familiarity with the conventions of their *Umwelt*, the micro-environment to which they belong. They have no difficulty in seeing in her things that have not yet crystallized in her own awareness. Her body language instantly betrays her: the phrase 'elle paroissoit un peu embar-rassée' implies kinesic effects (such as blushing) that are only perceivable within the fictional world (they are not specified by the narrative itself). She is betrayed, too, by her unreflective evasion of Mme la Dauphine's question: this is a mind-reading effect that again operates within the fictional world but is also available to the reader by inference.

What seems to be suggested by such examples is, first, that where authors imagine their fictional scenarios in terms of instinctively plausible motor and mind-reading models, the impact they achieve is likely to be at least equivalent to what can be done by the aggrega-tion of descriptive detail.[14] Secondly (and this point is not unrelated to the first), such effects are highly economical: they can deliver a great deal in a few words. We return here to the underspecification that is endemic in the cognitive domain. Cognition has evolved to enable the

organism to act swiftly in reponse to salient or relevant features of
the environment, and mental or linguistic representations operate
according to the same economy. Thirdly, both perception and
imagination are always mobile; static representations are not the
currency of cognition. Shakespeare's language, and his actors, take
us *towards* the edge of an imagined cliff, get us to imagine the sensation
of *falling*. Nemours's impetuous athleticism is dynamic and highly
enactive, a leap of the extended mind that creates a reality in transit.
Fourthly, it should be understood that, whether we are speaking of
teddy's bathtime, the Dover Cliff scene or the ballroom scene, the
critical model works best as an imaginative whole. For the purposes of
analysis, one can separate perceptual modelling from kinesic effects,
and both these from mind-reading, but in the reading process, which
is cognitively seamless, they are as intimately conjoined as mind is
with body. Finally, since these texts activate instinctive and powerful
processes that have been 'designed' by millions of years of evolution to
give individuals an at least partly reliable sense of the mind- and body-
states of others, they do something which is also profoundly parti-
cularized, culturally and historically. They give us access to other
people's environments and cultures, to their angles of perception,
their scales of values, their languages, and their most intimate feelings
about the world. Thanks, in addition, to the extended memory that
writing affords, they operate as miniature time-capsules. The windows
they open on other times and cultures are always partial and subject to
correction, but those are fundamental constraints of all perception
and cognition. A cognitive approach is also in that sense a thoroughly
historicizing approach.

Mimesis, kinesis, and empathy

I return now briefly to the question I left hanging. The difference
between mimesis and diegesis, as defined by Aristotle, is of course
fundamental. The presence of the actors' bodies walking on the stage
as if it were a hill, the noises they make (the sound of their voices, their
footfalls, their breathing under stress, not to mention Gloucester's
body thudding on the boards if indeed he falls), all these things deliver
a kinesic immediacy which, if the performance is skilful, make for
a more painfully embodied response than is afforded by a 'mere'

reading of Shakespeare's text. Yet Nemours's stride and the narrated conversation that follows are certainly neither mere text nor a two-dimensional transcription. For an attentive reader, written language does its very efficient work as kinesic proxy. It provides enough information to allow the reader to enter the ecology of the storyworld and thereby rehearse an imagined event—not a picture (or movie) in the mind, but a complex echo of real-world movements, voices, gestures, postures. I would be inclined to call this a mental representation or simulation, but the word itself doesn't matter. What matters is that something of this kind happens, or we wouldn't bother to read such texts at all.

All this, of course, is 'just' the kinesic ecology that affords the possibility of reflective engagement, and thus of a richer empathetic immersion. In Conrad's *Lord Jim*, as we shall see in Chapter 8, the kinesic ecology proper to the novel as a whole contains as one of its focal points a veranda where listeners adopt what I call a 'posture of reading'. *Their* dramatically heightened kinesic intelligence assists the story to reach out to other cultures and other listeners or readers, carrying with it ever-widening—yet no less precise—implicatures.

Mme de Lafayette was familiar with a story-telling ecology too, even though she used it to invent a 'new' narrative affordance (something like what we would call a novel). *La Princesse de Clèves* famously features four intercalated stories, narrated orally to the Princess herself. Each of them is exemplary, in that it provides a model of what can happen in this particular world if people lose control of their feelings. At one point, an earlier real-world story-teller is evoked: Marguerite de Navarre, sister of the King and author of the sixteenth-century collection known as the *Heptameron*. In that collection, as in its fourteenth-century model, Boccaccio's *Decameron*, a group of ten noble men and women, cut off from the world by accidental disasters, spend their enforced leisure in telling each other stories *and then discussing them*. Much more could be said about this sequence of works, but the essential thing is that a practice of collective oral story-telling and reflection reaches on into the era of printed books and private reading. *La Princesse de Clèves* is a printed novel, purchased and read for the most part in solitude; but within its pages, it still contains the oral model, with its message of shared attention and cognitive enrichment. And so, as we shall see, does *Lord Jim*.

The point for the Princess, of course, is how *she* listens to the four exemplary stories, what their downstream effects are on her. The short answer is that they do change her cognitive environment, but not enough, or not quickly enough, to prevent disaster.[15] They only afford a delayed moral transcendence (renunciation, removal from the world) at the furthest limits of the storyworld; they don't prevent her from unwittingly causing the death of her husband. She is too immersed in her perceptions, too responsive to the immediate pressure of the world around her; she is forced onto the back foot and lacks the experience to take the initiative, despite the evidence that accumulates in those stories. The reader can infer all this under the guidance of the author, although it can be amplified by knowledge of the cultural and intellectual milieu to which Lafayette belonged. The key factor is the circulation in contemporary society of a pessimistic view of psychology and ethics according to which moral intention is always liable to be undermined or called into question by a profoundly embedded self-interest. As Kirsti Sellevold has pointed out, this view, associated above all with Lafayette's friend the Duc de La Rochefoucauld, anticipates in important respects the diagnosis of human cognitive dissonance put forward by modern cognitive scientists such as Daniel Kahneman, George Ainslie, and Chris Frith. What they would say is that the initial (pre-reflective) cognitive response, primed on the one hand by the environment and by ancient priorities such as sexual desire, fear, self-protection, and on the other by deeply embedded procedural memories, is automatic and therefore very swift; reflection can't keep up and comes too late.[16] In other words, the assumed psychological conditions of the Princess's mistake apply to everyone: when you're in a situation of duress, when the world presses in on you, you're likely to act according to sub-reflective impulses rather than reflective ones. Lucidity is only available when it is no longer effective.

This will also be the problem of Lord Jim (the character). The young would-be hero is so overwhelmed by sensation and emotion that he can't assess the ethical demands of his situation and act in accordance with them. He acts instinctively, and Conrad's novel will be devoted on the one hand to making his readers *feel* kinesically how that comes about, and on the other to using that feeling as the affordance for a long process of reflective mind-reading.

8

The Posture of Reading

The veranda: a cognitive vantage point

No one who has read *Lord Jim* will have forgotten this scene, where a master story-teller's audience prepares to listen to his narrative:

> Perhaps it would be after dinner, on a veranda draped in motionless foliage and crowned with flowers, in the deep dusk speckled by fiery cigar-ends. The elongated bulk of each cane-chair harboured a silent listener. Now and then a small red glow would move abruptly, and expanding light up the fingers of a languid hand, part of a face in profound repose, or flash a crimson gleam into a pair of pensive eyes overshadowed by a fragment of an unruffled forehead; and with the very first word uttered Marlow's body, extended at rest in the seat, would become very still, as though his spirit had winged its way back into the lapse of time and were speaking through his lips from the past.[1]

The scene is dramatically underspecified. As in a theatre or cinema, darkness removes all but the most marginal visual cues. The foliage frames the veranda as if it were a stage, although here the stage too is dark, since it is inward and imaginary. The story will be told, not enacted by visible bodies. We infer the listeners' presence from the lighted tips of their cigars, then their posture from the 'elongated bulk' of the cane chairs. The glowing cigar-ends draw attention to tiny bodily movements, the synecdochic glimpse of fingers or a part of a face, the gleam of eyes, a 'fragment' of forehead. The one insistent note is repose, the induced languor of a tropical night, and with it a pensive *attentiveness*. We know little about these listeners except that they listen profoundly, unruffled by emotions or anxieties of their own.[2] Even the foliage is motionless. Then a word is uttered and the speaker becomes incarnate, embodied like the listeners, stretched out in repose and still as they are. This shared embodied stillness of narrator and listeners indicates the profundity and reach of their communicative mind-reading. Nothing, it is implied, will be lost here, none of the implicatures of the complex story that will be told. That Marlow is assigned the function of a 'medium', a mere receptor for an earlier voice that was and is also his own, is continuous with the bodily passivity of the story-telling community. The narrative must in some sense tell itself, be passive and unreflective, if it is to remain faithful to the fictionally lived events, which in turn is the condition for those events becoming a fruitful object of reflection.

The very stillness implies expectation of that outcome. Reflection is what the group is there for. They all know (so we reliably infer from the underspecified scene) that a deeply serious kairos will ensue,[3] pregnant with ethical implications and implicatures: a social act of gathered appraisal and judgement. Jim's leap from the perilously immobile ship, the moment when the body makes its own decision before reflective awareness can intervene, is already beginning to become a possibility for these receptive listeners, whose collective experience guarantees a sustained but also suspended ethical consciousness both before and after the act. And beyond the leap, as if by feedback from the future listeners to his story, Jim's later desperate desire to enact a heroic 'nature' is already prefigured.

The second-level readers, the readers of the novel *Lord Jim*, know from the start that this intensely realized and intensely lived scene plays out in one of a set of parallel thought-worlds: this is what the modalizing word 'Perhaps' tells us.[4] The play of imaginative cognition around the story has been re-enacted over and over again, fortuitously, contingently, by later readers and critics. Few of them have sat in the dark on tropical verandas. Few of them were smoking cigars. Many of them have been women, challenging the notion that Jim's failure to live up to his own schoolboy vision of heroism could only be judged by an all-male all-white jury. Some of them have been native speakers of German, or Arabic, or Malay. But somehow the model provided here is translatable into all those other modes, just as King Henry's soldiers and his modern audiences can imagine imitating the action of the tiger. Everyone can imagine Jim's leap: you feel it in your bones, in your muscles, in that headlong downward vision that Edgar induced in Gloucester's dark soul somewhere not so very far from Dover Cliff. And everyone knows that it is a matter of the utmost seriousness, testing our very idea of what ethical responsibility is, what a moral act might and might not be. Those values are of course also embodied in the hearing which delivers a formal verdict on Jim's culpability. The cognitive fluidity implied by the single modalizing word 'perhaps' is what affords the very possibility and nuanced repeatability of moral judgement. The implicatures spelt out in those parallel worlds are divergent yet commensurate; conversely, the very exemplarity of the tale depends on the multiple chances of narrative.

Or one could put it this way: Conrad designs a perfect immersive ecology, an extended mental or cognitive arena in which the participants know their roles, are nothing but those roles. A single author conjures up a collective imagining that allows the reflective resonances of the story to reverberate back and forth as in a fine-tuned instrument. Kinesis is there, in the feel of a cigar held in a *languid* hand, in the transmitted sensation of a reclining posture (so different from Alfred's trouble with the chaise longue in Franzen's *The Corrections*). Memory is there too, procedural as well as episodic, in its access to significant detail, dialogues, listening bodies, states of mind.[5] And, since Marlow's words come mysteriously out of the darkness of past time, this is indeed a conjuring, an art of enactive mimesis that is as lawful as eating. Chaucer, Boccaccio, and Marguerite de Navarre stage their collective story-telling differently, but they surely belong to that same ancient strand of cultural evolution.

A narrative frame for cognitive dissonance

I suggested a moment ago that, listening to Lord Jim's story, one might think also of the story of Gloucester and his imaginary fall. They are of course unlike in many ways, but so are the two *comparanda* of a metaphor: my lawyer may be a shark, but she doesn't have gills or fins. Once one strips them down, a lot of stories are like a lot of other stories. Lear is literally stripped down, stripped naked, until his predicament looks like the existential *degré zéro* of the human story. The fall is both a prototypical metaphor and a recurring plot across 'Western' narrative, from the book of Genesis and its avatars (including anti-Christian ones like Philip Pullman's *His Dark Materials*) or the story of Icarus via the tragic canon to Gibbon, Evelyn Waugh,[6] Conrad, Hitchcock's *Vertigo*, and *King Kong*.

Story-tellers have always been aware of the repeatability of proto-typical plots, and story-collectors of one kind and another have exploited it for their own ends. For a thousand years, Christian mythographers pointed out parallels between Graeco-Roman myths and Christian stories as a way of annexing the culture of classical antiquity to their own culture; projecting Orpheus or Bacchus onto Christ presented few problems for them. Their latter-day representa-tives make the crucial shift from a theologically based interpretation to a more neutral historical one—George Eliot's Mr Casaubon, in search of a *Key to All Mythologies*, is a proponent of the Christian method who finds himself stranded in a secularizing age—and thus open the way to collections based on other corpora, notably folk-stories. Twentieth-century criticism, drawing on the insights of Jung and Frazer, explored the notion of *archetypal* plot-types in terms of thematic content (Maud Bodkin, Northrop Frye), while the structur-alist narratologists (Propp, Todorov, and their heirs) advocated a formalistic classification that was largely context- and even content-free. The fascination with the origins of story has proved remarkably persistent: Carlo Ginzburg's brilliant identification of the 'cynegetic' or hunting plot as the archetype of recognition plots of all kinds, from *Oedipus* to the detective novel, is just one instance that demonstrates how rich such an anthropological perspective can be.[7]

The urge to uncover baseline stories in this way is now receiving new energies from cognitive approaches to story-telling. Brian Boyd's *The Origin of Stories* remains one of the most comprehensive: it offers a broad-based explanatory frame of reference for the human urge to tell stories, drawing on theories (or perhaps one should say hypotheses) of cognitive evolution, and focuses on the value of fictional narration as a form of play as well as on the social value of story-telling as a vehicle for cooperation, collective problem-solving, and so on.

In another productive mode of cognitive narratology, the conver-gence of metaphor and narrative structure or plot turns out once more to be central. The metaphors we live by, to use Lakoff's phrase, all take the form of a nuclear story: a journey, a battle, an erotic encoun-ter, a family quarrel or reunion.[8] The various kinds of associative translation that such prototypical plots and plot-metaphors lend themselves to is currently being explored in considerable detail, and across a broad chronological and cultural spectrum, by narratologists such as Patrick Colm Hogan.[9] David Herman, by contrast, investigates the modalities of 'storyworlds', their intentionalities and internal logics, together with the ways in which they lend themselves to construction by the everyday cognitive processing faculties of their readers.[10] These various methodologies constitute a broad-based, loosely connected family and are for the most part compatible, in principle at least. None of them is purely formal, precisely because cognitive narratologists would all agree that mental functioning is a network of relations and is not reducible to a single logic; Hogan, for example, focuses in particular on the emotional 'systems' that drive plot invention. Such methodologies are, however, designed to detect recurrent structures and deep structures and elicit from these narrative 'rules' and principles. Literary criticism in that mode becomes in essence an attempt to devise a new narrative poetics guaranteed (or at least authorized) by the cognitive sciences.

These studies have staked out such a broad terrain that one finds oneself crossing and recrossing its external and internal borders at every turn. In *Lord Jim*, for example, one might easily reflect on the 'conceptual blending' of a series of archetypal or prototypical stories: the sailor's yarn, the enduring fascination of which Conrad evokes in his authorial preface of 1917;[11] the narrative metaphor of a fall, or again a dangerous leap into the unknown; a story of honour irreparably lost and of the exile (ejection from the tribe) that follows; and a story of absorption into an alien world or culture (the 'going native' story).[12]

I prefer here, however, to look at some of the ways in which one could say that Conrad's narrative is cognitively rich, even cognitively saturated. We may begin with the placing of the passage we have already considered. It is a kind of narrative *incise*, replicating at the level of narrative sequence the micro-intercalations that are used in syntactical language when one wants to make manifest the second-order reflective context within which the utterance is to be understood.[13] 'Listen now', it says; 'focus your attention: you are on the threshold of fascination, immersion, but also judgement.'

The reading scene is also, famously, the synapsis (point of cognitive transference) that substitutes Marlow the intradiegetic story-teller for the anonymous narrator who himself saw Marlow at the inquiry, saw him gaze at Jim, saw Jim seeing Marlow.[14] That prior moment of underspecified seeing is the heart of the dark yet lucid mind-reading that traverses the fiction as a whole, the place where it is communicated tangibly (kinesically) to the consciousness of the reader. And since the moment occurs at the inquiry into the *Patna* incident, (mind-)reading is from the outset charged with the duty and burden of making a judgement.

The exchange of glances is underspecified because, manifestly, it doesn't tell the actors or the reader all they want to know. Instead, it affords a specific set of coordinates for the prolonged act of mind-reading which will constitute the novel: A watches B watching C, who is aware of the gaze of B (but not A). Jim is always conscious from this point on of the possibility of being 'seen'; it haunts him, pursues him half-way across the world, across the seas, through the coastal towns of South-East Asia, and eventually into the rainforest as a last hiding-place. Marlow, with his empathetic desire to understand, will follow him all the way (through the telling of stories, if not in person) until Jim's death brings the enterprise of mind-reading to a close. The position of A is that of author and reader, who can enter and leave the fictional world (specifically, via the cognitive affordance named Marlow) and who therefore, as visitors to it, can see the actors within it but are not seen by them.

So much is self-evident. Yet to separate narrative 'voices' theoretically (or ontologically, for that matter) is to counter the cognitive fluidity of the narration. Rather than speaking of extra- and intradiegetic narrators, omniscient narrators, or 'reflectors' whose point of view is strictly confined, it may be more helpful here to speak of the fluid, mutually interpenetrable vectors of mind-reading.[15] The anonymous narrator of *Lord Jim* clearly belongs to Marlow's story-world, and therefore to Jim's. Even Conrad the author says in his preface that he has 'seen' Jim. It is true that he means he has seen him in the real world, not the fictional one, but the whole point is that cognitively the only difference is that fictional worlds open themselves up for exploration to a degree that is not possible in the real world. Thus, for example, the narrator tells us what Jim felt, physically and mentally, during the hearing:

fair of face, big of frame, with young, gloomy eyes, he held his shoulders upright above the box while his soul writhed within him. He was made to answer another question so much to the point and so useless. His mouth was tastelessly dry, as though he had been eating dust, then salt and bitter as after a drink of sea-water. He wiped his damp forehead, passed his tongue over his parched lips, felt a shiver run down his back.

These details—Jim's proprioceptive sensations—are not simply invented externally and pasted on to a fictional puppet. They belong to the domain of fully kinesic mind-reading, where motor resonance, affective empathy, and more reflective modes of inference operate seamlessly together to render a living model of the other's 'subjective' experience—what it felt like at that moment to be Jim.[16] Looked at from that angle, the narrator doesn't need to be 'omniscient': he is deploying the suite of cognitive affordances that are at the disposal of humans when they want or need to know how others feel. Marlow will do the same: how else would he guess his way towards an understanding of Jim's story? That the story is fictional makes, again, no difference.

The court scene plays a pivotal role in the cognitive construction of the story and how it is told. The narrative of the *Patna* incident has been taken up to the point where the ship passes over a hidden obstruction. We know nothing yet of Jim's response to that accident, or why he is here in court to explain it. The factual questions Jim is forced to answer are unspecified, although the reader can already draw inferences on the basis of earlier scenes where he has failed to live up to his own expectations. All the attention here is on his moral and hence physical discomfort, the motor responses and somatic reflexes that accompany the sense of an irremediable failure. In a moment, he will, arrestingly, see Marlow looking at him, looking through him—perhaps already towards that group of readers sitting in the dark on the veranda, or some other unspecified reader ('one of us'). As that moment approaches, the apparently well-informed narrator of the opening pages of the book begins himself to adopt the inferential mode. As in the passage just quoted, he construes Jim's feelings from his stance, the way he licks his lips, the agonized pauses in his response to the questions he is asked. In other words, the narrator, who had previously preferred the standard diegetic mode ('Jim did this, felt that, thought such and such'), begins to use both the inferential mind-reading mode and kinesic intelligence. He begins, as it were, to become Marlow, the character in the storyworld who can actually *see* Jim, not just narrate him. And Jim, by the same token, begins to emerge here as something other than a character in an exemplary fiction. He becomes, for the reader, a fully sentient being.

This account needs to be inflected, however, by the glimpse of Jim we are offered in the opening pages. This Jim is the figure in the story that follows the hearing (the one already *seen* at the hearing), the marine officer exiled from the sea and constrained to work as an agent in East Asian seaports. The way Conrad presents him is not merely 'descriptive': it is cognitively underspecified (the reader has to guess what sort of a person he is), and at the same time *mobilized*:

> He was an inch, perhaps two, under six feet, powerfully built, and he advanced straight at you with a slight stoop of the shoulders, head forward, and a fixed-from-under stare which made you think of a charging bull.

The 'stoop' and the 'stare' scan this representation with an alliteration that links the two bodily postures: the stoop means that the stare is 'fixed from under'. These are twin sensorimotor habits formed by—rather than simply symbolic of—the experience of disgrace, and consequently by the instinct both to evade the onlooker's gaze and to defy it. As he 'advances' towards you (the reader sees Jim, according to the order of the fiction, even before Marlow does), you feel that stoop, that stare, in the muscles of your neck and face. The result is that the implicatures of the ad hoc image that follows ('charging bull') are strictly confined. This 'advance' is not threatening to the viewer; Jim is not a dangerously violent man. The image, like the rest, bespeaks Jim's cognitive dissonance: he has performed, publicly and irreversibly, an action which seems to define his 'character' but which runs counter to the belief-systems he and his culture adhere to.[17] Once a promising and talented young man with his life before him and his agency still intact, he has acquired the energy of an animal, a creature whose cognition is saturated with feelings of pain and anger.

Cognitive dissonance, in fact, becomes the implied motif of the micro-biography of the young Merchant Navy officer that the narrator subsequently offers us. It contains two episodes that might come from the standard stock of sailor's yarns: both feature spectacularly hostile maritime weather. The first is the episode on the training ship, where Jim fails to grasp the opportunity to particpate in a quasi-heroic rescue; in the second, he is also sidelined or disabled (he breaks his leg) and is forced to sweat out a horrendous storm in his cabin, suffering extreme pain and fever. Both register, in descriptive rather than inferential mode, the resonance of Jim's physical sensations, and at the same time the strangely dislocated movement of his mental reflections. What happens here is that he experiences the brute force of the natural world as something other than, and resistant to, the imagined world in which he believes his capacity for action will be demonstrated. He finds himself involuntarily living out a skewed version of the sailor's yarn, one in which a young sailor, primed by conventional sea-stories, imagines himself as a hero, but is overwhelmed by the impersonal physicality of circumstance and his own instinctive responses. He finds that he can't *choose* to be a hero; even Jim's co-student from the training ship who rescued the drowning seamen is not, when he subsequently boasts of his exploit, an authentic hero (he invents the most favourable story for himself). Imagination appears here, quite explicitly, in a negative light: the world is resistant to the reassuring or inspiring stories humans tell themselves.[18] Jim imagines himself to be heroic, but the horror of the storm at sea and the horror of death it carries with it—a horror of the unknowable, like Kurtz's—offer a counter-imagination, one that undermines his ethical conception of himself.

The irony, of course, is that when the decisive event occurs, the one that will test Jim's moral worth, it comes in disguise. Jim's disaster hides itself, the way the beast in the jungle hides itself in Henry James's tale; it creeps up on him unawares, undoes yet again his chance of seizing the heroic moment. He had imagined that this moment would come in the form of some recognizable cataclysm, but it emerges from a dead calm, a sea so smooth, a weather so clement, that Jim is luxuriating in this easy ride. If he had in earlier episodes been paralysed by the sheer brutal force of a storm at sea, he is now disarmed by the very absence of the standard indications of adventure and the heroic. He takes action, observes the danger to the ship, but it is as if he has been *primed* by the calm[19] and fails to recognize that moral responsibility is independent of particular circumstances and storylines. In a storm, one feels, he might not have made his fatal leap and abandoned ship. Nor would he have done so, certainly, had the passengers been Europeans. The ultimate irony is that he does what his body wants, takes flight, when in fact the ship will remain afloat. There *was* no adventure, no disaster, no occasion for heroism. And so the alien malevolent world tricks Jim into betraying his fear of death and thus revealing the cognitive dissonance that seals his fate. The story the world tells him and the stories he tells himself, the ones he wants to live by, are incompatible.

This interpretation could be enhanced by a further cognitive perspective. Famously, Jim doesn't know why he jumped from the ship. He simply can't grasp the story the world tells him, because he has no conception of the calculations his mind (and thus also his body) might make sub-reflectively at a moment of crisis. His conscious intentions are sharply dissonant with the embodied intentionality of his leap into the lifeboat. He doesn't understand that his action was primed by the behaviour of the other members of the crew, and beyond that by his sense that this ship isn't his kind of ship, the kind of ship in which a story of courage and honour would be told. One could say that his instinctive calculus of possibilities, at the moment of decision, was already skewed by those preconceptions.[20] Of course that reading implies that somehow Conrad had grasped this point, despite having no access to modern cognitive science. I see no problem in asserting that he understood it by means of an enriched reflection on human behaviour, and more specifically an enriched fictional imagination. The example argues again for the hypothesis advanced in this study as a whole, namely that cognitively enriched fiction offers a mode of intelligence—at once kinesic and reflective—not available to other kinds of discourse.

The mode of cognitive dissonance Conrad presents us with here places *Lord Jim* squarely in the category of fictions that show the dangerous potential of fiction to offer temptingly simplified or erroneous accounts of the world: *Madame Bovary*, *Northanger Abbey*, and *Don Quijote* are a small canonic sub-set of these, but they display the wide range of possibilities open to a fictional critique of fiction-induced cognitive distortions and disruptions.[21] At the broadest level, what is at issue is epistemic vigilance, the balancing system one has to presuppose in order to explain why the human capacity for counterfactual, hypothetical, or generally 'imaginative' thinking isn't normally a one-way ticket to Hotel California.[22] Fiction, as the mode of thinking which *de jure* suspends the need to serve practical ends or proffer verifiable propositional content, is always vulnerable to rational-minded critics, some of whom are inclined to see the hotel round every corner. It has many modes of epistemic vigilance at its disposal. One is precisely the move made by Conrad in showing the havoc that can be wrought on impressionable minds by simplistic fictions. Another is to draft into the narrative a figure whose attention is maximally focused and who demands an equivalent focus from his readers: who better than a master story-teller? In that sense, Marlow could be said to be the epitome, even the personification, of epistemic vigilance, and all the more because he couples vigilance with empathy. The scene of reading we began with thus provides the focal frame for this complex and finely calculated set of moves. Only a fiction could achieve that degree of cognitive transcendence of the fictional. Thirdly, an ending must be calculated, a probable outcome, that allows the character to handle the dissonance in his own way. Jim's way is not to take a safe subordinate position in 'his' world, his culture, but to seek out an alternative world of the imagination that provides him with the affordance he needs to move beyond shame and despair. For the reader, no doubt, Jim's quasi-heroic death doesn't in itself eradicate dissonance, except in the simplest and most obvious sense. It is the task of the novel, in the space between the narrator's intentionality and the character's, to uncover it as a hidden malaise, to explore it with an almost scientific precision, and to counter it with a kind of reflective consonance.

When Conrad ends his authorial preface with the remark that Jim is 'one of us', it is easy to assume that the remark is almost casually racist.[23] Only the white European male, he seems to be saying, understands the code of honour according to which Jim's life was broken and crudely remade. Perhaps that *is* what he's saying. But Conrad must have known that other cultures recognize a code of honour. Perhaps it would be more pertinent to read the remark ironically, as a twentieth-century counterpart to the last sentence of Montaigne's essay on the 'cannibals': 'So what?' he says, having provided ample illustration of the value, even superiority, of the culture of the native inhabitants of South America; 'they don't wear breeches.'[24] The phrase is echoic:[25] it's what prejudiced people say. The 'white man's' code of honour in *Lord*

Jim is no great shakes, after all. It is usually reduced to a formulaic
conception or a knee-jerk reaction, and as such is liable to do more
harm than good. If Jim is one of us, we're like Jim. One is reminded
here of another classic reversal of values, a sharp prefatory stab from
a poet whose work Conrad undoubtedly knew well: 'Hypocrite lecteur,—mon semblable,—mon frère!'[26] Which brings us back, with an
additional twist of epistemic vigilance, to the white males sitting
comfortably on their veranda, lighting their cigars in preparation
for a good yarn.

Jim charges into that scene like a bull, frightened rather than angry,
although he is angry too. His spectral form is already on the veranda
in the midst of the listeners, because according to the fictional chron-
ology Marlow has already encountered him on more than one veranda, and the listeners will soon hear those episodes related. One
scene in particular has all the resonances of the proverbial bull in a
china shop. Jim has been talking with Marlow over dinner at a
veranda restaurant about the frantic scenes on the *Patna* before the
'white' crew members abandoned ship; one of them, both servile and
bullying, called him a coward for *not* wanting to save his own life. Jim
repeats the word and breaks into laughter:

> 'I had never in my life heard anything so bitter as that noise.…Along
> the whole dim length of the gallery the voices dropped, the pale
> blotches of faces turned our way with one accord, and the silence
> became so profound that the clear tinkle of a tea-spoon falling on the
> tessellated floor of the veranda rang out like a tiny and silvery scream.'
>   '"You mustn't laugh like this, with all these people about,"
> I remonstrated. "It isn't nice for them, you know."'[27]

You hear with crystal clarity not only the tinkling of the spoon as it hits
the floor, but by extension, as it were, the breaking of fine porcelain.
There is empathy with Jim in this scene, undoubtedly, thanks to
Marlow's gaze and his ironic remark. But the irony is directed at the
other diners, sitting in their comfortably closed world of European
decorum. Suddenly, *you* are one of *them*, looking up in alarm, all
conversation extinguished, hearing from somewhere deep inside yourself the tiny scream a teaspoon might make. You feel the ship lurch
beneath your feet, the level stage turn into a cliff; and for a moment,
you share again the horror of Jim's leap into the dark.

Towards a reflective consonance

Since this chapter has been primarily a close reading rather than an account of particular cognitive topics or effects, I offer here some provisional conclusions at that secondary level.

First, much has been made of embedded mind-reading, of the affordances and constraints of social cognition. The complexity of mind-reading in *Lord Jim* far exceeds the classic chain of embedded 'clauses' (P knows that X believes that Y suspected that Q …). In the end, it takes us to the outermost limits of what it is to read another person's mind. You can do it, using all the kinesic intelligence, all the cultural and personal experience you can muster, provided that your attention is unwaveringly focused yet at the same time relaxed, passive, receptive. At that outermost limit, you will necessarily encounter the unknowable. It may be represented as a blur, as a fog, or as an inscrutable darkness, but it is always there: absolutely transparent persons do not exist. La Rochefoucauld is right to say that others can read you better than you read yourself, and that is certainly true of *La Princesse de Clèves* and of *Lord Jim*, but he also sees the inscrutable darkness. Which is not to say that the whole project of mind-reading is compromised, only that human cognition has evolved to handle the world pragmatically, not to juggle with abstractions or essences. Other people are in the end part of that disconcertingly intractable ecology that the Princess finds herself entangled in on the very threshold of adulthood, and that Jim first encounters on the training ship when the wind rises up like an alien agent and he can only look on, disempowered.

Secondly, it is a mistake to think that immersion and reflection are antithetical poles. As ecologically evolved beings, we are always immersed in the world: there is nowhere else for cognition to go. We can imagine things that are not in the world—counterfactuals, hypotheses, fictions, and the like—but the only way we can imagine them successfully is by first giving them the credit of reality. Mimesis is the necessary condition of reflection. There can then be critical reflection, appraisal, suspicion, discrimination, and it may be that in consequence the imagined world reveals its inadequacy, or its hidden power to delude and betray. But in principle, reflection is not immersion's enemy: the novels we have looked at, and the whole canon of Shakespeare's plays, make that insistently clear. The reciprocal action of mimesis and reflection is just how human cognition works, and literature is the mode of thinking where it is capable of the freest and furthest reach.

Thirdly, the examples we have been considering are all located in their own historical and cultural moment. The little cluster of court figures who feature centrally in *La Princesse de Clèves*, and the indiscriminate crowd of other nobles who surround them, form a cognitive ensemble with its own cultural constraints, as do the actors, storytellers and imagined readers of *Lord Jim*. The affordances the novel shares with prototypical narratives are likewise specifically shaped by their own moment: Mme de Lafayette and Conrad work within (though also on the outer edge of) the narrative instruments they inherited. To write those histories collectively is to write a social, cultural, and literary history. One could therefore argue that there is no such thing as a specifically cognitive history. However, the cognitive processes that govern both action and narration, the processes that make literature imaginable and communicable, are only available to us, for the most part, through the particular forms they take. It would be possible to imagine a new version of Auerbach's *Mimesis* (for example) which would analyse along a historico-cultural axis (i) the culturally mediated kinds of thinking about thinking that literature does, (ii) the prehistories of cognitive understanding that literature itself affords.[28] Mme de Lafayette's storyworld shows how much she and her contemporaries knew about deception, self-deception, misinterpretation, and the constant, exhausting struggle to maintain epistemic vigilance; Conrad knew a lot about cognitive dissonance, about the glories and illusions of story-telling. Both were expert in mind-reading and kinesic intelligence. It is precisely because of what they have in common with each other and with earlier and later tellers of stories that one could calibrate with some precision the affordance-enhanced possibilities of thought in such and such a period or cultural environment and thus (potentially) write a history of culturally constrained cognition.

Finally, I return to my suggestion that the task of the novel is both to reveal the nature of cognitive dissonance (or, more generally, of cognitive malfunction) and to provide a comprehensive and robust frame of reflective consonance. I was referring at that point to the novel *Lord Jim*, but one might ask whether that description might not be pertinent to the novel as a genre, and by extension to fictional story-telling in general. Narrative fiction is capable of affording a special kind of epistemic vigilance that is communicated to readers and shared with them: they create it collectively, not least through critical commentary. This does not mean that literature should be assigned an ethical task, or expected to conform to a particular cultural or even universal norm, still less supply a reassuringly didactic 'message'. It is not the business of literature to be the emissary of an ethical (or political, or ideological, or philosophical) master. It is not unconstrained, but it must be given the space and freedom to see past the constraints of the cognitive and cultural processes from which it arises. A strong fiction is not always an ethically strong fiction: literature, as I have argued throughout, is an instrument for thinking with, not in itself a safeguard of ethical values. We shall look more closely at these issues in Chapter 9.

9

Literary Values in a Cognitive Perspective

Fungible images

In the aftermath of her daughter's murder, the 65-year-old Sylvia, a minor character in Jonathan Franzen's *The Corrections*, watches pornography on the web for the first time:

> She wondered: How could people respond to these images if images didn't secretly enjoy the same status as real things? Not that images were so powerful, but that the world was so weak. It could be vivid, certainly, in its weakness, as on days when the sun baked fallen apples in orchards and the valley smelled like cider, and cold nights when Jordan had driven to Chadds Ford for dinner and the tires of her Cabriolet had crunched on the gravel driveway; but the world was *fungible* only as images. Nothing got inside the head without becoming pictures.[1]

This last sentence is not strictly true, because of course language can do it too. There is also an apparent confusion between first-order and second-order representations: the 'pictures' in question are mediated, precisely, by the media. But it is true that the circulation or communication of kinesic effects (and other sensations or indeed imaginings) requires an initial conversion into a fungible form, whether images on a screen or words spoken or on a page: Franzen's fallen apples and crunching pebbles are no less 'pictures' than are the pornographic images watched by Sylvia. It might indeed be argued that literature itself is a theatre of powerfully and pleasurably fungible representations.

Franzen's own success on the literary market can certainly be ascribed in large measure to his skills in making the everyday world fungible through language. But what is the going rate on the literary market? How is that rate determined? Are the values it embodies in any sense ethical as well as aesthetic? Could it be that literature is merely, as Gregory Currie has suggested, a form of cognitive pornography, peddling illusory pleasures?[2] We need now to ask whether a cognitive approach to literature can help us to answer such questions.

What is literature for?

Western culture has long taken it for granted that literature can be an object of knowledge. Aristotle's *Poetics* is only the most obvious ancient example, and many other cultures have similar traditions. You can teach it and study it in more or less systematic ways at school and university. You can write its history, you can analyse its formal properties or traditions, you can construct theories of literature and of literary criticism, you can treat it philosophically as an aspect of aesthetics or ethics. In the broadest sense of the word, 'literature' can become an object of anthropological and cognitive study, a human phenomenon operating within the constraints of human phylogenetic and cultural evolution. And since it draws on the same cognitive apparatus as the rest of our thinking, it may be explored as a special manifestation of human thought.

Yet anyone who is literate can read novels and poems or go to the theatre, and it is often claimed that critical analysis spoils the experience, over-complicates it. As we saw in Chapters 2 and 3, there is an observable difference between pre-reflective reading and critical reflection, although the borders are impossible to draw precisely. The reading of Dante or Virginia Woolf can hardly be unreflective or even pre-reflective; yet it is clear that we *want* to read unreflectively: we want to be immersed in a narrative fiction or a theatrical enactment, or to feel directly the affect with which a lyric poem is charged. That's what reading is for, isn't it? But the argument of the literary critic and a fortiori the literary theorist has to be that extensive and iterated reflection must in the end inform, be prior to, be absorbed into the unreflective mode. This feedback process is after all one of the two principal ways in which we learn things, the other being pre-reflective observation and imitation (as with many manual skills).

So you can make an argument for the proposition that literature is a legitimate object of knowledge, but it won't look very strong unless literature is perceived as worthy of being studied in the first place. Plato wouldn't have thought so, if his attack on dramatic poetry in the *Republic* is anything to go by,[3] and versions of his argument have been repeated down to the present day by philosophers, theologians, and others.

So let's look at the wide-angle question: what is literature for? What is its cognitive function (it may of course have many)? Why do humans inveterately tell stories, sing songs, enact characters and scenes? Here are some of the answers that have been given, starting with the negative or dismissive ones:[4]

- Literature is merely an accidental spin-off of language, a side-effect. Like language, it comes cheap, in the sense that it doesn't require physical labour or risk. Most people wouldn't endanger their lives in order to hunt a virtually inedible beast; there has to be a serious benefit if the potential costs are high, but if they are low, the benefit could be marginal.

- The role of literature (and other arts) in human evolution is comparable with the peacock's tail: it's a showy appendage that demonstrates to potential sexual partners that the individual who produced it can survive and flourish even with that handicap. Sexual advantage here may of course be transmuted into the competition for power and money (cf. patronage as a display of power, whether one is speaking of the visual illusions of the Palazzo Te or the avant-garde art flaunted by captains of industry and commerce).[5]

- It's a means of wish-fulfilment, fantasy, escapism ('cognitive pornography'), or at best a form of self-indulgence or entertainment (like eating chocolate, or having sex without procreative intent).

- It has affinities with delusion; major writers ('geniuses') have traditionally been regarded as in some sense delusional ('inspired'), emotionally and morally volatile, etc.

- It can be shown to promote deviance, crime, violence (see in particular the impact of fictional representations of sex and violence on children).

- With appropriate state control, it can be deployed as a means of ideological enforcement, or used as a mass drug, a way of distracting people from the oppression to which they are subject.

- It can serve as a force of political destabilization or subversion.
- It offers puzzles to be solved. This feature is prominent in detective novels, thrillers, and any fiction dependent on suspense, but it could also be attributed to many kinds of poetry. Human cognition thrives on the solving of puzzles (including pattern detection and other hermeneutic activities), but there is as yet no firm evidence that the cognitive abilities of people who regularly play chess or solve crosswords, Sudokus, and other problems are significantly sharpened.
- Story-telling is a form of social glue, a kind of gossip extended through the imagination: it is above all in origin a collective activity, and even if it is nowadays often consumed in private, it promotes conversation, enhancing social solidarity and facilitating collective calibration of social and ethical values. Poetry, for its part, has its origin in collective singing, which helps the group to coordinate important activities; it too, in its own way, promotes cooperation. Drama can combine both of those functions.
- Literature of many kinds can bring about a form of psychological release (catharsis) and restore the balance of the emotions. This conception appears in various guises from Aristotle's *Poetics* onwards: Wordsworth's famous adage that poetry arises from 'emotion recollected in tranquillity' is one among many.
- In the perspective of cultural history (or cultural studies more generally), literature is a major constituent of collective cultural memory. Its themes and stories are icons of the prevailing imagination of given societies and periods; it is strongly marked by mnemonic affordances (including metre and rhyme in poetry, but also script and print as modes of conservation) and by explicit appeals to memory.
- Literary fictions draw on 'folk psychology', both explicitly (in narrative and dramatic representations of the dialogue, the reflections, and the motivation of characters) and implicitly (in fictional representations of behaviour and action). They have the function of appraising, testing, and evaluating folk psychology, and in some cases affording counter-intuitive or defamiliarizing alternatives (for example, modernist techniques such as 'stream of consciousness').
- Literature of all kinds can be a vehicle for knowledge or ideas that can be expressed in other ways and other media (didactic literature, satirical literature, utopias and dystopias, etc.).

- Literature can be an instrument of thought; for example, it can be used as a 'thought-experiment', allowing embodied represen- tations of social, political, or ethical ideas and thus testing those ideas in approximations to real-world situations; but it might also be claimed that the mode of thought it affords is *sui generis* and self-sufficient, i.e. not simply an auxiliary for other more literal- rational modes of thought.

The first thing to say here is self-evident but essential: literature as an evolved human activity is a multiple phenomenon, a coral reef whose ecology encompasses an extraordinary diversity of forms, expressive possibilities, and potential functions. It's hardly surprising, then, that it's possible to put forward so many accounts, both positive and negative, of what it's for. Like many other human instruments, it offers a constantly expanding range of possibilities for use, some of which may be beautiful and enriching, others sinister, subversive, repulsive. It seems unlikely that its evolutionary role is confined to a single phylogenetic function (such as the 'peacock's tail' hypothesis), or a fortiori to a single mode of cultural evolution.

Another way of putting this point is to say that literature is by its nature overdetermined and underspecified. It's important to note that this pair of apparent opposites are really twins, two aspects of the same phenomenon. The plurality of implied inputs and intentions is matched by the proliferation of affordances, the possibilities that a given work offers for cognitive realization. Just as single interpret- ations rarely exhaust the hermeneutic use-value of literary works, so more broadly any particular literary phenomenon (let's say, for example, a television soap opera) will lend itself to several overlapping frames of explanation. Some of these will be compatible with others, some may be partially or potentially incompatible. Overdetermin- ation in this sense is a function of the kind of language that literature uses, combined with the fact that it is intrinsically permissive: it can take all kinds of risks, explore all kinds of alternatives, without signifi- cant consequences in the real world.

When I speak of a 'kind of language' here, I mean that literature uses what one might call a cognitively mixed language. It is charac- teristically an embodied language in its rich exploitation of its intrin- sically situated ecology and in its preference for kinesic palpability and figurative elaboration; similarly, at the broader level of plot, fictional 'characters' are by definition embodiments, living their fictional lives in situated environments (storyworlds) that may be represented in concrete detail. It follows that mental processes as they appear in literature—the beliefs and imaginings of characters, the social, ethical, or political conceptions that are enunciated or implied within a given work, whether they are attributed to fictional character, narrator, or author—are always entangled with modes of embodiment. Even gnomic or didactic poems that appear to enunciate single abstract conceptions submerge those conceptions in palpable sounds and rhythms more salient than those one would expect in everyday speech.

We return here to a recurrent refrain and founding supposition of this study: literature partakes of the fluid connectivity of human cognition, and retains some at least of the unresolved complexity to which that connectivity gives rise. Like the human mind, it's a market-place of competing embodied conceptions. To this extent (but critic-ally), it's unlike the rationally delineated debating chamber of philosophy or the trial by verification conducted by the sciences. A philosopher's thought-experiment is carefully designed to test the truth value of a particular proposition or position. Blue-skies research in particle physics has to be rigorously tested against experimental data of the kind currently being produced by the Large Hadron Collider at CERN. The simulations that are used to teach pilots to fly jet aircraft are entirely different in their purpose and function from *King Lear* as a simulation of human action. Literary works are too rich in implications, too densely fabricated, to allow a controlled 'experi-ment' in which the proposition that is to be tested can be clearly tagged and tracked. Their import can't be finally verified or discon-firmed. But the costs of entanglement are outweighed in their case by the benefits of their ability to let imaginative propositions (let's call them that, to avoid assuming that literature deals in propositions in the analytic sense) behave in ways that are precisely not controlled in advance according to a rationalizing criterion. They improvise, or rather perhaps they model improvisation, in their own cognitive mode. Since humans wouldn't have got very far, as Cosmides and Tooby have argued, without improvisation, it may be that, in the evolution of imaginative affordances, what we are here calling litera-ture may have been more central and more productive than the protocols of philosophy and science, which are after all a recent invention in the history of culture.[6] To attempt to harness literature to specific propositional content or truth values is to deprive it of its distinctive character and force: the licence to think more variously, more plurally, more many-strandedly.[7]

Those moves towards a conception of the distinctiveness of the literary imagination should, however, not be understood to separate literature from the real world; on the contrary. It has been my argument throughout that literature, in the broadest sense, participates fully in a *spectrum* of counterfactual imaginings and arises from the same fundamental cognitive capacity, namely the capacity to entertain mental representations (simulations, projections) that are not mapped onto immediate perceptual contexts and uses, and to multiply and compare those representations. The different types mentioned above, and many others, would then be arranged rather on a spectrum that would begin with those that are closest to empirical reality or to truth-conditions and move out towards the realms of fiction (science fiction, fantasy, surrealist poetry). But note that fictions still have to be in some sense believable, like the coat that you hang on the vacuum cleaner—they still have to work with real-world affordances, because that is how our cognitive systems have evolved, in response to real-world needs. Conversely, we know that scientists who try to infer which sub-atomic particles will be needed to explain the behaviour of the particles that are already known and understood also have to make an enormous imaginative leap away from the conditions of the everyday world.

What is important here for a cognitive approach to literary study is, first, that the products of thought too can become affordances, moving between mind and world (which includes in particular other people's minds) via the medium of the oral performances and written texts that are afforded by the technologies of script, print, and electronic media. This is also true of mathematics, philosophy, history, do-it-yourself books, travel guides, and everything else you see on the shelves of bookshops or in online catalogues. But that way of thinking about the products of the mind can, I think, potentially give us a more specific purchase on the *range of cognitive affordances* that moves out towards literature: blue-skies thinking, counterfactual scenarios, thought-experiments, fictions of all kinds, and poetry.

Of course you can't do the same things with a fiction as you can with the real world. What it affords is not what is afforded by the real, or at least it operates in a different mode. It's helpful to remember here the point about perceived and imagined 'images' (see Chapter 5). You can't resolve the immanent three-dimensional structure of a Necker cube in your imagination, or fail to notice something in an imagined representation, or imagine something that doesn't originate in perceptual experience. But those intractabilities are richly compensated for by the alternative plasticities of imagined representations.

Downstream conversations

In a recent review, Gregory Currie ends with this sharp riposte to claims that literature can mediate knowledge:

> We are apt, in our pleasantly conversational way, to hear two people say they learned different things, indeed contradictory things, from the same novel and think it impolite to say 'That's extraordinary—how can we work out which one of you is right?'[8]

There is an immediate question here about 'learning': what would it mean to 'learn' something from a novel? It wouldn't count, presumably, to say that we learnt that Elizabeth Bennett ended up by marrying Mr Darcy, or that people in Jane Austen's day thought of marriage primarily in terms of wealth, property, and status. But let's say that Currie means something altogether more complex, for example that these two people propose incompatible interpretations of the same novel. One doesn't need to be an out-and-out relativist to say that people might 'learn' different things from the same literary work without having to insist that only one of these different perspectives can be right. Even in polite conversation (let alone professional literary criticism) one might have a useful discussion about the relative merits of the readings, and—if it emerges that one is implausible, or that each may validly modify the other—expect either or both parties to move, by the time they have finished talking about it, to a further perspective that is more productive. Of course philosophical works also lend themselves to such interpretative debates, but literary works thrive on it: their capacity for generating further conversation represents a major part of the value we assign to them. As we saw earlier, the story-tellers in Chaucer's *Canterbury Tales* and Boccaccio's *Decameron* knew this very well.

Modern media fictions, it might be argued, operate in just this way. Soap-operas, thrillers, and crime fiction openly rehearse contemporary 'issues' such as gender politics and race relations; Lisbeth Salander in Stieg Larsson's *Millennium* trilogy and Saga Norén in *The Bridge* are fictionally characterized as in some sense autistic; Carrie in *Homeland* is explicitly if implausibly bipolar; torture as used by US state agents is problematized in *24*. In *The Archers*, there was a sequence of episodes in which the middle-aged couple Mike and Vicky Tucker had a Down's Syndrome child, and the culling of badgers was also an ongoing story-line. Do these fictions change the ethical beliefs or behaviour of the audience? Is that what the writers are trying to do? Their agenda appears to be 'liberal', but perhaps they're simply exploiting trends in current society to create feel-good stories that will attract a wide audience.[9]

Chris Frith has suggested that such materials are affordances for collective metacognition.[10] Individual experience is necessarily extremely limited, which in turn limits the possibilities of individual metacognition. The sharing of experience enables this limitation to be circumvented; conjectural and fictional representations provide affordances for yet wider collective reflection. Whatever Chaucer or Boccaccio or the writers of soap-operas and crime fiction think they're doing (they may not reflect on it in much detail), they are responding to that need and providing materials for collective metacognitive feedback. One may reasonably assume that, however unevenly and imperfectly, the outcome creates value for society at large and for the individuals of which it's composed.

That argument suggests that it's not essential to a case for the value of literature that we should be able to demonstrate the positive ethical effects of literary experience (reading fiction or poetry, watching drama). Any claim made on those grounds is vulnerable to the objection that even the most publicly valued works cannot be relied on to produce beneficial effects; devoted readers of high-quality literature may be and remain nasty people. However, it's hard to deny that literary experience can be a vehicle for ethical reflection, offering far more examples than readers are likely to have access to through their everyday experience of the world.

Another thing that literary fictions can do is to undermine our confidence in our perceptual and cognitive tools and challenge the illusions we harbour in respect of our own and other people's behaviour. This is the kind of thing that cognitive psychologists like to do, and they do it with refreshing verve, but there is a long prehistory of cognitive reflection that features remarkably penetrating insights into the ethical and perceptual self-deceptions that humans are prone to, and proposes models of embodied cognition that would not be rejected out of hand by modern cognitivists. I am thinking, for example, of Diderot's powerful attempts to imagine ways in which a material mind would function, using metaphorical models such as a swarm of bees.[11] Seventeenth-century French writers such as Mme de Lafayette and La Rochefoucauld relentlessly exposed the slippage between conscious intention and prior motivation, and George Eliot was no less aware of the ways in which the self-interested body pre-empts the decisions of the reflective self: she speaks of the small misdeeds that are 'like the subtle muscular movements which are not taken account of in the consciousness, though they bring about the end that we fix our mind on and desire'.[12] The word 'muscular' in that sentence is particularly telling, implying as it does an embodied response that normally passes unnoticed, like the gorilla in the famous change blindness experiment. Such examples make it impossible to speak of literature as merely retailing the errors and illusions of folk psychology.

Similarly, the defence of literature and literary studies in a cognitive perspective doesn't and shouldn't depend on a restriction of 'literature' to its canonic manifestations, or to any other sub-set considered as embodying 'good literature'. The calculus of literary value, whether aesthetic, ethical, or more broadly cultural, is a universal feature of literate cultures (and no doubt oral cultures too); it arises from the sense that fiction, poetry, theatre, and their analogues are potential goods and potential evils, so that it becomes a matter of urgent concern to calibrate those values in relation to the wider values of the culture in question. This calculus is therefore intrinsic to the cognitive behaviour surrounding literature; it is often pre-reflective, but with persistent reflective feedback. If a specific act of calibration (such and such is 'good literature', such and such is 'trash') becomes a prior move or presupposition, it will therefore pre-empt the whole discussion of literature as a cognitive resource. Some people think that *Downton Abbey* is trash, or even morally pernicious, but others disagree, and it will not help to exclude such instances from our enquiry.

The calculus of value is one version of the calculus of the imagination that must be taken to be fundamental to the operation of human cognition. Let's rehearse the argument one last time. Human cognition thrives on improvisation, on flexibility as embodied in predicting, planning, the imagining of alternative scenarios, counterfactuals, thought-experiments, and the like. We characterize this domain loosely as that of the 'imagination', which is reciprocally characterized by deviation from the pressures and constraints of action in the real world. Such deviations can be calibrated on a gradient of closeness to or distance from empirical reality or truth (for these purposes, the important distinction between those two is only secondary). Some cognitive mechanism or mechanisms must be presupposed if the gradient is to be effective: tagging, decoupling, and other metaphors have been put forward as candidates for this function. The tagging may be internal to the imagined representation or external to it, but it allows the mind in normal circumstances to remain in sufficient pragmatic control of its representations. Delusional imagination would be an obvious exception: in that case, one must presume that the tagging process is deficient.

It's essential to grasp here that cognitive tagging is not just a mode of inhibition. Like censorship, it actually licenses the imaginative excursion: it provides the passport for a move into potentially risky territory. Fiction is clearly an extreme case, since it demands the right to go anywhere, do anything that is humanly imaginable (including the highly improbable or the impossible). So in the case of fiction, the external tagging must be unambiguous. The internal tagging may be less so (for example, in a historical novel or a 'faction'), but that is a possibility already included in the small print of the external licence ('this is a novel', 'this is a faction').

Why is this argument so central to the question of literary value? First, because it evaluates literature as a central human cognitive activity, rather than as a side-issue or a side-effect: it provides an account of fictional representations (which may include lyric poetry) as lying on a continuum with other imagined representations of which the use-value is already acknowledged. Some of those are apparently trivial imaginings ('I imagine that my aunt wouldn't like chocolate cake for tea'); others are creative, but have demonstrable effects in the real world ('Einstein imagined laws of physics radically different from those imagined by Newton'). But that's just what one would expect of an inclusive gradient; there seems to be no reason to create some decisive cut-off point between the trivial and the important, the 'scientific' and the fictional, or indeed to assume that the gradient is in itself value-based. 'Trivial' imaginings may be non-negligible: decisions about whether to serve chocolate cake to an aunt might conceivably affect the terms of her will. Equally, scientific imaginings aren't intrinsically more or less important than literary ones, even if it would be reasonable to think that *Fifty Shades of Grey* is less likely to have long-term real-world effects than the theory that led to the discovery of the Higgs–Boson particle.[13]

I have always felt uneasy about the notion, widespread since the eighteenth century, of a fundamental separation of the aesthetic domain from other realms or modes of knowledge. The gradient (or spectrum) argument is offered here as an alternative. The aesthetic imagination is in principle insulated from the pressures of utility and functionality, but that doesn't mean that it has no uses or functions beyond itself. Similarly, the fact that pleasure (in a broad sense) is a constituent feature of the aesthetic domain doesn't mean that reading literature or looking at paintings or listening to music is just 'fun'. For obvious reasons, feelings of pleasure accompany most of the activities that are important for the survival of the species. Reason, as *Star Trek*'s Mr Spock is regularly reminded by the other characters and indeed the story-lines themselves, is disabled if it lacks the motivating power of emotion. But the uses and functions of literature should not be sought, in the main, *upstream* of literary experience. If you can get the value without the literary work, why bother with all that reading? And if the values that come after are thereby less easy to grasp as distinct, rational propositions, that's no reason to assume they don't exist. All that one need assume is that literature, with its peculiarly complex and tangled nature, is the only way of obtaining access to them. That assumption is the foundation of any defence of literary studies that is likely to have any chance of success.

Literature as a cognitive affordance

What this amounts to is a set of arguments that focuses on the use and value of literature as an *instrument* of thought, while acknowledging that it may also be (or be read as) a *vehicle* of thought or even of knowledge. Recent work on Montaigne, Descartes, Locke, and Darwin (to mention only a handful) has demonstrated that thinkers use salient metaphor and other procedures normally associated with literature in order to perform thought, not just to exemplify it. If you removed those features, the thought would be different—philosophically as well as imaginatively impoverished. It follows that, a fortiori, the value of works that advertise themselves as fictions or poems is not likely to be best measured in terms of propositional content or a verifiable change in the reader's beliefs. Shakespeare's intelligence is palpably not that of a philosopher; it is communicated through imaginative stagings of human action. The same can be said of Dante, George Eliot, and Henry James. Although one can no doubt elicit interesting and valid truth-values from their works by asking the 'What?' questions that analytic philosophers like to ask, their value lies rather in their function as instruments of thought, that is to say in the 'How?' questions they raise, where process, shift of perspective, angle of vision, and the like are paramount.

The idea that literary works are instruments capable of adjustment to high levels of precision is consonant with the claim (put forward by Lisa Zunshine, among others) that literature affords a cognitive callisthenics. It stretches cognitive processes beyond the requirements of the everyday, much as the manual and cognitive skills of performers and (kinesically) listeners are fine-tuned in demanding musical works. Zunshine is concerned primarily with the complex forms of mind-reading that characterize narrative fiction and drama, especially those where the reader is required to handle several layers of embedded intention. But one could without difficulty expand the repertory to include all the modes of imaginative simulation, with their calculated underspecifications and their complex sub-routines. Without these, and the equally varied modes of immersion they promote, there would be no empathy, no embodied ecology affording 'downstream' ethical or social imaginings. And more fundamentally still, literature of course stretches the cognitive boundaries of language itself, whether one is thinking of its syntax (the poems of Horace or Mallarmé, the prose of Montaigne, Thomas Mann, or Proust), its figurative acrobatics, or its pragmatic functions (irony being a salient example). Western modernism has taken this type of exercise to its virtual limits, but similar processes are apparent in the literatures of other times and cultures. An analysis of procedurals or second-order expressions according to the principles of cognitive pragmatics is capable of demonstrating the finely tuned instrumentality (the 'how-ness') of literary communication in comparison with the approximations of everyday language.

At higher levels of organization, considering literature as an instrument of thought would entail looking at the way in which the afterlives of canonic literary works (Sophocles' Oedipus plays, Homer's epic poems) may be read as micro-mutations or inflections not in respect of ethical or ideological content on the one hand or of literary form on the other but of the cognitive uses that particular downstream cultural contexts make of their shifting interaction. One example I have worked with recently is the scene of a tarantella danced by a young woman with an interested male spectator; there are salient instances in the writings of Goethe, Mme de Staël, and Ibsen (with possible extensions into Henry James, Wedekind, and others). In each case, the position of dancer and spectator is reconfigured in order to deliver a way of *imagining*—rather than analysing or commenting on—a particularly fraught encounter that sets up a reciprocal relation between desire, affect, sensorimotor perceptions, and kinesic effects on the one hand and social and ethical preoccupations on the other. In other words, the scene becomes a cognitive affordance that is adjusted to local cultural contexts and intentions.

A sense of wonder: Eeyore's birthday presents

According to Aristotle (*Metaphysics* 982b), the desire for philosophical knowledge begins with wonder, the emotion that accompanies the sense of not-quite-knowing. Wonder is where cognition begins, and is thus prior to reflective reason. Here is Paul Harris again on the role of fictional and counterfactual imagining in human development:

> To the extent that absorption in fiction is not a short-lived phenomenon of childhood but a capacity that endures a lifetime, it is appropriate to ask

what it is about the cognitive and emotional make-up of human beings that disposes them toward such sustained involvement in other people's lives—including the lives of fictional characters.[14]

Imagination is fundamental to human cognition from early childhood and remains so throughout adult life. Absorption in fictions (not only fictional characters, but also imagined storyworlds and poetic modes of thought) is consequently not just a pastime played on the margins but one of the key strategies humans use in order to think creatively about other humans and about the world in general.

If literature occupies a distinctive position in the spectrum of imaginative alternatives, taking every possible advantage of the cognitive fluidity afforded by human cognition, it follows that literary study properly belongs to the spectrum of academic disciplines that investigate human cognition and its evolution. Like them, it's an institutionalized form of collective metacognition. Unlike them, however, one of the main functions of its object of knowledge is precisely to *promote* collective reflection, or what I've called downstream effects. In that sense, it has a double claim to the status of a cognitive discipline.

It has been a premise of this study that literature is cognitively mixed and not easily reduced to a set of distinct strands. It covers the whole gradient from richly embodied language to 'abstract'[15] reflection, but presents this gradient as continuous rather than hierarchical: embodied language hovers between the pre-reflective (kinesic effects and the like) and the reflective, while the conceptual thought it offers, whether in the form of authorial or narratorial discourse, or of the cerebrations of characters, is always inflected by the imaginative environment of the fiction and saturated in the traces of embodiment that literary language distinctively exploits. Another way of putting this is that literature always operates via the particular: as extended mind, an affordance for thought, it flourishes in local habitats and finds exquisitely fine-tuned modes of responding to human ecologies.

As Flaubert famously put it, 'La bêtise consiste à vouloir conclure' ('Stupidity consists in wanting to reach conclusions'). Literary works are not vague, they are not undecidably open-ended in the postmodern sense, but they resist attempts to pin them down and frame them. They favour 'How?' questions rather than 'What?' questions, and their very uniqueness—each literary work is a hapax—fosters the tightly constrained yet mobile and flexible downstream effects that emerge as afterlives. They constitute, in other words, one of the prime instruments of cultural improvisation, an embodiment of human cognition striving to overreach itself.

Since balloons have provided a recurrent motif for this study, another episode from the first book of Winnie-the-Pooh stories featuring a balloon and its uses will allow a kind of conclusion Flaubert might not have disapproved of. In this episode, Pooh and Piglet plan to take Eeyore a birthday present. Pooh takes a jar of honey, Piglet takes a balloon. On the way, Pooh gets hungry and eats the honey; Piglet falls over and bursts the balloon. They're embarrassed, but they give Eeyore their presents anyway. As they leave, Eeyore is happily occupied in putting the burst balloon into the empty jar and taking it out again.

Winnie-the-Pooh was published in 1926, not so long after Yeats's poem 'The Balloon of the Mind', and this episode could almost be seen as an ironic comment on it. Both scenes enact the fundamental human gesture of using hands to bring two apparently incompatible affordances (balloon and jar, balloon and shed) into relation with one another:

> When Eeyore saw the pot, he became quite excited.
> 'Why!' he said. 'I believe my Balloon will just go into that Pot!'
> 'Oh, no, Eeyore,' said Pooh. 'Balloons are much too big to go into Pots. What you do with a balloon is, you hold the balloon—'
> 'Not mine,' said Eeyore proudly. 'Look, Piglet!' And as Piglet looked sorrowfully round, Eeyore picked the balloon up with his teeth and placed it carefully in the pot; picked it out and put it on the ground; and then picked it up again and put it carefully back.[16]

In the story itself, Eeyore uses his teeth, as any self-respecting four-legged animal should, and one of E. H. Shepard's original illustrations depicts just this. But another shows Eeyore sitting upright, his gaze fixed on what his hooves are doing as they hold the pot. This is an archetypal human gesture: the freeing up of the hands to use and make tools with close visual control is now thought to be one of the key moments in the shift from primate to hominin, pre-dating the rise of language perhaps by millions of years. In the pretend world of Milne's stories, as we saw in Chapter 3, the animals have rudimentary but recognizably human cognitive faculties. Pooh himself is 'a bear of very little brain', and sees things for the most part through a comfortable honey-coloured haze. Eeyore may not have much more brain, but he has enough to make a difference here—he can improvise, imagine alternatives. Of course, his absorbing game with the burst balloon and the empty jar is 'useless', remote from the world of practical needs and functions. But it delivers a powerful and unexpected ethical benefit: Pooh and Piglet are released from their guilt and embarrassment so that they can go back home contented. The game enshrines an oblique but unmistakable act of kindness. Perhaps that downstream consequence is accidental: there is nothing in the story to indicate that Eeyore invents the game to produce any such effect. But the consequence is there nonetheless. Furthermore, Eeyore himself achieves contentment, and not only because he has, against his own expectations, received a double birthday present. For all its deflationary implicatures, the game opens up a new possibility, a tiny but sharply framed window on to undreamt-of uses of the jar and the balloon. In Eeyore's imaginary eyes, one might think, there is the gleam of cognitive excitement that, for Aristotle, was the beginning of knowledge.

Virtual Manifesto for a Cognitive Approach to Literary Studies

A cognitive approach to literary study will be anthropological in essence, recognizing that literature (in the broad sense) is an ancient and quasi-universal feature of human cultures, widely respected and indeed prized by them, but also widely held in suspicion. It will ask the questions 'What is literature doing in human cultures? What is it for? What does it enable humans to do that they couldn't do otherwise?'

A cognitive engagement with literature will focus primarily on the kinds of thinking that are afforded by literature, where 'thinking' means cognitive activity that includes emotion, imagination, kinesic response, and (not least) interaction with other humans and the world at large.

It will require a broad explanatory framework constructed in an interdisciplinary context. It will be alert to suggestive and potentially paradigm-changing new work in neuroscience, evolutionary science, cognitive psychology, developmental psychology, philosophy (both analytic and phenomenological) and linguistics; but it will be cautious in drawing on conjectures that may be controversial or prove short-lived.

A framework so constructed will give priority to the kinds of question that literature itself poses, since those questions might well challenge some of the positions and perspectives put forward by other disciplines. It will thus acknowledge the power of scientific methodologies without renouncing the ambition (some might say the duty) to devise methodologies specific to literature as an object of knowledge.

A cognitive engagement with literature as a collective and collaborative project will aim, ideally, to be comprehensive: it will not be directed merely at certain effects, literary modes, or genres. Human cognitive activity is apparent in everything that literature does and says.

The programme sketched out thus far will in addition entail

1. The tracing of cognitive prehistories as exhibited in literary works and as made explicit in other kinds of discourse (philosophical, rhetorical, etc.);

2. an engagement with the ways in which 'folk' accounts of the cognitive domain (folk psychology, etc.) are reflected but also challenged or disrupted by literary enactments of human cognition;

3. a mode of analysis in which the dichotomy of (conventional) form and (propositional) content is set aside in favour of a focus on the dynamic instrumentality of literary form as an affordance for productive modes of thought and communication, and hence on the continuity between the affordance and what it makes happen;

4. an adherence to the principle that cognition (mind), body, language, and their products, including culture in general and literature in particular, are continuous aspects of 'nature', such that there can be no rupture between (for example) language and world that is not itself a second-degree product of the cultural imagination;

5. a constant awareness of the relation between historico-cultural particulars and their longer-term infrastructures (both ways round);

6. a recognition of the insight that literature does what the human mind (cognition) does best—it specializes in cognitive fluidity, the tangled connectivity and capacity for improvisation that enable it to engage with the world in 'decoupled' mode;

7. a willingness to accept the anthropological focus in cognitive work on individual and collective agency, the viability (as well as the problems) of mutual communication and understanding, the role of language as a cognitive affordance;

8. a thoroughgoing reappraisal of central issues in literary study such as 'representation' (mimesis) in fiction and drama, the construction of viable storyworlds, the processes governing 'immersion' in literary experience, the relation of literary images to everyday language use, the communicative function and value of literature, the

constraints operating on literary interpretation, the processes of cultural transference (tradition, imitation, translation, etc.), and many more;

9. a use of intuitively viable terminology derived from adjacent disciplines in order to make salient aspects of literary works that have either seemed 'self-evident' or been otherwise neglected (mind-reading, extended/distributed cognition, enactive engagement, kinesic response, Bayesian calculus, underspecification/underdeterminacy, ad hoc concepts, strong and weak implicatures, affordance, decoupling, confirmation bias, cognitive dissonance, etc.);

10. a commitment to using this instrumentation in ways that further the mainstream understanding of texts, eschewing technical language and allusions where they are not strictly required, and drawing also on the skills that good readers of literature have always drawn on;

11. a commitment to preserving the special character of literature and literary study while being ready to move out into dialogue with other disciplines and with the public at large;

12. the belief that thinking with literature is a resource which has strong social and ethical implications and which therefore requires from those who promote its cause a willingness to engage in both academic and public debate.

Terence Cave
April 2015

Notes

Preface

1. Readers who are interested in acquiring a more comprehensive overview of the scene in cognitive literary studies should consult Liza Zunshine (ed.), *The Oxford Handbook of Cognitive Literary Studies* (New York: Oxford University Press, 2015).
2. To these can be added many others which, while fully meeting the criteria for a specialist research study, are also accessible to a wider public: I am thinking in particular of Paul Harris's prize-winning *The Work of the Imagination* and his subsequent study *Trusting What You're Told: How Children Learn from Others*.
3. Rebecca Elson, *A Responsibility to Awe* (Manchester: Carcanet Press, 2001), p. 71.

1. Openings

1. The game he is referring to is 'real tennis' (*jeu de paume*), which is something like a cross between modern tennis and squash, but the analogy works equally well if one thinks of it as the modern form of tennis.
2. Michel de Montaigne, *Les Essais*, ed. Jean Céard et al. (Paris: Livre de Poche, 2001), pp. 1694–5 (III.13). I have used the feminine pronoun in the second sentence in accordance with a clever convention adopted by relevance theorists: the imagined speaker is always feminine gender, the imagined interlocutor always masculine (but see Ch. 2 n. 7).
3. Magical events in fiction may seem to transcend physical laws, but they do so in ways that are constrained by the way we think about the world: imagining a fairy, or a spaceship flying at the speed of light, for example, is a perfectly normal use of a skill of human cognition, the capacity to handle counterfactuals, and it draws on what we know about the world we live in.
4. Montaigne, *Les Essais*, p. 1465 (III.8).
5. As will be clear from the examples used here, the inferential process is to a large extent invisible to cognitive inspection: we just do it, most of the time, although of course, when the going gets tough, it moves to the conscious or reflective level.
6. This proposition would of course require exhaustive substantiation, which is not possible here. It would begin, I think, with a study of the minute but insistent uses of procedural and modalizing phrases throughout the *Essais* that insistently tweak the reader's cognitive attention and point it in possible new directions; see Kirsti Sellevold, *'J'ayme ces mots…': expressions linguistiques de doute dans les* Essais *de Montaigne* (Paris: Champion, 2004); also Ch. 5 of the present study, n. 18.

7. Or of philosophy at large which thrives on constraints, rules, self-denial—an ascesis that literature is impatient with. This requires another set of arguments, about the respective domains of literary study and philosophy, which this study cannot undertake.

8. Edward Lear, *The Complete Nonsense of Edward Lear*, ed. Holbrook Jackson (London: Faber and Faber, 1947 and reprints), p. 5. I have adopted here the standard modern practice of breaking the third line of Lear's 'limerick' into two shorter lines.

9. I use the word in an extended sense that includes any imagination that is 'decoupled' from, or strictly impossible in, the real world. This includes the standard sense, namely 'something that might have happened in the real world but did not': historical counterfactuals such as the imagination of what would have happened if Napoleon had won the battle of Waterloo, or if Henry VIII had died before his daughter Elizabeth was conceived, belong to this class.

10. Is 'literary archipelago' a false collocation? Probably not, since there is a bridge via 'domain', 'landscape', etc. I use this metaphor, rather than that of a continuous territory, in order to allow for the plurality of human ecologies or cultures, a plurality that remains, however, *connected* (especially nowadays), with endless crossings, bridges, modes of communication, trading possibilities, etc.

11. John Milton, *Complete Prose Works*, vol. 2, ed. Ernest Sirluck (New Haven: Yale University Press, 1959), p. 492.

12. See <www.stephenmottram.com>.

13. See for example Chris Frith, *Making Up the Mind: How the Brain Creates Our Mental World* (Chichester: Wiley-Blackwell, 2007), pp. 140–1.

14. See Frith, *Making Up the Mind*, pp. 141–4.

15. See Montaigne, *Essais*, pp. 267–71 (I.25; I.26 in some editions).

16. *Essais*, p. 1327 (III.5), after Juvenal, *Satires* VI.196.

2. Cognitive Conversations

1. Among recent examples, one of the best-known is Martha Nussbaum's *Love's Knowledge: Essays on Philosophy and Literature* (New York: Oxford University Press, 1990).

2. There are also a number of new projects which are beginning to make a significant impact: in the United Kingdom, the Balzan project (see Preface) is one of these, and the annual 'Cognitive Futures in the Humanities' conferences which began in 2013 have been extremely well attended, although, again, mainly by people who are already working in these areas.

3. This approach begins with the work on fundamental metaphorical concepts by George Lakoff and Mark Johnson, *Metaphors We Live By* (Chicago and London: Chicago University Press, 2003 (first published 1980)) and has been developed in studies such as Patrick Colm Hogan, *The Mind and*

Its Stories: Narrative Universals and Human Emotion (Cambridge: Cambridge University Press and Paris, Éditions de la Maison des Sciences de l'Homme, 2003). See also Brian Boyd, *On the Origins of Stories: Evolution, Cognition, and Fiction* (Cambridge, Mass., and London: Belknap Press, 2009).

4. Cognitive psychologists and philosophers use a range of different terms for these phenomena: some distinguish between 'personal' and 'subpersonal', others continue to use the always problematic word '(un)conscious'. I have for the most part chosen to speak of 'reflective' and 'pre-reflective' cognition, partly because these terms seemed better suited to the character of literature and literary study, and partly because they raise fewer philosophical problems. As for the prefix 'pre-', it points towards the notion of a gradient, avoiding both the sharply antithetical effect of 'un-' and the hierarchical implications of 'sub-'.

5. Daniel Kahneman's study *Thinking, Fast and Slow* (London: Penguin Books, 2011) explores this opposition brilliantly, but is arguably open to the objection that it tends to over-polarize these modes of cognition. A similar effect arises in studies of the two hemispheres of the brain: see Ian McGilchrist's remarkably comprehensive exploration of this polarity, *The Master and His Emissary: The Divided Brain and the Making of the Western World* (New Haven and London: Yale University Press, 2009), which I shall return to briefly in Ch. 5.

6. Joseph Conrad, *Lord Jim*, ed. Jacques Berthoud (Oxford: Oxford University Press, Oxford World's Classics, 2002), p. 3.

7. A further comment on pronouns (see also Ch. 1 n. 2): I have used here the convention adopted among relevance theorists according to which the feminine pronoun is used for the speaker, the masculine pronoun for the interlocutor. This device doesn't work well when the interlocutor becomes 'the reader': literary specialists talk a lot about readers, and authors, of course, usually have a specific gender of their own. So I have chosen elsewhere in this study to assign gender randomly when that and similar issues arise.

8. This phrase refers to the set of cognitive resources available to the interlocutor at a given moment, considered as a constantly shifting environment or ecology. My own use of the expression in Chapter 1 of this study and elsewhere is probably more elastic, less precise, than relevance theorists would like, but such elasticity is germane to the very notion of an intervention that modifies a person's cognitive environment.

9. See Dan Sperber and Deirdre Wilson, *Relevance: Communication and Cognition* (Oxford: Blackwell, 1995; 1st edn 1986), 'Postface', p. 270. The 'ostensive stimulus' is the utterance as it is brought to the attention of the interlocutor (i.e. the utterance must not only be delivered, it must also be manifestly intended as a communicative act); this ostensive aspect was already pointed out by Paul Grice.

10. Paul Grice, *Studies in the Way of Words* (Cambridge, Mass., and London: Harvard University Press, 1989), pp. 26–7.

11. Most of the time: of course the process slows down and becomes reflective rather than automatic where obstacles, difficulties, or uncertainties emerge.

12. Robyn Carston, *Thoughts and Utterances: The Pragmatics of Explicit Communication* (Oxford: Blackwell, 2002), p. 206.

13. This formulation appears in Carston's article 'Metaphor: ad hoc concepts, literal meaning and mental images', *Proceedings of the Aristotelian Society*, 110 (2010), pp. 295–321 (p. 305 n. 11), where she refers the reader to the 'particular view of the language–thought or word–concept relation' presented in *Thoughts and Utterances*.

14. The landmark study of autism, despite considerable controversy, remains Simon Baron-Cohen's *Mindblindness: An Essay on Autism and Theory of Mind* (Cambridge, Mass.: The MIT Press, 1995). Lisa Zunshine's *Why We Read Fiction: Theory of Mind and the Novel* (Columbus, Oh.: Ohio State University Press, 2006) marked a corresponding watershed in cognitive literary studies. For a recent example of the impact of autism studies on literary studies with specific reference to mind-reading, see Kirsti Sellevold, 'Cognitive deficits in literary fictions: Faulkner's *The Sound and the Fury* and Vesaas' *The Birds*', *Comparative Critical Studies*, 12 (2015), pp. 71–88.

15. Some anticipatory observations of this phenomenon by past thinkers such as David Hume and Adam Smith are cited by Alvin Goldman, *Simulating Minds: The Philosophy, Psychology, and Neuroscience of Mindreading* (New York: Oxford University Press, 2006), pp. 17–18.

16. Adrian Pilkington argues for a broader, more inclusive view in *Poetic Effects: A Relevance Theory Perspective* (Amsterdam: John Benjamins, 2000). The issue is at the centre of the forthcoming volume *Relevance in Literature*, ed. Terence Cave and Deirdre Wilson.

17. See in particular the highly influential work of Antonio Damasio, *Descartes' Error: Emotion, Reason, and the Human Brain* (London: Penguin Books, 2005; first published 1994) and *The Feeling of What Happens: Body and Emotion in the Making of Consciousness* (New York: Harcourt Brace, 1999). Among those who have taken up the challenge of explaining 'consciousness', Daniel Dennett's *Consciousness Explained* (Boston: Little, Brown, 1991) and subsequent contributions have generated a good deal of controversy.

18. Andy Clark, *Supersizing the Mind: Embodiment, Action, and Cognitive Extension* (Oxford: Oxford University Press, 2008), provides a detailed and comprehensive exploration of this range of concepts.

19. The term 'enactive' was brought into prominence by Francisco Varela and his colleagues in the early 1990s; see Francisco Varela, Evan Thompson, and Eleanor Rosch, *The Embodied Mind: Cognitive Science and Human Experience* (Cambridge, Mass.: MIT Press, 1991); also Emily Troscianko, 'Reading Kafka enactively', in Terence Cave, Karin Kukkonen and

Olivia Smith (eds), *Reading Literature Cognitively*, special edition of *Paragraph*, 37 (2014), pp. 15–31.

20. Guillemette Bolens, *Le Style des gestes: Corporéité et kinésie dans le récit littéraire* (Lausanne: Éditions BHMS, 2008; English version: *The Style of Gestures: Embodiment and Cognition in Literary Narrative*, Baltimore: Johns Hopkins University Press, 2012).

21. Bolens's study *The Style of Gestures* belongs in spirit to one of the most fruitful twentieth-century 'schools' of criticism, the Geneva school; among the forerunners of her book is the Genevan critic Jean Starobinski's essay 'L'Échelle des températures: lecture du corps dans *Madame Bovary*', in *Le Temps de la réflexion*, 1, ed. J.-B. Pontalis (Paris: Gallimard, 1980), pp. 145–83, where an excruciating scene from Flaubert's novel is analysed kinaesthetically.

22. The sense of this word is engagingly illustrated by various currently available YouTube videos of metronomes 'entraining'. There remains the question of the relation (if there is any) between mechanical and biological entrainment. Phenomena such as dancing induced by rhythmic drum-beats, synchronized clapping, marching, and crowd behaviour of all kinds, from chanting, singing, and Mexican waves to panic and stampede, bear a family likeness to entrainment, but the mechanisms of motor resonance that are arguably common to all these are not necessarily dependent on the physics of entrainment.

23. My insistent use of the word 'gradient' in this book arises from my sense that antithetical formulations, while they can be a useful heuristic tool, are nearly always inappropriate in the human cognitive ecology. Among other things, it is an antidote against various forms of essentialism, including the so-called 'Cartesian dualism' which no one wants to defend but nearly everyone is accused of. The work of George Lakoff, Eleanor Rosch and others on categories as fuzzy-edged instruments that are more suited than sharply defined concepts to the tangled nature of cognition is relevant here; see in particular George Lakoff, *Women, Fire and Dangerous Things: What Categories Reveal About the Mind* (Chicago and London: Chicago University Press, 1987). I made some preliminary use of that approach in my study *Mignon's Afterlives: Crossing Cultures from Goethe to the Twenty-First Century* (Oxford: Oxford University Press, 2011), pp. 23–6.

24. More specifically: 'The literary mind is not a separate kind of mind. It is our mind. The literary mind is the fundamental mind' (Mark Turner, *The Literary Mind: The Origins of Thought and Language* (Oxford and New York: Oxford University Press, 1996), p. v).

3. The Balloon of the Mind

1. W. B. Yeats, 'The Balloon of the Mind' in *Collected Poems* (London: Macmillan, 1955), p. 175; from *The Wild Swans at Coole* (1919).

2. The verb 'to prime' is used by cognitive psychologists such as Christopher Frith to refer to the way in which an individual's perspective or choice is inflected in advance by perceptual or affective factors, states of belief, etc.

3. See Carston, *Thoughts and Utterances*, pp. 28–32, on 'eternal sentences'. Carston provides a reductio ad absurdum of the idea that a proposition, given enough words, could be exhaustively articulated.

4. See Ch. 1, on the general aims of relevance theory, and Ch. 6 for further clarification and examples. For a basic but thorough guide to relevance theory and its terminology, including the distinction between explicature and implicature, see Billy Clark, *Relevance Theory* (Cambridge: Cambridge University Press, 2013).

5. This is the procedure proposed for biblical reading and interpretation by St Augustine in his *De doctrina christiana*, Book II.

6. The term was coined in 1917 by Viktor Shklovski.

7. It's interesting what a difference it makes when one speaks of the activities performed by hands and those that are afforded by fingers: playing instruments, sewing, making fine-tuned adjustments, skilful erotic touching, and the like. When Montaigne says that poetry has fingers (see Ch. 1), he triggers a kinesic response that is quite different from the one set in motion by Yeats's 'hands'.

8. The importance of the haptic domain, and more generally the question of how cognitive engagements with the environment are enacted via the body, is brilliantly developed by Maurice Merleau-Ponty in his *Phénoménologie de la perception* (first published in 1945), recently translated by Donald Landes as *Phenomenology of Perception* (London and New York: Routledge, 2013). For reasons given in my preface, the phenomenological perspective has for the most part been omitted from this book, although it is evoked at many points in the work of Guillemette Bolens, which remains my primary point of reference here.

9. For a succinct account of motor resonance, see Bolens, *The Style of Gestures*, Introduction.

10. These findings have been in the public domain for some considerable time since they were put forward by a group of Italian neuroscientists, notably Giacomo Rizzolatti and Vittorio Gallese; for the classic statement of the 'mirror neuron' hypothesis, see Vittorio Gallese, Luciano Fadiga, Leonardo Fogassi, and Giacomo Rizolatti, 'Action recognition in the premotor cortex', *Brain*, 119 (1996), pp. 595–609. The hypothesis, and the mirror metaphor, have provoked considerable controversy, but the basic phenomenon of motor resonance has proved relatively robust. It is perhaps helpful to introduce here the related notion of 'canonical neurons', which fire when an object is observed that invites a certain kind of motor action (the sight of a cup of a particular shape and size primes the motor system for the grasping of such an object); this would be relevant to Bolens's opening account of the Chardin painting of a boy

watching a spinning top, and more specifically of the way his right hand and fingers are rendered.

11. Relevance theorists remain on the whole sympathetic to this view, although with important modifications.

12. See Lawrence W. Barsalou, 'Situated simulation in the human conceptual system', *Language and Cognitive Processes*, 18 (2003), pp. 513–62. For a discussion of other aspects of this approach, see Ch. 4.

13. It is not by accident that verbs and adverbs are often the focus of kinesic effects.

14. See Bolens, *Le Style des gestes*, p. 1, citing Ellen Spolsky, 'Elaborated knowledge: reading kinesis in pictures', *Poetics Today*, 17 (1996), pp. 157–80.

15. The definition I develop here emerged from a series of conversations with Guillemette Bolens on the possible implications of Spolsky's phrase.

16. Kinesic intelligence needs also to be mastered by those who invent and design commercials and other advertising materials: these concentrated miniature artefacts show in exemplary manner how important it is to draw on kinesic response in order to alter the cognitive environment of the spectator, reader, or interlocutor.

17. Speaking of his own youth and his lack of aptitude for school work, Yeats uses the same image: 'My thoughts were a great excitement, but when I tried to do anything with them, it was like trying to pack a balloon into a shed in a high wind' (*Autobiographies* (London: Macmillan, 1955), p. 41). I am grateful to Deirdre Wilson for pointing this reference out to me.

18. I am speaking here of short lyric poems, but the same argument applies, *mutatis mutandis*, to longer narrative poems. See also Ch. 4, on affordances. The view I am offering here is not intended to be reductive, or dismissive of the imaginative reach of poetry: on the contrary, my aim is to bring about a shift of perspective that opens up 'imaginative reach' as a powerfully embodied phenomenon.

19. The etymologies of words denoting mind or spirit consistently retain this connection: Latin *animus* and *anima* derive from Greek *anemos* ('wind'); inspire, spirit, etc. refer back to the breath of life; German *atmen* ('to breathe') is cognate with Sanskrit *atman* ('breath, soul, self').

20. In this context, we only need a pragmatic guide to what 'full consciousness' might be: it would be represented by a considered exposition, oral or written or possibly 'mental' (i.e. neither oral nor written), of the text in question.

21. For an accessible survey of recent research on the functioning of memory, see Larry Squire and Eric R. Kandel, *Memory: From Mind to Molecules* (2nd edn; Greenwood Village, Colo.: Roberts & Company, 2009).

22. It has even been claimed that musical expression and communication is the immediate precursor of hominin language; see Stephen Mithen, *The Singing Neanderthals: The Origins of Music, Language, Mind and Body* (Cambridge, Mass.: Harvard University Press, 2005).

23. A. A. Milne, *Winnie-the-Pooh* (London: Egmont, 2004; first published 1926), pp. 1–18 (this reference covers the whole chapter; I have not thought it necessary in this case to provide individual page numbers).

24. I find myself wanting to compare this inaugural passage with one of Montaigne's earliest chapters (*Essais* I.8), where he embarks on the project of imagining his own thought-processes: he puts his head between his hands, as it were, and begins to think about thinking.

25. See Paul Harris, *The Work of the Imagination* (Oxford: Blackwell, 2000), ch. 2. For the broader notion of shared pretence, see n. 29 in this chapter.

26. See Ch. 5 for a more detailed account.

27. Cf. the flying bicycles in the closing episode of Stephen Spielberg's film *ET*. I remember being fascinated as a child by the 'fairy-cycle' of another bear, Rupert Bear of the *Daily Express* strip cartoon, which was capable of flight. I recall that there was in those days a kind of cycle for small children that was called 'fairy-cycle', and that I wanted one because I conflated it with Rupert's imaginary version, somehow believing that it would afford magic flight. In the mid-1940s, this dream was brutally incapable of being realized.

28. The notion of ad hoc concepts and metaphors can be understood in ordinary-language terms, but it has been creatively exploited by relevance theorists, as we shall see in Ch. 6. As for the notion of a resemblance in relevant respects, I have adapted it here from the translation theory of Ernst-August Gutt, which itself draws heavily on relevance theory. See Gutt, *Translation and Relevance: Cognition and Context* (2nd edn; Manchester: St Jerome Publishing, 2000).

29. The notion of shared pretence (together with a required 'stipulation of pretence') was put forward by the philosopher Kendall Walton in his landmark study *Mimesis as Make-Believe: On the Foundations of the Representational Arts* (Cambridge, Mass., and London: Harvard University Press, 1990); it was picked up and productively extended by Jean-Marie Schaeffer in *Pourquoi la fiction?* (Paris: Seuil, 1999; English version *Why Fiction?*, trans. Dorrit Cohn, University of Nebraska Press, 2010).

30. But note that there is another gradient effect here: one can of course mind-read non-fictional animals, too. Bees have intentions, albeit unreflective ones, and the way they are represented in this story is entirely naturalistic.

4. Literary Affordances

1. Jonathan Franzen, *The Corrections* (London: Fourth Estate, 2002), pp. 63–4.

2. The repetition of the word 'blind' ('blind backwards free fall', 'blind pivot') draws attention to Alfred's loss of this embodied memory: it's as if he can't see any more.

3. James J. Gibson, 'The Theory of Affordances', in *The Ecological Approach to Visual Perception* (Hillsdale, NJ: Lawrence Erlbaum Associates, 1986), pp. 127–43.
4. See for example Nathan Crilly, 'The design stance in user-system interaction', *Design Issues*, 27 (2011), pp. 16–29.
5. *The Ecological Approach*, p. 127.
6. See the Edward Lear limerick quoted in Ch. 1.
7. For a brilliantly prescient description of this process, and of what one might call the 'affordance explosion' of modern times, see Paul Valéry, 'Le Bilan de l'intelligence', in *Œuvres*, ed. Jean Hytier, vol. 1 ([Paris]: Gallimard, Bibliothèque de la Pléiade, [1957]), pp. 1058–83 (p. 1067). This essay, which dates from 1935, originated as a lecture given under different titles in the early 1930s; I have chosen the most relevant version.
8. *The Ecological Approach*, pp. 134–5. The French neuroscientist Alain Berthoz translates 'affordances' (for which there is no direct equivalent in French) as 'faisabilités' ('feasibilities'), while at the same time characterizing these as 'invariants'; see Alain Berthoz, *La Simplexité* (Paris: Odile Jacob, 2009), p. 190. The notion of 'simplexity', as a way of conceiving the pragmatic compromises between the general and the particular that shape the functioning of human cognition, is in fact germane to Gibson's coinage. See also the work of Eleanor Rosch, George Lakoff, and others on categories: as Emily Troscianko helpfully summarizes it, 'the most cognitively basic level [within the general-to-specific hierarchy] is in the *middle* of the hierarchy, that is, "bed", not "furniture" or "futon"'; see Emily Troscianko, 'Reading Kafka enactively', in *Reading Literature Cognitively*, special edition of *Paragraph*, 37 (2014), p. 21. Troscianko provides detailed references to Rosch and Lakoff, and goes on to connect this cognitive principle with the linguistic underspecification (underdeterminacy) which is central to relevance theory accounts of language.
9. For a detailed account of this notion, see Clark, *Supersizing the Mind*. For an interesting alternative view of the way in which agency may be assigned to objects, see Alfred Gell, *Art and Agency: An Anthropological Theory* (Oxford: Clarendon Press, 1998).
10. These problems are of course a local variant of those that traverse the whole conceptual domain of 'embodied cognition', which is haunted by the phantom of 'Cartesian dualism'. As I suggest elsewhere, this fear seems in most cases to be purely imaginary: anyone working on cognition has to account for the range of intractably complex phenomena which are commonly ascribed to 'the mind', whether one uses that word or 'cognition', or some other term.
11. Gibson, *The Ecological Approach*, p. 137, refers briefly to this exponential outgrowth of human affordances. See Clark, *Supersizing the Mind*, pp. 58–60; Clark uses the suggestive expression 'linguaform resources' (p. 58) to characterize this view of language. Referring to this passage while drawing heavily on the sceptical perspective of Stanley Cavell, Ellen

Spolsky expresses an important reservation: 'Literature and art', she says, 'are study houses of the creative heights, *of the failures and of the creative evasion of failure*' that characterize cognition ('An embodied view of misunderstanding in *Macbeth*', *Poetics Today*, 32 (2011), pp. 489–520 (p. 515); my italics). In order to avoid falling into a naive optimism about the human capacity for imaginative invention, I have woven a parallel thread of caution into my own account of such matters, especially in the later part of this book.

12. In addition to the work by Barsalou mentioned in Ch. 3, see Arthur M. Glenberg and Michael P. Kaschak, 'Grounding language in action', *Psychonomic Bulletin and Review*, 9 (2002), pp. 558–65. For a dissenting view, see Bradford Z. Mahon and Alfonso Caramazza, 'A critical look at the embodied cognition hypothesis and a new proposal for grounding conceptual content', *Journal of Physiology*, 102 (2008), pp. 59–70; note, however, that Mahon and Caramazza accept many of the findings associated with Barsalou and others and propose, in effect, a modified version of the embodiment thesis that allows more space for cognitive abstraction.

13. The phrase was famously coined by Fredric Jameson in his book *The Prison-House of Language* (1972), but it chimes also with Foucault's conception of a controlling 'discursive order', with its connotations of surveillance and punishment.

14. The articulation of the sonnet and the possibilities it offers have of course been analysed many times, both in general and via particular cases: the point here is to redescribe that known form in a less familiar perspective.

15. For a lively account of the Shakespearian sonnet in a comparable perspective, see Brian Boyd, *Why Lyrics Last: Evolution, Cognition, and Shakespeare's Sonnets* (Cambridge, Mass.: Harvard University Press, 2012).

16. It is perhaps prudent to point out here that the word 'evolution' as used here and elsewhere in this book is meant to be value-neutral.

17. The essay is still seen as a peculiarly English genre; in French, the word *essai* is rarely used in that sense.

18. See n. 8.

19. See the discussion of this opera in Jessica Waldoff, *Recognition in Mozart's Operas* (New York: Oxford University Press, 2006), ch. 6; cf. also Richard Strauss's cross-generic counterpoint in *Ariadne auf Naxos*.

20. The word 'afford' is etymologically related to the verb and adverb 'further'.

5. Literary Imaginations

1. The French word *âme* can have either meaning.

2. Alfred de Vigny, *Œuvres complètes*, ed. F. Baldensperger, vol. 1 ([Paris]: Gallimard, Bibliothèque de la Pléiade, [1955]), p. 816.

3. See for example the satirical examples of interdisciplinary prejudice and misunderstanding that form a quasi-narrative thread in Chris Frith's *Making Up the Mind*.

4. Marina Warner, *Stranger Magic: Charmed States and the* Arabian Nights (London: Chatto & Windus, 2011).

5. John Milton, *Poetical Works*, ed. Douglas Bush (London: Oxford University Press, 1966), p. 107.

6. Pierre de Ronsard, *Œuvres complètes*, ed. Jean Céard, Daniel Ménager, and Michel Simonin ([Paris]: Gallimard, Bibliothèque de la Pléiade, 1994), vol. 2, p. 601.

7. Letter to Karl Ludwig von Knebel, 17 November 1784, in Johann Wolfgang Goethe, *Sämtliche Werke*, vol. 29 (II.2), ed. Hartmut Reinhardt (Frankfurt am Main: Deutscher Klassiker Verlag, 1997), p. 554. I am grateful to Jim Reed for suggesting this example.

8. Henry James, *The American* (New York: Charles Scribner's Sons, 1922), pp. xvii–xviii; James is talking here at length about romance and the romantic in relation to the plot of his novel.

9. In Teutonic languages, the Latinate English word 'imagination' has two equivalents: *Vorstellung* (Ger.), *forestilling* (Norw.), etc., and *Einbildung, innbildning*, etc.: the first is neutral and has roughly the sense of 'representation', the second often has negative connotations of the kind associated with the English word 'fantasy'.

10. Harris, *The Work of the Imagination*, p. 3.

11. Harris, *The Work of the Imagination*, pp. 6, 7. The revival of interest in the imagination among psychologists and philosophers is richly illustrated by the contributions to *Imaginative Minds*, ed. Ilona Roth (Oxford and New York: Oxford University Press for the British Academy, 2007).

12. See Alison Gopnik, *The Philosophical Baby: What Children's Minds Tell Us About Truth, Love & the Meaning of Life* (London: The Bodley Head, 2009).

13. The fundamental importance of improvisation as a distinctive feature of human evolution is proposed by Leda Cosmides and John Tooby in their paper 'Consider the source: the evolution of adaptations for decoupling and metarepresentation', in Dan Sperber (ed.), *Metarepresentations: A Multidisciplinary Perspective* (Oxford: Oxford University Press, 2000), pp. 53–111.

14. See the paper by Leda Cosmides and John Tooby cited in n. 13. It is perhaps necessary to emphasize here that my references to the work of Cosmides and Tooby do not entail adherence to all their hypotheses about human evolution. For example, I regard their advocacy of the 'massive modularization' argument, according to which the human brain is constructed like a Swiss army knife, with a large number of domain-specific phylogenetically acquired gadgets, as too extreme and insufficiently nuanced, allowing little room for cultural plasticity and hence cultural evolution. But we need to recall again here that all these debates are still in their infancy; it will be a long time before they are definitively resolved, if indeed they ever are.

15. Deirdre Wilson's distinction between 'external' and 'internal' relevance offers one productive tool for thinking about the relation of these different

reading levels; see her 'Relevance and the interpretation of literary texts', *UCL Working Papers in Linguistics*, 23 (2011), pp. 69–80.

16. See Schaeffer, *Pourquoi la fiction?* (Paris: Seuil, 1999; English version *Why Fiction?*, trans. Dorrit Cohn, Lincoln, Nebr.: University of Nebraska Press, 2010), especially pp. 159–62. Schaeffer is aware of the work of Kendall Walton and others who speak of the 'stipulation of pretence' as a marker of entry into a given fictional or imagined domain.

17. This association between fiction and pretence is fundamental to Schaeffer's argument. He derives it from a scenario of phylogenetic evolution which includes the deceptive markings on the bodies of insects, birds, and animals (the eyes on a peacock butterfly's wings, for example). See *Pourquoi la fiction?*, pp. 147–8.

18. 'Modalizing expressions' are words and expressions like 'perhaps', 'arguably', 'it seems that', which allow the speaker to avoid taking full responsibility for the proposition she is advancing. 'Procedurals' are the broader set of words and expressions that give guidance to the interlocutor as to how to understand the proposition: 'Alice is right'; 'Alice is *always* right'; 'Alice is *almost always* right'.

19. I use the phrase 'literary criticism' here in its broadest sense, encompassing all the modes of reflection and discussion which have always accompanied the personal and social uses of literature.

20. A caveat here, to avoid a possible misunderstanding: epistemic vigilance is not equivalent (or reducible) to 'reason'.

21. One of the most famous examples of such a diagram is Robert Fludd's early seventeenth-century representation of the human mind as a microcosm. Reproductions of this can easily be found on the internet, but see especially the website of the project 'Evolution and the Social Mind', based at the University of California, Santa Barbara (<http://www.anth.ucsb.edu/projects/esm/>).

22. As indicated in Ch. 3, 'Thinking with Pooh' (reference in note 21), Squire and Kandel's study *Memory* provides a comprehensive and reliable account of current research on this topic. Squire and Kandel speak in detail about the several different kinds of memory that characterize human cognition, including short-term or working memory, as well as 'episodic' and 'procedural' memory, although they prefer a somewhat different terminology ('declarative' for 'episodic', for example). On the relation between memory and imagination, see the more specialized paper by Daniel L. Schacter (with Donna Rose Addis and Alana T. Wong), 'Remembering the past and imagining the future: common and distinct neural substrates during event construction and elaboration', *Neuropsychologia*, 45 (2007), pp. 1363–77.

23. Iain McGilchrist, *The Master and His Emissary: The Divided Brain and the Making of the Western World* (New Haven and London: Yale University Press, 2009).

24. See George Ainslie, *Picoeconomics: The Strategic Interaction of Successive Motivational States within the Person* (Cambridge: Cambridge University Press, 1997).

25. See Peter Hacker, *The Intellectual Powers: A Study of Human Nature* (Oxford: Wiley-Blackwell, 2013), ch. 11.

26. It is only present in the second of the Germanic equivalents mentioned in n. 9. Other languages segment this conceptual field in quite different ways; see for example Geert Jan van Gelder and Marlé Hammond (eds), *Takhyīl: The Imaginary in Classical Arabic Poetics* (n.p.: Gibb Memorial Trust, 2008).

27. On conceptions of language as grounded in sensorimotor awareness, see Ch. 3.

28. A sensible account of what is meant by 'representation' in contexts of this kind, and in relation to higher-order 'metarepresentations', is provided by Daniel Dennett, 'Making tools for thinking', in Dan Sperber (ed.), *Metarepresentations: A Multidisciplinary Perspective* (New York: Oxford University Press, 2000), pp. 17–29.

29. I must here acknowledge my debt to Jennifer Gosetti-Ferenci, with whom I was fortunate enough to be able to discuss this and other issues arising from the study of the imagination while she was an Associate Researcher in the Balzan project 'Literature as an Object of Knowledge'. Dr Gosetti-Ferenci is currently preparing an important study of the imagination and its literary uses in relation to phenomenological philosophy.

30. Aristotle, *Rhetoric* I.xi.

31. Frith, *Making up the Mind*, p. 137. Frith is speaking here of perceptual reversals of the Necker cube diagram, not of the creative imaginations of literature, but if inflexibility is proper to imaginary representations, it must also be apparent in so-called 'creative' instances. We can't, for example, imagine what isn't there in a 'realist' description of a fictional room unless the writer sets the representation up in that way, inviting us to notice an absence. This is an area that needs to be explored further.

32. Temple Grandin, *Thinking in Pictures and Other Reports from My Life with Autism* (London: Bloomsbury, 2006; first published 2006).

33. Among the many recent studies on immersion, see Jennifer Anna Gosetti-Ferenci, 'The mimetic dimension: literature between neuroscience and phenomenology', *British Journal of Aesthetics*, 54 (October 2014), pp. 425–48. For a more general study of mental imagery in a narrative perspective, see Anežka Kuzmičová, *Mental Imagery in the Experience of Literary Narrative: Views from Embodied Cognition* (Stockholm: Stockholm University, 2013).

34. See also Kendall L. Walton, *Mimesis as Make-Believe: On the Foundations of the Representational Arts* (Cambridge, Mass., and London: Harvard University Press, 1990). Walton's seminal analysis of 'make-believe' and its value in the formation of an imaginative capacity out of which grows, among

other things, the feeling for literature and the arts has made a major impact on work by psychologists and philosophers across this whole field. See also Gregory Currie and Ian Ravenscroft, *Recreative Minds: Imagination in Philosophy and Psychology* (Oxford: Clarendon Press, 2002), and Gregory Currie, *Arts and Minds* (Oxford: Oxford University Press, 2004).

35. Harris, *The Work of the Imagination*, pp. 9–10. I have slightly modified the details of the story as he tells it.

36. Cf. the many variants on the game of Monopoly that are now available.

37. See also the work of the 'cognitive puppeteer' Stephen Mottram, referred to in Ch. 1.

38. See Elaine Scarry, *Dreaming by the Book* (New York: Farrar, Strauss & Giroux, 1999), pp. 11–13.

6. Cognitive Figures

1. Guillemette Bolens, 'Les styles kinésiques. De Quintilien à Proust en passant par Tati', in Laurent Jenny (ed.), *Le Style en acte. Vers une pragmatique du style* (Geneva: Métis Presses, 2011), pp. 59–85 (p. 77).

2. But see Terence Cave and Deirdre Wilson (eds), *The Long-Legged Fly: Relevance in Literature*, in progress. Adrian Pilkington's *Poetic Effects* was a pioneering study in this field; Ian MacKenzie's *Paradigms of Reading: Relevance Theory and Deconstruction* (London: Palgrave Macmillan, 2002) argues in favour of replacing the deconstructionist view of language and literary interpretation with the relevance theory view. Among other cognitive approaches to poetry and poetics, see for example Reuven Tsur, *Towards a Theory of Cognitive Poetics* (Brighton: Sussex Academic Press, 1992).

3. Dan Sperber and Deirdre Wilson, 'A deflationary account of metaphors', in Ray Gibbs (ed.), *The Cambridge Handbook of Metaphor and Thought* (New York: Cambridge University Press, 2008), pp. 84–105; Deirdre Wilson and Robyn Carston, 'Metaphor, relevance and the "emergent property" issue', *Mind & Language*, 21 (2006), pp. 404–33; and Robyn Carston, 'Metaphor: ad hoc concepts, literal meaning and mental images', *Proceedings of the Aristotelian Society*, 110 (2010), pp. 297–323.

4. Charles Baudelaire, *Œuvres complètes*, ed. Y.-G. Le Dantec and Claude Pichois ([Paris]: Gallimard, Bibliothèque de la Pléiade, 1961), p. 71 (*Les Fleurs du mal*, 'Spleen').

5. See the section 'Poetic effects', in Sperber and Wilson, 'A deflationary account of metaphors'.

6. Psychologically, A would almost certainly not experience the process as a two-stage logical exercise. Such routines are so practised, so embedded in the cognitive faculties of adult humans, that they become automatic or pre-reflective: reflective awareness of the process only arises when problems are encountered. What is at issue here, then, is a form of procedural memory (see Ch. 5 n. 22).

7. It's perhaps necessary to say yet again here that phrases like 'inferential work' are not meant to refer to a clunky reflective procedure. They presuppose that much cognitive processing, even where it is automatic ('unconscious'), can be assumed to have an inference-like structure; the reflective variant is merely the topmost branch of this structure.

8. See Sperber and Wilson, 'A deflationary account', pp. 101–3. With Deirdre Wilson's assent, I have paraphrased and simplified their argument here in order to avoid terminological overload.

9. The original Japanese of Bashō was composed in 1680. I have taken this translation from Joan Giroux, *The Haiku Form* (North Clarendon, Vt: Tuttle Publishing, 1974). There are many competing English versions of this text.

10. On procedurals, see Ch. 5 n. 18.

11. These effects are also encouraged by the punctuation (specifically the dash at the end of line 2). Crow and dusk are placed in apposition, such that the crow just *is* the dusk (hence the melancholy, solitude, etc.). This would be another reason why it's odd to call the haiku purely 'literal'. (I am grateful to Tim Chesters for this comment.)

12. This term was originally proposed by Lawrence Barsalou and subsequently adopted by relevance theorists.

13. Relevance theorists adopt the convention of using capitals to designate a concept; when an asterisk is added, it indicates that it is an ad hoc concept in the sense defined here.

14. See Wilson and Carston, 'Metaphor, relevance and the "emergent property" issue'.

15. For relevance theory, ad hoc formations are fundamental to the pragmatics of language use; they occur every time the speaker improvises in her choice of words, makes things happen on the wing as opposed to using a stable lexicon.

16. Donald Davidson, 'A nice derangement of epitaphs', in Ernest Lepore (ed.), *Truth and Interpretation: Perspectives on the Philosophy of Donald Davidson* (Oxford: Blackwell, 1986), pp. 433–46. It should be borne in mind that Davidson was not a relevance theorist, and that any application of his notion of a 'passing theory' to the issues discussed by Carston and her colleagues inevitably modifies the sense of the expression.

17. Paul Verlaine, 'Clair de lune' (first published 1867), in *Œuvres poétiques*, ed. Jacques Robichez (Paris: Garnier, 1969), p. 83.

18. The implicatures of the French word 'choisi' in this context are complex. Other possible renderings would be 'elective', as in Goethe's notion of 'elective affinities', 'exquisite', in an etymological sense which has now effectively been erased, or 'select'. I am grateful to Guillemette Bolens for her comments on this word.

19. I have used square brackets here because it seems to me that the rich implicatures of 'chosen' are operative at the level of both the metaphor's literal meaning and the proposition itself (the addressee is 'chosen' as a

beloved by the speaker). In other words, although the metaphor and its emergent properties are arguably limited to the noun 'landscape', rather than to the noun phrase, one could also say that the adjective acts as a bridge between the two levels, is instrumental in creating the desired emergent properties.

20. See Carston's 'Metaphor: ad hoc concepts', pp. 307–12. This approach is further developed in Robyn Carston and Catherine Wearing, 'Metaphor, hyperbole and simile: a pragmatic approach', *Language and Cognition*, 3 (2011), pp. 283–312.

21. Carl Sandburg, 'Fog', in *Chicago Poems* (New York: Henry Holt, 1916), p. 71.

22. A more detailed analysis of this poem would certainly include an account of the kinesic effects that arise not only from the particular kinds of movement that are common to fogs and cats, the way they come and sit and go, but also from the affordances of line division: this is a poem full of soft spaces and pauses.

23. John Ashbery, 'A Call for Papers', in *Hotel Lautréamont* (Manchester: Carcanet, 1992), pp. 69–70.

24. Donald Davidson, 'What metaphors mean', in Donald Davidson, *Inquiries into Truth and Interpretation* (Oxford: Clarendon Press, 1984; first published 1978), pp. 245–64.

25. Paul Éluard, 'La terre est bleue' (first published 1929), in *Capitale de la douleur; L'Amour la poésie* (Paris: Gallimard, 1966), p. 153.

26. An analogous argument is made with regard to the use of procedurals in La Rochefoucauld's maxims in Kirsti Sellevold, 'Reading short forms cognitively: mindreading and procedural expressions in La Rochefoucauld and La Bruyère', in Cave, Kukkonen, and Smith (eds), *Reading Literature Cognitively*, pp. 104–6.

27. 'Metaphor: ad hoc concepts', pp. 305, 306, 317.

28. See Chs. 3 and 4. Cf. also Shaun Gallagher's phenomenological study of gesture in *How the Body Shapes the Mind* (Oxford: Clarendon Press, 2005), ch. 5, although Gallagher has little to say about verbal language.

29. See also Markus Tendahl and Raymond W. Gibbs Jr, 'Complementary perspectives on metaphor: cognitive linguistics and relevance theory', *Journal of Pragmatics*, 40 (2008), pp. 1823–64, and Deirdre Wilson's reply, 'Parallels and differences in the treatment of metaphor in relevance theory and cognitive linguistics', *Studia Linguistica Universitatis Iagellonicae Cracoviensis*, 128 (2011), pp. 195–213; however, it should be noted that this exchange refers to the cognitive linguistics of Lakoff, Fauconnier, and others, which has a more formalistic character.

30. It might be argued that the response is inferential in a weak sense, namely 'B is remembered as usually following A; therefore when A is experienced, the system responds with action appropriate for B.' A dog that smells a rat will run in the direction of the smell. But we would not normally say that the dog infers from the smell the presence of a rat. The

Bayesian calculus (see Ch. 8 n. 20) is potentially relevant here as an alternative for the inferential calculus.

31. 'Relevance and the interpretation of literary works', p. 78 (see also Sperber and Wilson, *Relevance*, p. 55).

32. The word 'qualia' is used by some to denote radically personal (subjective) experience: what it feels like to find something you thought you'd lost, to smell lilacs in the spring, to drink a glass of cool water when you're hot and thirsty, or, more adventurously, to be a bat or a cat. See Thomas Nagel's famous paper 'What is it like to be a bat?', *Philosophical Review*, 83/4 (1974), pp. 435–50; also Peter Hacker's response, 'Is there anything it is like to be a bat?', *Philosophy*, 77 (2002), pp. 157–74. For a discussion of the concept in a literary context, see Pilkington, *Poetic Effects*, ch. 7.

33. I am referring here, of course, to J. L. Austin's foundational distinction between locutionary, illocutionary, and perlocutionary acts. Students of literature may well feel inclined to baulk at Austin's rigid lines of demarcation, especially as he was also famous for regarding literary examples, whether derived from poetry or from narrative fiction, as useless for philosophical purposes.

34. Emily Dickinson, 'My Life had stood', in *The Complete Poems*, ed. Thomas H. Johnson (London: Faber and Faber, 1982; first published 1863), pp. 369–70. This example is proposed and skilfully analysed by Robyn Carston in 'Metaphor: ad hoc concepts', p. 311.

35. See Sperber and Wilson, *Relevance*, pp. 38–46 (for a definition of 'cognitive environment') and 58–60 (on modifying the interlocutor's cognitive environment).

36. See Colin McGinn, *Mindsight: Image, Dream, Meaning* (Cambridge, Mass.: Harvard University Press, 2004), to which Carston refers. McGinn's view of 'mental imagery' is useful, but in my view too exclusively focused on the visual rather than on other proprioceptive and kinesic processes.

37. Gustave Flaubert, *Madame Bovary*, ed. C. Gothot-Mersch (Paris: Garnier, 1971), p. 196 (II.12).

7. Cognitive Mimesis

1. For two recent analyses of this scene, see Raphael Lyne, 'Shakespeare, perception and theory of mind', in Cave, Kukkonen, and Smith (eds), *Reading Literature Cognitively*, pp. 82–4, and Philip Davis, *Reading and the Reader* (Oxford: Oxford University Press, 2013), pp. 112–18. Raphael Lyne and I participated in a discussion of the text which he initiated in the framework of the Balzan project; I am indebted to his unpublished as well as his published remarks. Philip Davis's reading, which focuses on how Shakespeare 'thinks' in this scene, is also one that I find persuasive, and his project as a whole is in fact germane to my own.

2. William Shakespeare, *King Lear*, ed. R. A. Foakes (Walton-on-Thames: Thomas Nelson, 1997; The Arden Shakespeare), pp. 326–8.

3. More precisely, modern audiences know it perfectly well. The conventions of Shakespeare's day, which relied on what the characters say rather than on the physical properties (in both senses) of the stage, might have led his early audiences to wonder at first whether they were to suppose that Edgar and Gloucester were 'really' climbing a hill.

4. I hope it is clear that this phrase is intended in a figurative sense, the sense it has in folk descriptions of such feelings.

5. One is reminded, for example, of Pascal's reflection on the imagination, where the spectacle of a philosopher on a plank above a precipice is used to dramatize both the power and the potential dangers of imaginative immersion; see Blaise Pascal, *Les Pensées*, ed. Philippe Sellier ([Paris]: Mercure de France, 1976), fragment 78. In a different perspective, Alfred Hitchcock's invention in his film *Vertigo* of the now-standard 'vertigo-shot' (simultaneous rapid-zoom and backward tracking) constitutes a nice example of a kinesic story-telling affordance.

6. The colleagues of Dan Sperber have recently proposed the notion of 'emotional vigilance', according to which 'unintentional' responses such as blushing may be motivated in evolutionary terms by the needs of the group; this would allow such signals to be included in a full account of communication, whereas relevance theory previously regarded them as excluded. See Guillaume Dezecache, Hugo Mercier, and Thomas C. Scott-Phillips, 'An evolutionary approach to emotional communication', *Journal of Pragmatics*, 59 (2013), pp. 221–33.

7. Readers of fiction also respond to bodies, of course, where those bodies are appropriately described by the author; this is the primary thesis of Bolens's *Le Style des gestes*, where it is illustrated with a wide range of wonderfully well-chosen examples.

8. Robin Dunbar, 'Why are good writers so rare? An evolutionary perspective on literature', *Journal of Cultural and Evolutionary Psychology*, 3 (2005), pp. 17–18.

9. Lisa Zunshine, 'Theory of mind and experimental representations of fictional consciousness', in Lisa Zunshine (ed.), *Introduction to Cognitive Cultural Studies* (Baltimore: Johns Hopkins University Press, 2010), p. 208 (205–9 for the analysis of this passage as a whole).

10. This is perhaps a suitable moment to mention an important precursor of the 'theory of mind' approach to fiction. Dorrit Cohn's *Transparent Minds: Narrative Modes for Presenting Consciousness in Fiction* (Princeton: Princeton University Press, 1978), which cuts across the grain of the literary theory flourishing at that time, provides a fine-tuned account of fictional minds. More recently, Alan Palmer's studies *Fictional Minds* (Lincoln, Nebr., and London: Nebraska University Press, 2004) and *Social Minds in the Novel* (Columbus, Oh.: Ohio State University Press, 2010) explore the same terrain but from a perspective inflected by recent cognitive psychology.

11. On this concept, see Ch. 5. That Gloucester is not naive is shown by the fact that he expresses suspicions about Edgar's reference to the steep slope and his changing mode of speech.

12. Mme de Lafayette, *The Princesse de Clèves*, trans. Terence Cave (Oxford: Oxford University Press, 1992), pp. 23–4. The reader should consult the *original for a view of the scene as a whole.

13. There are other details here that help to direct the attention of the reader along the axis of the Princess's perception of the scene, above all other *sounds* (the King calling out to her, the 'murmure de louanges' that surrounds the dancing couple).

14. It is important, however, not to turn such observations into fixed criteria of literary value. Readers expect, and pay attention to, kinds of effect in ways that depend to a significant extent on cultural habits. Besides, the aggregation of descriptive detail that one finds in a Balzac or a Dickens is often saturated with kinesic prompts, lexical items that mime the actual engagement of bodies with the world. A whole new phase of work in a cognitive perspective on the mimetic writing of so-called 'realist' writers would be required in order to move this question forward. For a detailed study of the mimetic modes of a 'modernist' writer in a cognitive perspective, see Emily Troscianko, *Kafka's Cognitive Realism* (London: Routledge, 2014).

15. For a more detailed account of the set of questions sketched here, see *The Princesse de Clèves*, Introduction, pp. xv–xvi, xviii–xx.

16. Sellevold, 'Reading short forms cognitively', pp. 106–7.

8. The Posture of Reading

1. Joseph Conrad, *Lord Jim*, pp. 24–5.

2. It's of course possible to infer a good deal about the sort of people they are likely to be: male, white, European, etc.—the sort of people referred to as 'us' in the recurrent phrase '(he was) one of us'. I shall return to these issues later.

3. The word 'kairos' means something like 'opportune moment', a moment when something significant happens, or is expected to happen, as in these famous lines from Brutus' speech in Shakespeare's *Julius Caesar*. 'There is a tide in the affairs of men | Which, taken at the flood, leads on to fortune; | Omitted, all the voyage of their life | Is bound in shallows and in miseries' (*Julius Caesar* IV.3). Jim's leap is itself such a moment, and Marlow's audience know that Marlow will deliver for them an equivalent narrative kairos. See also Frank Kermode, *The Sense of an Ending: Studies in the Theory of Fiction* (Oxford: Oxford University Press, 1967).

4. On modalizing expressions, see Ch. 1 n. 6, and Ch. 5 n. 18. The modalizing sense of the word is clarified by the sentence that precedes the quoted passage: 'And later on, many times, in distant parts of the world, Marlow showed himself willing to remember Jim, to remember him at

length, in detail and audibly.' Jakob Lothe offers a close reading of this sentence in *Conrad's Narrative Method* (Oxford: Oxford University Press, 1991), pp. 145–8.

5. The sentence quoted in n. 4 makes salient the iterative operation of memory, and thus 'primes' the implicatures of the concluding segment of my opening quotation.

6. I refer here, of course, to Waugh's satirical novel *Decline and Fall* and its allusion to Gibbon.

7. For an account of Ginzburg's argument, see my *Recognitions: A Study in Poetics* (Oxford: Clarendon Press, 1988), pp. 250–2.

8. The convergence of metaphor and plot was anticipated long ago by Maud Bodkin, Northrop Frye, and their followers. Patricia Parker's seminal paper 'The metaphorical plot', in David S. Miall (ed.), *Metaphor: Problems and Perspectives* (Brighton: Harvester, 1982), pp. 133–57, is one instance; similarly, Paul Ricœur's magisterial work on narrative, *Temps et récit*, 3 vols (Paris: Seuil, 1983–5), is consonant with, and complementary to, his account of metaphor in *La Métaphore vive* (Paris: Seuil, 1975).

9. Patrick Colm Hogan, *The Mind and its Stories: Narrative Universals and Human Emotion* (Cambridge: Cambridge University Press, 2003).

10. See David Herman, *Story Logic: Problems and Possibilities of Narrative*, Frontiers of Narrative (Lincoln, Nebr.: University of Nebraska Press, n.d.); also his useful online account of cognitive narratology (accompanied by a rich bibliography), 'Cognitive narratology', in Peter Hühn et al. (eds), *The Living Handbook of Narratology* (Hamburg: Hamburg University Press), URL = <hup.sub.uni-hamburg.de/lhn/index.php ?title=Cognitive Narratology &oldid=2058> (view date: 19 Jan. 2015).

11. The sailor's yarn has its own recurrent sub-stories: the storm at sea, the dead calm which is its polar opposite, landfall in strange places, and alien encounters of various kinds.

12. Jakob Lothe, in an important essay on *Lord Jim*, shows that Conrad's narrative method draws on a wide range of generic templates (the sketch, the tale, the episode, the legend, the letter, the romance, the parable, the lyric, and the tragic). This complex web of narrative affordances, as I would call them, could be regarded as the support for the higher-order conceptual overlappings, that which makes them possible. See Jakob Lothe, 'Conrad's *Lord Jim*: narrative and genre', in Jakob Lothe, Jeremy Hawthorn, and James Phelan (eds), *Joseph Conrad: Voice, Sequence, History, Genre* (Columbus, Oh.: Ohio State University Press, 2008), pp. 236–55.

13. Such *incises* often express the degree of the speaker's commitment to, or responsibility for, the proposition in question: '..., as I see it, ...'; '..., according to many psychologists, ...'; '..., one might claim, ...'. While such phrases may appear anywhere in the sentence, or be reduced to a single word such as 'arguably' or even 'perhaps', the *incise*, by interrupting the flow of the proposition, makes the second-order reflection, one might

say, especially salient. (There are of course other kinds of *incise* which don't have a second-order or reflective function.)

14. See *Lord Jim*, p. 24.

15. Gregory Currie's analysis of 'character-focused narration' and other aspects of narrative voice in *Narratives and Narrators: A Philosophy of Stories* (Oxford: Oxford University Press, 2011), chs 7–8, provides a cogent account of such phenomena, framed in what is in essence a cognitivist perspective.

16. I use scare quotes for 'subjective' because the last thing I want to do here is to suggest an opposition (ontological or otherwise) between 'subjective' and 'objective'. The whole point about mind-reading is that a given individual's feelings about the world are not radically incommunicable or unguessable, even though they may often be ultimately elusive. Conrad's 'heart of darkness' is an imaginative representation of that which goes beyond understanding, but it is also a way of provoking reflection on that which does not, and on the prejudices that result in a premature foreclosure of understanding.

17. An initial version of the theory of cognitive dissonance was proposed by Leon Festinger as early as 1956.

18. On Jim's early fantasies of heroism, see *Lord Jim*, p. 5; on 'Imagination, the enemy of men, the father of all terrors', see p. 9.

19. The verb 'to prime' is widely used by cognitive psychologists to refer to the way that appropriate stimuli can unconsciously inflect the ensuing response of an individual (their action, moral choice, etc.). One trivial but nonetheless striking example that is often cited is evidence that holding a warm cup of coffee in your hand may make you more inclined to make morally benevolent choices. 'Priming' is also the purpose of prefaces, prologues, author's notes, and other similar paratexts: they set the reader up to think and feel in a particular way and thus be more receptive to the book's content. It would not be difficult to link this phenomenon to the history of rhetoric and its emphasis on persuasion, *captatio benevolentiae*, and so on—what one might call 'the poetics of suggestibility'.

20. I refer here to the Bayesian calculus, which, according to some experimental psychologists, is the model for the way the brain makes choices in relation to past experience and projected future possibilities. A function of evolution itself, it is highly fallible, but also the best instrument living creatures have developed for achieving survival. See Frith, *Making Up the Mind*, pp. 119–25; for an interesting application to fiction, see Karin Kukkonen, 'Quixotic reasoning: counterfactuals, causation and literary storyworlds', in Cave, Kukkonen, and Smith (eds), *Reading Literature Cognitively*, pp. 47–61.

21. Karin Kukkonen's Bayesian reading (see n. 20) focuses on just this kind of story.

22. 'Hotel California' is the title track from a famous Eagles album; it was released as a single in 1977. The song tells of a female figure who entices a

weary wanderer into a fantasy hotel which he subsequently discovers that he can never leave (the story thus has some affinities with the Lorelei legend). I owe this reference to Shaun Gallagher, who used it to illustrate his talk at a Balzan project workshop organized by Tim Chesters at Royal Holloway, University of London, in January 2013.

23. This phrase is repeated some ten times in the course of the novel and forms a key leitmotif.

24. Montaigne, *Les Essais*, p. 333 (I.30).

25. This term is used in relevance theory to refer to utterances that echo a previous utterance, whether allusively, ironically, or for other illocutionary effects. See Sperber and Wilson, *Relevance*, 4.9.

26. This is the closing line of the prefatory poem ('Au lecteur') of Baudelaire's *Les Fleurs du mal*, echoed at the end of the first section of T. S. Eliot's 'The Waste Land'.

27. Conrad, *Lord Jim*, p. 72.

28. The possibility of other variants of Auerbach's project has been raised elsewhere in this study (for example in Ch. 4); I find this kind of conjecture an attractive way of imagining the potential of particular cognitive perspectives.

9. Literary Values in a Cognitive Perspective

1. Franzen, *The Corrections*, p. 306.

2. Gregory Currie, 'Literature and the psychology lab', *Times Literary Supplement* (31 Aug. 2011), available online at <http://www.the-tls.co.uk/tls/public/article765921.ece>.

3. Strictly speaking, his argument is that 'poetry' (by which is meant public fictional representations of human feeling and behaviour) can be dangerous for people with suggestible minds, unfortified by a philosophical education. So perhaps Plato would not have objected to the *study* of literature. But the simplified version of his position which I have presented here, like other philosophical simplifications ('stoic', 'sceptic', 'epicurean'), has persisted, and it has done so because it embodies a suspicion that is widely felt. So perhaps it doesn't matter if 'Plato' as cited here is in some sense a fictional philosopher.

4. A generous sample of the negative and dismissive ones is provided by Stephen Pinker, *How the Mind Works* (New York and London: W. W. Norton, 1997), ch. 8 (similar explanations are proposed for music and the fine arts).

5. This hypothesis provides a central strand of argument in Boyd, *Why Lyrics Last*.

6. That argument has a well-known genealogy, in which Nietzsche occupies one particular niche; other niches are represented by E. R. Dodds (on irrationality in Greek civilization) and by Claude Lévi-Strauss and his followers.

7. Perhaps it is still necessary, even at this late stage, to insist again on the distinction between this view and the postmodern claim that meaning in a literary work is 'undecidable'.

8. Gregory Currie, review of Gregory Tate, *The Poet's Mind: The Psychology of Victorian Poetry 1830–1870*, in *Times Literary Supplement* (19 July 2013). I hope it will be clear that my argument with Greg Currie is one that I have found extremely productive, precisely because he likes at times to be provocative. Also that I have simplified and perhaps caricatured his position, as I earlier simplified and caricatured Plato's.

9. When the BBC website ran a poll asking whether listeners thought Mike and Vicky should go ahead with the pregnancy, there were strong moral objections and the BBC was forced to apologize.

10. See Christopher D. Frith, 'The role of metacognition in human social interactions', *Philosophical Transactions of the Royal Society: Biological Sciences*, 367 (2012), pp. 2213–23.

11. I am referring here in particular to Diderot's *Le Rêve de d'Alembert*. For a recent account of Diderot's metaphors of the material mind, see Kate Tunstall,'The early modern embodied mind and the entomological imaginary', in Mary Helen McMurran and Alison Conway (eds), *Mind, Body, Motion, Matter: Eighteenth-Century British and French Literary Perspectives* (Toronto: University of Toronto Press, forthcoming 2016), ch. 7.

12. George Eliot, *Middlemarch* (Oxford: Oxford University Press, 1988; The World's Classics), p. 562 (ch. 68). I would like here to express my gratitude to Ben Morgan, to whom I owe this remarkable reference.

13. This argument looks stronger if one speaks of technological or medical innovations; but it seems to be a widely held view among scientists that, in the long term, the 'blue-skies' research of which particle physics is a paradigm leads to far wider and more transformative impacts than technological innovations driven by immediate needs.

14. Harris, *The Work of the Imagination*, p. 6.

15. I use quotation marks here because the everyday sense of the word suggests something disembodied. It is not clear that pure disembodied abstractions are possible: general concepts such as 'truth' and 'justice' are certainly not, and it is even a moot point whether the number 673,910.95201 or the notion of a fifth dimension is abstract in that sense. It's probably best, in fact, to remember the etymology of 'abstraction' here: the distinctly embodied gesture of 'drawing away' or 'drawing out' neatly captures the sense in which abstract concepts are always abstracted from, drawn out of embodied ones.

16. Milne, *Winnie-the-Pooh*, pp. 79–80.

Select Bibliography

In addition to works referred to in this book, I have included here a number of titles which, although not specifically cited, are of general importance for the perspective proposed here. On the other hand, a few works (especially literary works) mentioned only in passing have been omitted.

Literary works

Amis, Martin, *Time's Arrow or The Nature of the Offence* (London: Vintage Books, 2003; first published 1991).

Ashbery, John, *Hotel Lautréamont* (Manchester: Carcanet Press, 1992).

Bashó, *see* Giroux, Joan.

Baudelaire, Charles, *Œuvres complètes*, ed. Y.-G. Le Dantec and Claude Pichois ([Paris]: Gallimard, Bibliothèque de la Pléiade, 1961).

Conrad, Joseph, *Lord Jim*, ed. Jacques Berthoud (Oxford: Oxford University Press, Oxford World's Classics, 2002).

Dickinson, Emily, *The Complete Poems*, ed. Thomas H. Johnson (London: Faber and Faber, 1982).

Eliot, George, *Middlemarch* (Oxford: Oxford University Press, 1988).

Elson, Rebecca, *A Responsibility to Awe* (Manchester: Carcanet Press, 2001).

Éluard, Paul, *Capitale de la douleur; L'Amour la poésie* (Paris: Gallimard, 1966).

Franzen, Jonathan, *The Corrections* (London: Fourth Estate, 2002).

Goethe, Johann Wolfgang, *Sämtliche Werke*, vol. 29 (II.2), ed. Hartmut Reinhardt (Frankfurt am Main: Deutscher Klassiker Verlag, 1997).

James, Henry, *The American* (New York: Charles Scribner's Sons, 1922).

Lafayette, Mme de, *The Princesse de Clèves*, trans. Terence Cave (Oxford: Oxford University Press, 1992).

Lear, Edward, *The Complete Nonsense of Edward Lear*, ed. Holbrook Jackson (London: Faber and Faber, 1947 and reprints).

Milne, A. A., *Winnie-the-Pooh* (London: Egmont, 2004; first published 1926).

Milton, John, *Areopagitica*, in *Complete Prose Works*, vol. 2, ed. Ernest Sirluck (New Haven: Yale University Press, 1959).

Milton, John, *Poetical Works*, ed. Douglas Bush (London: Oxford University Press, 1966).

Mitchell, David, *Cloud Atlas* (London: Hodder & Stoughton, 2004).

Montaigne, Michel de, *Les Essais*, ed. Jean Céard et al. (Paris: Livre de Poche, 2001).

Pascal, Blaise, *Pensées*, ed. Philippe Sellier ([Paris]: Mercure de France, 1976).

Proust, Marcel, *A la recherche du temps perdu*, ed. Jean-Yves Tadié et al., 4 vols ([Paris]: Gallimard, Bibliothèque de la Pléiade, 1988–9).

Ronsard, Pierre de, *Œuvres complètes*, 2 vols, ed. Jean Céard, Daniel Ménager, and Michel Simonin ([Paris]: Gallimard, Bibliothèque de la Pléiade, 1994).

Sandburg, Carl, *Chicago Poems* (New York: Henry Holt, 1916).

Shakespeare, William, *The Complete Works*, ed. Stanley Wells and Gary Taylor (Oxford: Clarendon Press, 1986).

Shakespeare, William, *King Lear*, ed. R. A. Foakes (Walton-on-Thames: Thomas Nelson, 1997; The Arden Shakespeare).

Valéry, Paul, *Œuvres*, vol. 1, ed. Jean Hytier ([Paris]: Gallimard, Bibliothèque de la Pléiade [1957]).

Verlaine, Paul, *Œuvres poétiques*, ed. Jacques Robichez (Paris: Garnier, 1969).

Vigny, Alfred de, *Œuvres complètes*, vol. 1, ed. F. Baldensperger, ([Paris]: Gallimard, Bibliothèque de la Pléiade, [1955]).

Yeats, William Butler, *Autobiographies* (London: Macmillan, 1955).

Yeats, William Butler, *Collected Poems* (London: Macmillan, 1957).

Non-literary works

Ainslie, George, *Picoeconomics: The Strategic Interaction of Successive Motivational States Within the Person* (Cambridge: Cambridge University Press, 1997).

Armstrong, Paul B., *How Literature Plays with the Brain: The Neuroscience of Reading and Art* (Baltimore: Johns Hopkins University Press, 2013).

Austin, J. L., *How To Do Things With Words* (Oxford: Clarendon Press, 1962).

Baron-Cohen, Simon, *Mindblindness: An Essay on Autism and Theory of Mind* (Cambridge, Mass.: MIT Press, 1995).

Baron-Cohen, Simon, Helen Tager-Flusberg, and Donald J. Cohen (eds), *Understanding Other Minds: Perspectives from Developmental Cognitive Neuroscience* (2nd edn, Oxford: Oxford University Press, 2000).

Barsalou, Lawrence W., 'Situated simulation in the human conceptual system', *Language and Cognitive Processes*, 18 (2003), 513–62.

Barsalou, Lawrence W., 'Social Embodiment', in Brian H. Ross (ed.), *The Psychology of Learning and Motivation: Advances in Research and Theory*, vol. 43 (San Diego: Academic Press, 2003), pp. 43–92.

Bennett, Maxwell, Daniel Dennett, Peter Hacker, and John Searle, *Neuroscience & Philosophy: Brain, Mind, & Language* (New York: Columbia University Press, 2007).

Bolens, Guillemette, *Le Style des gestes: Corporéité et kinésie dans le récit littéraire* (Lausanne: Éditions BHMS, 2008; English version: *The Style of Gestures: Embodiment and Cognition in Literary Narrative*, Baltimore: Johns Hopkins University Press, 2012).

Bolens, Guillemette, 'Les Styles kinésiques. De Quintilien à Proust en passant par Tati', in Laurent Jenny (ed.), *Le Style en acte. Vers une pragmatique du style* (Geneva: Métis Presses, 2011), pp. 59–85.

Bolens, Guillemette, 'Kinaesthetic empathy in Charlie Chaplin's silent films', in Dee Reynolds and Matthew Reason (eds), *Kinaesthetic Empathy in Creative and Cultural Practices* (Bristol and Chicago: Intellect, 2012), pp. 143–56.

Boyd, Brian, *The Origin of Stories: Evolution, Cognition, and Fiction* (Cambridge, Mass.: Harvard University Press, 2009).

Boyd, Brian, *Why Lyrics Last: Evolution, Cognition, and Shakespeare's Sonnets* (Cambridge, Mass.: Harvard University Press, 2012).

Bruhn, Mark J., and Donald R. Wehrs (eds), *Cognition, Literature, and History* (New York and Abingdon: Routledge, 2014).

Burke, Michael, *Literary Reading, Cognition and Emotion* (New York and London: Routledge, 2011).

Carey, Susan, *The Origin of Concepts* (Oxford: Oxford University Press, 2009).

Carroll, Joseph, *Literary Darwinism: Evolution, Human Nature, and Literature* (New York and London: Routledge, 2004).

Carston, Robyn, *Thoughts and Utterances: The Pragmatics of Explicit Communication* (Oxford: Blackwell, 2002).

Carston, Robyn, 'Metaphor: ad hoc concepts, literal meaning and mental images', *Proceedings of the Aristotelian Society*, 110 (2010), 295–321.

Carston, Robyn and Catherine Wearing, 'Metaphor, hyperbole and simile: a pragmatic approach', *Language and Cognition*, 3 (2011), 283–312.

Cave, Terence, *Mignon's Afterlives: Crossing Cultures from Goethe to the Twenty-First Century* (Oxford: Oxford University Press, 2011).

Cave, Terence, Karin Kukkonen, and Olivia Smith (eds), *Reading Literature Cognitively*, special edition of *Paragraph*, 37 (2014).

Chalmers, David (ed.), *Philosophy of Mind: Classical and Contemporary Readings* (New York: Oxford University Press, 2002).

Clark, Andy, *Supersizing the Mind: Embodiment, Action, and Cognitive Extension* (Oxford: Oxford University Press, 2008).

Clarke, Billy, *Relevance Theory* (Cambridge: Cambridge University Press, 2013).

Cohn, Dorrit, *Transparent Minds: Narrative Modes for Presenting Consciousness in Fiction* (Princeton: Princeton University Press, 1978).

Cosmides, Leda and John Tooby, 'Consider the source: the evolution of adaptations for decoupling and metarepresentation', in Dan Sperber (ed.), *Metarepresentations: A Multidisciplinary Perspective* (New York: Oxford University Press, 2000), pp. 53–111.

Crane, Mary Thomas, *Shakespeare's Brain: Reading with Cognitive Theory* (Princeton: Princeton University Press, 2001).

Crane, Tim, *The Objects of Thought* (Oxford: Oxford University Press, 2013).

Crilly, Nathan, 'The design stance in user-system interaction', *Design Issues*, 27 (2011), 16–29.

Currie, Gregory, *Arts and Minds* (Oxford: Oxford University Press, 2004).

Currie, Gregory, *Narratives and Narrators: A Philosophy of Stories* (Oxford: Oxford University Press, 2010).

Currie, Gregory, 'Literature and the psychology lab', *Times Literary Supplement* (31 August 2011), at <http://www.the-tls.co.uk/tls/public/article765921. ece>.

Currie, Gregory, Review of Gregory Tate, *The Poet's Mind: The Psychology of Victorian Poetry 1830–1870*, in *Times Literary Supplement* (19 July 2013).

Currie, Gregory and Ian Ravenscroft, *Recreative Minds: Imagination in Philosophy and Psychology* (Oxford: Clarendon Press, 2002).

Damasio, Antonio, *The Feeling of What Happens: Body and Emotion in the Making of Consciousness* (New York: Harcourt Brace, 1999).

Damasio, Antonio, *Descartes' Error: Emotion, Reason, and the Human Brain* (London: Penguin Books, 2005; first published 1994).

Davidson, Donald, 'What metaphors mean', in Donald Davidson, *Inquiries into Truth and Interpretation* (Oxford: Clarendon Press, 1984; first published 1978), pp. 245–64.

Davidson, Donald, 'A nice derangement of epitaphs', in Ernest Lepore (ed.), *Truth and Interpretation: Perspectives on the Philosophy of Donald Davidson* (Oxford: Blackwell, 1986), pp. 433–46.

Davis, Philip, *Reading and the Reader* (Oxford: Oxford University Press, 2013).

Dennett, Daniel, *Consciousness Explained* (Boston: Little, Brown, 1991).

Dennett, Daniel, 'Making tools for thinking', in Dan Sperber (ed.), *Metarepresentations: A Multidisciplinary Perspective* (New York: Oxford University Press, 2000), pp. 17–29.

Dezecache, Guillaume, Hugo Mercier, and Thomas C. Scott-Phillips, 'An evolutionary approach to emotional communication', *Journal of Pragmatics*, 59 (2013), 221–33.

Dunbar, Robin, *Grooming, Gossip and the Evolution of Language* (London: Faber & Faber, 1996).

Dunbar, Robin, 'Why are good writers so rare? An evolutionary perspective on literature', *Journal of Cultural and Evolutionary Psychology*, 3 (2005), 17–18.

Fauconnier, Gilles and Mark Turner, *The Way We Think: Conceptual Blending and the Mind's Hidden Complexities* (New York: Basic Books, 2002).

Fludernik, Monika, *Towards a 'Natural' Narratology* (London and New York: Routledge, 1996).

Frith, Christopher D., *Making Up the Mind: How the Brain Creates Our Mental World* (Chichester: Wiley-Blackwell, 2007).

Frith, Christopher D., 'The role of metacognition in human social interactions', *Philosophical Transactions of The Royal Society: Biological Sciences*, 367 (2012), 2213–23.

Gallagher, Shaun, *How the Body Shapes the Mind* (Oxford: Clarendon Press, 2005).

Gallagher, Shaun and Dan Zahavi, *The Phenomenological Mind* (London and New York: Routledge, 2012; first published 2008).

Gallese, Vittorio, Luciano Fadiga, Leonardo Fogassi, and Giacomo Rizolatti, 'Action recognition in the premotor cortex', *Brain*, 119 (1996), 595–609.

Gell, Alfred, *Art and Agency: An Anthropological Theory* (Oxford: Clarendon Press, 1998).

Gibson, James J., *The Ecological Approach to Visual Perception* (Hillsdale, NJ: Lawrence Erlbaum Associates, 1986; first published 1979).

Giroux, Joan, *The Haiku Form* (North Clarendon, Vt: Tuttle Publishing, 1974).

Glenberg, Arthur M. and Michael P. Kaschak, 'Grounding language in action', *Psychonomic Bulletin and Review*, 9 (2002), 558–65.

Goldman, Alvin A., *Simulating Minds: The Philosophy, Psychology, and Neuroscience of Mindreading* (New York: Oxford University Press, 2006).

Gopnik, Alison, *The Philosophical Baby: What Children's Minds Tell Us About Truth, Love & the Meaning of Life* (London: The Bodley Head, 2009).

Gosetti-Ferencei, Jennifer Anna, 'The mimetic dimension: literature between neuroscience and phenomenology', *British Journal of Aesthetics*, 54 (October 2014), 425–48.

Grandin, Temple, *Thinking in Pictures and Other Reports from My Life with Autism* (London: Bloomsbury, 2006; first published 2006).

Grice, Paul, *Studies in the Way of Words* (Cambridge, Mass., and London: Harvard University Press, 1989).

Gutt, Ernst-August, *Translation and Relevance: Cognition and Context* (2nd edn; Manchester: St Jerome Publishing, 2000).

Hacker, Peter, 'Is there anything it is like to be a bat?', *Philosophy*, 77 (2002), 157–74.

Hacker, Peter, *The Intellectual Powers: A Study of Human Nature* (Oxford: Wiley-Blackwell, 2013).

Hacker, Peter and M. R. Bennett, *Philosophical Foundations of Neuroscience* (Oxford: Blackwell, 2003).

Hacker, Peter and M. R. Bennett, *History of Cognitive Neuroscience* (Oxford: Wiley-Backwell, 2008).

Harris, Paul, *The Work of the Imagination* (Oxford: Blackwell, 2000).

Harris, Paul, *Trusting What You're Told: How Children Learn from Others* (Cambridge, Mass., and London: The Belknap Press of Harvard University Press, 2012).

Herman, David, *Story Logic. Problems and Possibilities of Narrative*, Frontiers of Narrative (Lincoln, Nebr.: University of Nebraska Press, n.d.).

Herman, David, 'Cognitive narratology', in Peter Hühn et al. (eds), *The Living Handbook of Narratology* (Hamburg: Hamburg University Press), URL = <hup.sub.uni-hamburg.de/lhn/index.php ?title=Cognitive Narratology &oldid=2058> (view date: 19 Jan 2015).

Herman, David (ed.), *Narrative Theory and the Cognitive Sciences* (Stanford, Calif.: CSLI Publications, 2003).

Hogan, Patrick Colm, *The Mind and its Stories: Narrative Universals and Human Emotion* (Cambridge: Cambridge University Press, 2003).

Jameson, Fredric, *The Prison-House of Language* (Princeton: Princeton University Press, 1972).

Johnson, Christopher, 'Leroi-Gourhan and the limits of the human', *French Studies*, 65 (2011), 471–87.

Kahneman, Daniel, *Thinking, Fast and Slow* (New York: Farrar, Straus and Giroux; London: Penguin Books, 2011).

Kukkonen, Karin, 'Quixotic reasoning: counterfactuals, causation and literary storyworlds', in Cave, Kukkonen, and Smith (eds), *Reading Literature Cognitively*, special edition of *Paragraph*, 37 (2014), pp. 47–61.

Kuzmičová, Anežka, *Mental Imagery in the Experience of Literary Narrative: Views from Embodied Cognition* (Stockholm: Stockholm University, 2013).

Lakoff, George, *Women, Fire and Dangerous Things: What Categories Reveal About the Mind* (Chicago and London: Chicago University Press, 1987).

Lakoff, George and Mark Johnson, *Metaphors We Live By* (Chicago and London: Chicago University Press, 1980).

Lavocat, Françoise (ed.), *La Théorie littéraire des mondes possibles* (Paris: CNRS Éditions, 2010).

Lothe, Jakob, *Conrad's Narrative Method* (Oxford: Oxford University Press, 1991).

Lothe, Jakob, 'Conrad's *Lord Jim*: narrative and genre', in Jakob Lothe, Jeremy Hawthorn, and James Phelan (eds), *Joseph Conrad: Voice, Sequence, History, Genre* (Columbus, Oh.: Ohio State University Press, 2008), pp. 236–55.

Lyne, Raphael, *Shakespeare, Rhetoric and Cognition* (Cambridge: Cambridge University Press, 2011).

McGilchrist, Iain, *The Master and his Emissary: The Divided Brain and the Making of the Western World* (New Haven and London: Yale University Press, 2009).

McGinn, Colin, *Mindsight: Image, Dream, Meaning* (Cambridge, Mass.: Harvard University Press, 2004).

MacKenzie, Ian, *Paradigms of Reading: Relevance Theory and Deconstruction* (London: Palgrave Macmillan, 2002).

Mahon, Bradford Z. and Alfonso Caramazza, 'A critical look at the embodied cognition hypothesis and a new proposal for grounding conceptual content', *Journal of Physiology*, 102 (2008), 59–70.

Merleau-Ponty, Maurice, *Phenomenology of Perception*, trans. Donald A. Landes (London and New York: Routledge, 2013; original first published 1945).

Mikkonen, Jukka, *The Cognitive Value of Philosophical Fiction* (London and New York: Bloomsbury, 2013).

Milner, Brenda, see autobiographical chapter in *The History of Neuroscience in Autobiography*, vol. 2, ed. Larry R. Squire (San Diego, London, etc.: Academic Press, 1998), pp. 276–305.

Mithen, Stephen, *The Singing Neanderthals: The Origins of Music, Language, Mind and Body* (Cambridge, Mass.: Harvard University Press, 2005).

Mottram, Stephen, <www.stephenmottram.com>.

Nagel, Thomas, 'What is it like to be a bat?', *Philosophical Review*, 83 (1974), 435–50.

Nichols, Shaun (ed.), *The Architecture of the Imagination: New Essays on Pretence, Possibility, and Fiction* (Oxford: Clarendon Press, 2006).

Noë, Alva, 'Is the visual world a grand illusion?', *Journal of Consciousness Studies*, 9/5–6 (2002), 1–12.

Nussbaum, Martha C., *Love's Knowledge: Essays on Philosophy and Literature* (New York: Oxford University Press, 1990).

Oatley, Keith, *Such Stuff as Dreams: The Psychology of Fiction* (Oxford: Wiley-Blackwell, 2011).

Olsen, Jon-Arild, *L'Esprit du roman. Œuvre, fiction et récit* (Berne: Peter Lang, 2004).

Palmer, Alan, *Fictional Minds* (Lincoln, Nebr., and London: Nebraska University Press, 2004).

Palmer, Alan, *Social Minds in the Novel* (Columbus, Oh.: Ohio State University Press, 2010).

Parker, Patricia, 'The metaphorical plot', in David S. Miall (ed.), *Metaphor: Problems and Perspectives* (Brighton: Harvester, 1982), pp. 133–57.

Pavel, Thomas, *Fictional Worlds* (Cambridge, Mass.: Harvard University Press, 1986).

Pilkington, Adrian, *Poetic Effects: A Relevance Theory Perspective* (Amsterdam: John Benjamins, 2000).

Pinker, Stephen, *How the Mind Works* (New York and London: W. W. Norton, 1997).

Ricœur, Paul, *La Métaphore vive* (Paris: Seuil, 1975).

Ricœur, Paul, *Temps et récit*, 3 vols (Paris, Seuil, 1983–5).

Roth, Ilona (ed.), *Imaginative Minds* (Oxford and New York: Oxford University Press for the British Academy, 2007).

Ryan, Marie-Laure, *Possible Worlds, Artificial Intelligence, and Narrative Theory* (Bloomington, Ind.: Indiana University Press, 1991).

Scarry, Elaine, *Dreaming by the Book* (New York: Farrar, Strauss & Giroux, 1999).

Schacter, Daniel L. (with Donna Rose Addis and Alana T. Wong), 'Remembering the past and imagining the future: common and distinct neural substrates during event construction and elaboration', *Neuropsychologia*, 45 (2007), 1363–77.

Schaeffer, Jean-Marie, *Pourquoi la fiction?* (Paris: Seuil, 1999; English version *Why Fiction?*, trans. Dorrit Cohn, University of Nebraska Press, 2010).

Sellevold, Kirsti, *'J'ayme ces mots . . . ': expressions linguistiques de doute dans les Essais de Montaigne* (Paris: Champion, 2004).

Sellevold, Kirsti, 'Cognitive deficits in literary fictions: Faulkner's *The Sound and the Fury* and Vesaas' *The Birds*', *Comparative Critical Studies*, 12 (2015), 71–88.

Sellevold, Kirsti, 'Reading shortforms cognitively: mindreading and procedural expressions in La Rochefoucauld and La Bruyère', in Terence Cave, Karin Kukkonen, and Olivia Smith (eds), *Reading Literature Cognitively*, special edition of *Paragraph*, 37 (2014), 96–111.

Sperber, Dan (ed.), *Metarepresentations: A Multidisciplinary Perspective* (New York: Oxford University Press, 2000).

Sperber, Dan and Deirdre Wilson, *Relevance: Communication and Cognition* (Oxford: Blackwell, 1995; 1st edn 1986).

Sperber, Dan and Deirdre Wilson, 'A deflationary account of metaphors', in Ray Gibbs (ed.), *The Cambridge Handbook of Metaphor and Thought* (New York: Cambridge University Press, 2008), pp. 84–105.

Sperber, Dan, et al., 'Epistemic vigilance', *Mind and Language*, 25 (2010), 359–93.

Spolsky, Ellen, *Gaps in Nature: Literary Interpretation and the Modular Mind* (Albany, NY: SUNY Press, 1993).

Spolsky, Ellen, 'Elaborated knowledge: reading kinesis in pictures', *Poetics Today*, 17 (1996), 157–80.

Spolsky, Ellen, 'An embodied view of misunderstanding in *Macbeth*', *Poetics Today*, 32 (2011), 489–520.

Squire, Larry and Eric R. Kandel, *Memory: From Mind to Molecules* (2nd edn; Greenwood Village, Colo.: Roberts & Company, 2009).

Starobinski, Jean, 'L'Échelle des températures: lecture du corps dans *Madame Bovary*', in J.-B. Pontalis (ed.), *Le Temps de la réflexion*, 1 (Paris: Gallimard, 1980), pp. 145–83.

Tallis, Raymond, *Aping the Brain: Neuromania, Darwinitis and the Misrepresentation of Humanity* (Durham: Acumen, 2011).

Tendahl, Markus and Raymond W. Gibbs Jr., 'Complementary perspectives on metaphor: cognitive linguistics and relevance theory', *Journal of Pragmatics*, 40 (2008), 1823–64.

Troscianko, Emily, *Kafka's Cognitive Realism* (London: Routledge, 2014).

Troscianko, Emily, 'Reading Kafka enactively', in Terence Cave, Karin Kukkonen, and Olivia Smith (eds), *Reading Literature Cognitively*, special edition of *Paragraph*, 37 (2014), pp. 15–31.

Tsur, Reuven, *Towards a Theory of Cognitive Poetics* (Brighton: Sussex Academic Press, 1992).

Tunstall, Kate, 'The early modern embodied mind and the entomological imaginary', in Mary Helen McMurran and Alison Conway (eds), *Mind, Body, Motion, Matter: Eighteenth-Century British and French Literary Perspectives* (Toronto: University of Toronto Press, 2016).

Turner, Mark, *The Literary Mind: The Origins of Thought and Language* (Oxford and New York: Oxford University Press, 1996).

Varela, Francisco, Evan Thompson, and Eleanor Rosch, *The Embodied Mind: Cognitive Science and Human Experience* (Cambridge, Mass.: MIT Press, 1991).

Waldoff, Jessica, *Recognition in Mozart's Operas* (New York: Oxford University Press, 2006).

Walton, Kendall L., *Mimesis as Make-Believe: On the Foundations of the Representational Arts* (Cambridge, Mass., and London: Harvard University Press, 1990).

Warner, Marina, *Stranger Magic: Charmed States and the* Arabian Nights (London: Chatto & Windus, 2011).

Whiten, Andrew, Robert A. Hinde, Christopher B. Stringer, and Kevin N. Laland, *Culture Evolves* (Oxford: Oxford University Press, 2011).

Wilson, Deirdre, 'Parallels and differences in the treatment of metaphor in relevance theory and cognitive linguistics', *Studia Linguistica Universitatis Iagellonicae Cracoviensis*, 128 (2011), 195–213.

Wilson, Deirdre, 'Relevance and the interpretation of literary texts', *UCL Working Papers in Linguistics*, 23 (2011), 69–80.

Wilson, Deirdre and Robyn Carston, 'Metaphor, relevance and the "emergent property" issue', *Mind & Language*, 21 (2006), 404–33.

Wynn, Thomas and Frederick L. Coolidge, *How to Think Like a Neandertal* (New York: Oxford University Press, 2012).

Zunshine, Lisa, *Why We Read Fiction: Theory of Mind and the Novel* (Columbus, Oh.: Ohio State University Press, 2006).

Zunshine, Lisa (ed.), *Introduction to Cognitive Cultural Studies* (Baltimore: Johns Hopkins University Press, 2010).

Zunshine, Lisa (ed.), *The Oxford Handbook of Cognitive Literary Studies* (New York: Oxford University Press, 2015).

Index of Names

Well-known works (e.g. *Henry V, Madame Bovary*) cited in the text by title, without mention of an author, are included here under the name of the author. Fictions best known by their title or written by a group of script-writers (e.g. *Fifty Shades of Grey, 24, The Archers*) are, however, included under the name of the work.

Index of Concepts and Terms